On Language

PLATO to von HUMBOLDT

Edited by

PETER H. SALUS
University of Massachusetts

Holt, Rinehart and Winston, Inc.
New York · Chicago · San Francisco · Atlanta
Dallas · Montreal · Toronto · London · Sydney

Preface

This anthology is not intended to trace the entire course of linguistics to the beginning of the nineteenth century: among other things, the Indic, Hebrew, and Chinese grammarians and phoneticians have been intentionally omitted. Nor does this book pretend to be all-inclusive where Western linguistics is concerned. It merely presents what the anthologist considers the most important and most influential works of the period from Plato to von Humboldt; the Introduction attempts to suggest just why these works were influential and how they fit into the development of Western thought about language.

The selection has been purely personal, but the anthologist would like to thank James E. Cathey, Gary Bevington, and Mrs. Mary L. Greenwood (of the University of Massachusetts), Michael C. Shapiro (of the University of Chicago), and Samuel Levin (of Hunter College) for their comments and assistance.

This anthology is dedicated to my colleagues and students at Queens College and the University of Massachusetts.

P. H. S.

Amherst, Massachusetts
January 1969

Contents

Preface   *iii*

Introduction   *1*

PLATO / Cratylus   *18*

ARISTOTLE / Poetics   *60*

M. T. VARRO / On the Latin Language   *64*

QUINTILIAN / Institutes of Oratory   *78*

DONATUS / The Ars Minor of Donatus   *92*

ST. ANSELM / De Grammatico   *104*

PETER OF SPAIN / Tractatus Suppositionum   *107*

ANTOINE ARNAULD / The Art of Thinking   *109*

JEAN-JACQUES ROUSSEAU / Essay on the Origin of Languages   *138*

J. G. HERDER / Essay on the Origin of Language   *147*

SIR WILLIAM JONES / Third Anniversary Discourse of the President of the Royal Asiatick Society ("On the Hindus")   *167*

SIR WILLIAM JONES / "Preface" to the Persian Language   *173*

WILHELM VON HUMBOLDT / "Introduction" to Concerning the Variety of Human Language and Its Influence on the Intellectual Development of Mankind   *178*

Bibliography   *199*

Introduction

And the whole earth was of one language, and of one speech.

And it came to pass, as they journeyed from the east, that they found a plain in the land of Shinar; and they dwelt there.

And they said to one another, Go to, let us make brick, and burn them thoroughly. And they had brick for stone, and slime had they for mortar.

And they said, Go to, let us build us a city, and a tower, whose top *may reach* unto heaven; and let us make us a name, lest we be scattered abroad upon the face of the whole earth.

And the LORD came down to see the city and the tower, which the children of men builded.

And the LORD said, Behold, the people *is* one, and they have all one language; and this they begin to do: and now nothing will be restrained from them, which they have imagined to do.

Go to, let us go down, and there confound their language, that they may not understand one another's speech.

So the LORD scattered them abroad from thence upon the face of all the earth: and they left off to build the city.

Therefore is the name of it called Babel; because the LORD did there confound the language of all the earth: and from thence did the LORD scatter them abroad upon the face of all the earth.

GENESIS 11:1–9 (KING JAMES VERSION, 1611)

The Egyptians, prior to the reign of Psammitichus, regarded themselves as the most ancient of mankind. But that prince, having come to the throne, resolved to ascertain what people were the first in existence: from that time the Egyptians have allowed that the Phoenicians existed before them, but that they themselves are anterior to all others. Psammitichus, finding it im-

1

possible to ascertain, by inquiry, any means of discovering who were the first of the human race, devised the following experiment. He delivered over to a herdsman two new-born children of humble parents, to rear them, with his flock, after this manner: his orders were that no one should ever pronounce a word in the presence of the children, who were to be kept by themselves in a solitary apartment; at certain hours, goats were to be brought to them; the herdsman was to see they sucked their fill of milk, and then go about his business. This was done and ordered by Psammitichus for the purpose of hearing what word the children would first utter, after they left off the unmeaning cries of infancy. And such accordingly was the result. For the pastor had continued during the space of two years to act according to these orders, when one day opening the door and entering, both the children fell upon him, crying "becos," and stretching out their hands. The first time that the shepherd heard this, he accordingly kept quiet; but the same word occurred repeatedly, every time he came to attend to them: he therefore let his master know, and was ordered to bring the children into his presence. Psammitichus heard himself the word; and inquired what people it was that called, in their language, any thing "becos:" he was informed that the Phoenicians give that name to "bread." In consequence, the Egyptians, having deliberately weighed the matter, gave place to the Phoenicians, and granted they were the more ancient than themselves.

HERODOTUS, HISTORY, II, 2 (TRANS. LAURENT, 1846)

Speculation as to the origin and development of language is as old as any other speculation in Western culture: the two citations just given are perhaps the oldest we preserve. Peculiarly—or, perhaps, not so peculiarly —both the Bible and Herodotus are based on the same idea: that primeval man spoke one language, and that all other tongues are somehow linked through this common ancestor. This volume attempts to trace man's thought about his most important tool from these early beginnings through the eighteenth century to the start of what we can now call linguistics, the scientific study of language.

The history of every discipline shows certain trends; in linguistics, these seem to be of two major types: philosophizing and classifying. Thus, we can oppose Plato to Aristotle, or von Humboldt to Rask and Grimm. The waxing and waning of these two activities delimit the interest in language (and languages) over the past two millennia: First we find speculation concerning the origin and ultimate meaning of language, then (for a thousand years or so) the emphasis is on the description of Latin and Greek and (later) on the use of these descriptions in describing the Western European languages. In the seventeenth century philosophizing again begins to find favor, only to be stifled in the early nineteenth century by the descriptive emphasis of historical comparative research. And finally, within the past decade, we see the interest in philosophical grammar begin to grow once more. This outline may be a bit stark, but —as will be seen further on—it is in general correct.

Ferdinand de Saussure, writing early in this century, felt that the study of language had passed through three stages: grammar, philology, and comparison of languages; and that the job of future linguists was to describe the histories of the languages of the world, to reconstruct the parent language of each family, and to seek out and recognize the universal forces which acted upon language to produce the several thousand individual languages spoken today.[1] Here we might add speculative philosophy to Saussure's three stages, for it is with *philosophia* that the formal study of language in the West began, and it is with philosophers that we will find ourselves concerned through most of this book.

The study of language among the Greeks grew out of the controversy over whether words are natural or conventional in their origin. The Platonic dialogue, the *Cratylus*, with which this volume begins, is devoted to a discussion of this question. Studded with bizarre and fantastic etymologies, the *Cratylus* nonetheless contains the seeds of a century-long controversy between the Analogists, who believed that language was natural, regular, and logical, and the Anomalists, who pointed at the irregularities of language as proof that such a theory could not be correct. Primary here, too, is the question of the origin of words. Socrates refuses to have anything to do with the notion that God handed the first words down to man. This is no reason, he declares, it is merely an excuse for having no reason. It must be noted here that for Socrates and Plato, for Aristotle, and for the later Greek grammarians, only Greek existed, and so a question such as "Why do we call a horse *horse*, while a German calls it *Pferd* and a Frenchman *cheval?*" could not arise. Those things which were outside Greek were not language, and that ended the problem. Thus all the pseudo etymologies in the dialogue make no attempt at relating Greek to non-Greek phenomena. Socrates ends by remarking that he does not feel that the speculations of the dialogue have given rise to any knowledge at all, but that Cratylus is "young and of an age to learn" and that when he has "found the truth" he should "come and tell" it to Socrates.

Plato lived from 428 B.C. to *ca.* 348 B.C.; Aristotle was born in 384 B.C. and died in 322 B.C. The actual dating of either the *Cratylus* or the *Poetics* is impossible, but as representatives of classical Greek thought about language, neither the precise dates, nor the probability that about half of the Aristotle fragment presented here is spurious, makes much difference. It is sufficient for us to know that at some time in the fourth century before Christ men thought in this way about their language.

Plato is usually given credit for first making the distinction between noun (that of which some action or condition was predicated) and verb (that which predicated something of it). Aristotle, too, seems to have begun by dividing words into nouns and verbs, calling everything else conjunctions. He did this because he felt that nouns and verbs had actual

[1] *Cours de linguistique générale* (Paris, 1915), 13f. and 20f.

isolable meaning, whereas other words had merely grammatical function. Aristotle defined the word as the minimum meaningful unit, thus coming quite close to the modern descriptivist's view of the morpheme. Following Protagoras, Aristotle divided the noun into three genders; and in the verb, he seems to have been the first person to consider tense in his definition. He also considered adjectives part of the verb class, for they predicated qualities of the noun, and he had unfortunate logical problems because of this. But nonetheless, Aristotle's categorizations had a profound influence upon later thought about language.

Aristotle goes to much greater lengths to define the various parts of speech and their functions in *On Interpretation* than he (or whoever wrote the section) does in the *Poetics*. The basic notions, however, are much the same. A point of interest, however, may be the opening of the *De Interpretatione*, wherein Aristotle defines his basic concepts.

> Let us, first of all, define noun and verb, then explain what is meant by denial, affirmation, proposition, and sentence.
> Words spoken are symbols of signs of affections or impressions of the soul; written words are the signs of words spoken. As writing, so also is speech not the same for all races of men. But the mental affections themselves, of which these words are primarily signs, are the same for the whole of mankind, as are also the objects of which those affections are representations or likenesses, images, copies. . . .
> As at times there are thoughts in our minds unaccompanied by truth or by falsity, while there are others at times that have necessarily one or the other, so also is it in our speech, for combination and division are essential before you can have truth and falsity. A noun or a verb by itself much resembles a concept or thought which is neither combined nor disjoined. Such as "man," for example, or "white," if pronounced without any addition. As yet it is not true nor false. And a proof of this lies in the fact that "tragelaphos," [= goat-stag, a fabulous animal—P. H. S.] while it means something, has no truth nor falsity in it, unless in addition you predicate being or not-being of it, whether generally (that is to say, without definite time-connotation) or in a particular tense.
>
> TRANS H. P. COOK (CAMBRIDGE, MASS., AND LONDON, 1938)

After Plato and Aristotle, the first real advances in grammatical theory were made by the Stoics, who made a real attempt at framing a theory of language. The Saussurian distinction between signifier and signified, between inner and outer form and meaning so important in modern linguistics finds its origin among the Stoics. The earliest Stoic writers expanded Aristotle's three classes to four (noun, verb, conjunction, and article), and later Stoics increased this to five (dividing noun into proper and common nouns). In the verb, the Stoics retained the Platonic concept of predication, but, though they developed a theory of tenses, they did not include time relationships in their definition of the verb. Within the group "conjunction," the Stoics seem to have differentiated between prepositions and conjunctions, and in the article category, between pronouns and articles. (There seems to have been no recognition of the difference between personal and relative pronouns.) The Stoics seem further to have been the first to study number and agreement in nouns and verbs, to study case in the noun, and voice, mood and tense in the verb. There were five cases distinguished: nominative, genitive, dative, accusative, and another—the position of the vocative was anomalous. The Stoic theory of tenses was a fairly elaborate one, based for the most part on the principle of opposition. The present and imperfect were opposed to the perfect and pluperfect; these four tenses as definites, were opposed to the two indefinites, aorist and future. The aorist in particular was opposed to the perfect and pluperfect. Finally, the present and imperfect were duratives, the perfect and pluperfect were completives, and the aorist and future were indeterminates.[2]

After the Stoics, the center of grammatical thought in the West shifted to Alexandria, and a whole school of Alexandrian grammarians arose during the first century B.C. Chief among these grammarians was Dionysius Thrax. His grammatical treatise classified and represented the findings of others, and became the standard textbook for the next 1800 years. It was during the Alexandrian period that grammar finally gained status as a discipline, but the knowledge of the difference between the literary and the spoken language led the Greeks down the unfortunate path of prescriptivism to the more unfortunate goal of preserving their language from decadent influences.

Dionysius Thrax emphasized the relationship between grammar and literature and totally ignored colloquial speech. In his grammatical system, there were eight parts of speech (the noun, the verb, the participle, the article, the pronoun, the preposition, the adverb, and the conjunction), certainly an improvement over Plato and Aristotle. Dionysius felt that the task of the grammarian was to discover the rules of the language, but his own grammar omitted any mention of syntax. This lack was made up by Apollonius Dyscolus, whose work—which no longer survives—is said to have been the most complete Greek grammar. It was the basis of a number of Roman grammatical treatises.

Just as Greek philosophy, art, and literature were adopted (and adapted) by the Romans, so too was Greek grammar. This grammar, exemplified by Dionysius and Apollonius, was used by the Romans with only minor modifications. Only one Latin grammarian seems to have re-examined the Greek systems in terms of Latin before attempting to use them. This was Marcus Terentius Varro, born in 116 B.C. in the Sabine country. Varro's treatise *De Lingua Latina*, originally in twenty-five books of which only five survive, is predicated upon the division of the

---

[2] Colaclides, "On the Stoic Theory of Tenses," *Quarterly Progress Report of the Research Laboratory in Electronics* (M.I.T.), no. 80 (January 15, 1966), 214–216.

study of language into three parts: etymology, morphology, and syntax. Varro also discusses the Analogist-Anomalist controversy, pointing out that the familiar domestic animals and the most familiar wild beasts have separate names for masculine and feminine, while the less familiar ones lack this distinction. Were the Analogist position valid, Varro seems to say, then all animals should have separate "names" for the male and female of the species, as all animal species comprise both sexes; only if the Anomalist position holds could the actual state of affairs come about.

Varro thought that Latin should have six cases (not five like Greek), calling his additional case the "ablative," and putting the vocative on the same plane as the nominative, genitive, dative, and accusative (it was Quintilian who added a seventh case, the instrumental). Varro's other major contribution was the attempt at working out a rule pattern for the active and the passive. The full contents of *De Lingua Latina* were:

> Book I: Introduction, including a dedication of the whole work to Cicero;
>
> Books II–VII: the *impositio vocabulorum*, how words originated and applied to things and ideas (Books V–VII start with a new dedication to Cicero.);
>
> Books VIII–XIII: derivation of words from other words, including stem derivation, declension of nouns, and conjugation of verbs (treating especially the problem of Analogy versus Anomaly);
>
> Books XIV–XIX: syntax;
>
> Books XX–XXV: stylistics and rhetorical embellishments.

Only Books V through X survive, and there are many lacunae in the manuscripts.

Varro was undoubtedly the most original and the most independent of the Roman grammarians, despite his obvious indebtedness to the Stoics. The Romans who followed him, for the most part, merely discussed already extant questions. One of these questions was the place of the interjection, and it was Remmius Palaemon in the first century A.D. who finally defined it as having no definite meaning, but indicating emotion.

Quintilian (A.D. 35–*ca.* 98) was a student of Remmius Palaemon, and though he is not customarily thought of as a grammarian, there is enough in his *Institutio Oratoria* concerning language to warrant his inclusion here. Quintilian felt that education began in the cradle and ended in the grave, and that the most important thing for a young man was for him to be able to handle himself verbally. As a result, the treatise on education deals at some length with questions of grammar and of rhetoric in the larger sense.

Quintilian's interests range from spelling (the need for both *u* and *v* in words like *servus* and *vulgus*—spelled *seruus* and *uulgus* in the first century—and *i* and *j*, as in *jacit*) and etymology through the theory of the parts of speech to the old Anomalist-Analogist controversy. Perhaps his greatest contribution was his attempt to have the instrumental set up as a separate case in Latin, not on the basis of inflection—for here it is not distinguished—but on purely semantic grounds. His suggestion of semantic rather than morphological distinction has stuck with us enough so that we can still actually use phrases like "dative of possession" without a qualm. Quintilian's *Institutes* were of tremendous influence over a span of nineteen centuries, but their popularity seems to have reached three great peaks.[3] First, there was his immediate influence, visible in Juvenal and Tacitus, as well as Christian leaders like Origen, Ambrose, Jerome, and Augustine. The second major period of Quintilian's influence came in twelfth-century France, during the so-called "renaissance of the twelfth century"; and finally, he awakened great interests in the Renaissance humanists of the fifteenth century. In England, Quintilian was a favorite of Pope, Disraeli, Macaulay, and Newman. For a solution to the questions of the parts of speech and grammar in general, however, we must turn from these notables to the lesser Aelius Donatus.

Donatus, writing *ca.* 350, composed two books which almost immediately became "best sellers." The first of these was a treatise *On The Parts of Speech* which helped set the parts of speech at eight over the next twelve hundred years. More important, however, may be the much shorter *Ars Minor*, printed here in its entirety. The *Ars Minor* attempted to present in a small compass and in the form of a catechism the basics of Latin grammar—and in this it succeeded brilliantly. These two little books became a standard and were used so widely that "Donat" or "Donet" became the word for "primer" or "first book" on any subject whatsoever.

The Latin grammars of today, however, are not based so much on those of Varro or Quintilian or Donatus as they are on the *Institutiones grammaticae* of Priscian (*ca.* A.D. 500).

Priscian's grammar, in eighteen books and extending to nearly a thousand pages, does its best to retain the classical system of eight parts of speech of Dionysius Thrax and Apollonius Dyscolus. Priscian omits the article and includes the interjection to keep the numbers the same. He reviews the work of earlier Greek grammarians, sets down the two "standard systems," and defines each class with reference to its formal categorization. This, and the examination of the sounds (*litterae*, "*letters*") —which Priscian duly defines as the smallest parts of articulate speech— and syllables, take up the first sixteen books, mainly because of the copiousness of Priscian's examples. The last two books are devoted to

[3] Murphy, "Introduction" to *Quintilian, On the Early Education of the Citizen Orator* (Indianapolis, Ind., 1965), xx–xxvi.

syntax. Robins [4] has compared Priscian's parts of speech with Apollonius', and concludes "that Priscian's definitions are substantially those of Apollonius, as is his statement that each separate class is known by its semantic content." Priscian makes it obvious that he is not plowing new ground, and that the place of grammar in education was the same for him as it had been for Dionysius Thrax and Quintilian. In the morphology, Priscian's disregard of Varro's insight into the difference between derivational and inflectional sets of words illustrates his indebtedness to the Greek tradition rather than to his Latin predecessors.

The next centuries saw little added to the grammarian's repertoire. The *Etymologiae* of Isidor of Seville in the seventh century, which featured some of the most bizarre etymologies yet concocted, though derivative in style and content, as well as the seventh- and eighth-century Latin grammars of Bede and Alcuin, the ninth-century Old Irish glosses on Priscian, the tenth-century Latin–Old English glossary of Aelfric, added to the literature of grammar but not to the theory.

The latter part of the Middle Ages was of much greater interest. The first excerpt from this period is not really grammatical, but logical: the *De Grammatico* of St. Anselm (mid-eleventh century). And the importance of this treatise becomes obvious only when we look at the importance of Saussure and his distinction between the signified and the signifier. It is the notion of linguistic sign that seems to find its roots here, and it is within the development of the field of semantics—the study of meaning—that Anselm becomes important.

Not only Latin, but the vernacular languages, too, were used in medieval grammatical writings. We possess grammatical works in Old Irish, Hebrew, and Arabic, to say nothing of the so-called *First Grammatical Treatise* in Old Norse. The First Grammarian—his real name is unknown —seems to have been an Icelander living in the middle of the twelfth century. He was an original thinker, pondering the intricacies of Icelandic orthography, and thereby arriving at a really detailed study of Icelandic phonology. Moreover, the First Grammarian was the first to use a tool which became of prime importance in this century: the notion of the minimal pair in phonological analysis. Lying in obscurity for over six hundred years, the *First Grammatical Treatise* was published by Rask in 1818, and from there was taken into the mainstream of nineteenth-century linguistic thought. The First Grammarian begins by recounting the inadequacies of the Latin alphabet when applied to Icelandic. He then goes on to analysis of the vowels and consonants, discussing thirty-six vowel segments: nine short, nine long, and each of these nasalized and nonnasalized. Among the consonants he distinguishes between the short

---

[4] *Short History of Linguistics* (London, 1967), 57ff.

and the long, geminated consonants. The *Treatise* is full of good, witty examples, and, in several points, foreshadows the phonological theories of the Prague School in this century.

At about the same time that the First Grammarian was writing in Iceland, we find Peter Helias in Paris beginning the eight-hundred-year history of what might be called philosophic grammar with his commentary on Priscian. In this commentary, Peter seeks philosophic explanation for the rules set down by Priscian, and affirms that "it is not the grammarian, but the philosopher who, carefully considering the specific nature of things, discovers grammar." Helias also wrote a summary of Latin grammar in hexameters which seems to have initiated the vogue of grammar texts in verse. One of these pedagogic grammars in verse is the *Doctrinale* of Alexander of Villedieu (*ca.* 1200), running to 2645 lines of execrable hexameters.

Philosophic grammar is the prime concern of the *Summulae Logicales* by Peter of Spain (Pope John XXI), written in the third quarter of the thirteenth century. In this treatise, Peter referred to the difference between the *significātiō*—the meaning of the word, the relation between the sign or word and what it signified—and the *suppositiō*—the "acceptance of a term . . . as denoting something." To Peter of Spain, as to many later philosophers and grammarians, there was an important difference between the "John" of "John is a man" and that of " 'John' is a name."

The last years of the Middle Ages and the first ones of the Renaissance do not offer the grammatical theorist much intellectual fodder. We do find such works as Thomas of Erfurt's modistic reinterpretation of Priscian's eight word classes, but they are still Priscian's categories; we find the beginnings of Hebrew grammars (such as those of Reuchlin, 1506, and Clénard, 1529); and we find the first attempts at the study of the Romance languages. This last may have been given its impetus by Dante's *De vulgari eloquentia* at the beginning of the fourteenth century. In this work Dante exalts the unconsciously learned vernacular at the expense of Latin, learned in the schools as a conscious acquisition. The first-known grammars of Spanish and Italian were written in the fifteenth century and the first French grammar at the outset of the sixteenth. Polish and Old Church Slavonic grammars were published at this time, too. Peter Ramus (born *ca.* 1515) is well known among the Renaissance grammarians. Ramus wrote Greek, Latin, and French grammars and set up a theory of grammar in his *Scholae*. He stressed the need to follow native speakers in modern languages as the key to usage. He is the most formal of the early grammarians, relying neither on semantics nor on logical categories, but on actual word forms. By the end of the sixteenth century, there were a reasonably large number of grammars of various languages available. But just as the Analogist-Anomalist controversy gave rise to much grammatical (linguistic?) work earlier, so now the philosophical questions of rationalist versus empiricist began to occupy men's minds, and the members of the Académie française, founded by Richelieu in 1635, became quite concerned with questions of thought and language.

All of the grammatical works mentioned here fall into two of the Saussurian classes mentioned at the beginning of this introduction: speculative philosophy and grammar. The latter is here to be read as basically prescriptive grammar on the model of the grammars of Dionysius Thrax and Priscian; the former is a more flexible concept. Beginning with Plato's pseudoetymologizing and passing through Peter of Spain's *Summulae*, we find the question of the difference between the sign for something and the thing itself occurring again and again, along with the question of the arbitrariness of the linguistic sign. These very basic queries recur innumerable times in the history of grammatical theory and linguistics, and are perhaps only dispensed with in this century because of the clear and concise statement of Saussure. But the questions were of sufficient interest in Victorian England to give rise to Alice's conversation with the White Knight.

> "The name of the song is called 'Haddocks' Eyes.' "
> "Oh, that's the name of the song, is it?" Alice said, trying to feel interested.
> "No, you don't understand," the Knight said, looking a little vexed. "That's what the name is *called*. The name really is '*The Aged, Aged Man*.' "
> "Then I ought to have said 'That's what the *song* is called'?" Alice corrected herself.
> "No, you oughtn't; that's quite another thing! The *song* is called '*Ways and Means*'; but that's only what it's *called*, you know!"
> "Well, what *is* the song, then?" said Alice, who was by this time completely bewildered.
> "I was coming to that," the Knight said. "The song really is '*A-sitting on a Gate*'; and the tune's my own invention."
>
> LEWIS CARROLL, THROUGH THE LOOKING GLASS AND
> WHAT ALICE FOUND THERE, CHAPTER 8.

However, in the seventeenth century in France other (philosophical) questions arose, and those of the Analogist-Anomalist controversy and those of the modistae were temporarily set aside. The sides of these new questions were personified by Descartes and Locke, though Locke was no Frenchman, and they were certainly not contemporaries. The two sides were called the Rationalists and the Empiricists, and the most basic question was whether all knowledge was observational in origin, or whether certainty lay not in the realm of the senses, but in the irrefutable truths of human reason. One of the most important concepts of the controversy revolved about the notion of innate ideas. Locke, Hume,

Berkeley, and the other Empiricists vigorously denied the existence of any ideas present in the human mind prior to experience; Descartes and the Rationalists regarded innate ideas as the basis of our knowledge, and included the ideas of number and figure and the elements of logical and mathematical reasoning as part of this basis.

Within the past few decades, the spoor of this controversy may be traced in the empiricist view of language taken by the psychologist B. F. Skinner and the rationalist ideas of language acquisition of Chomsky and the transformational-generative grammarians.

Robin T. Lakoff has recently shown that much of this work has its origin in the pre-Cartesian work of Sanctius (who was the prime influence on the Port Royal grammarians), but we shall continue to use the term "Cartesian" as a convenient label. When applied to language, the Cartesian philosophic notions gave rise to a slew of "philosophic grammars," *grammaires raisonnées*, the most important of which was the *Grammaire générale et raisonnée* of Lancelot and Arnauld (1660). Known widely as the Port Royal grammar, this grammar was most important for its attempt to reveal the basic unity of the grammar underlying not Priscian's Latin tomes but the separate grammars of different languages. For, it was felt, it was language which communicated thought, and thought was composed of perception, judgment, and reasoning. Thus, the basic elements of language—not of French or Chinese or Swahili, but of Language—were part of the reason and were innate. The Port Royal grammarians thus had little use for the classical word classes and redivided them on the basis of semantic categories, noun, article, pronoun, participle, preposition, and adverb relating to the objects of thought; verb, conjunction, and interjection relating to the form or manner of thought. The basic noun-verb dichotomy was thus preserved, but the patterns of Donatus and Priscian were no more.

It must be pointed out, however, that the *Port Royal Grammar* was not the first French grammar to deviate from the Latin norm—the laurels for that achievement must go to Claude de Vaugelas (1585–1650), whose *Remarques sur la langue française* (1647), according to Professor Keith Percival,[5] was the first grammar to incorporate a modern concept of usage.

Though Arnauld, Lancelot, Cordemoy, and others saw extreme beauty and grace in their native French, the Port Royal grammarians attempted to make their "universal" hypotheses as universal as possible. Examples were drawn not only from Latin, Greek, and the modern European languages, but also from Hebrew, the only non-Indo–European language

[5] Paper delivered at the Fourth Regional Meeting, Chicago Linguistic Society, April 20, 1968 and published in the *Proceedings* (Dept. of Linguistics, University of Chicago, 1968).

they knew. The Port Royal grammarians saw general grammar as the underlying base upon which all natural languages were founded. And in this, as generative grammar has shown us, they may not have been completely wrong.

Antoine Arnauld (1612–1694) may not have been the author of all of *La Logique ou l'Art de Penser* of 1662. Other *Messieurs* of Port Royal, doubtless Nicole among them, contributed sections to the text. Still, Arnauld was the chief author, and *The Art of Thinking* is usually attributed to him, though more often than not it is called the *Port Royal Logic*. The *Logic* is divided into four parts: Part I deals with conceiving, with having an idea; Part II treats judging; Part III deals with defective reasonings and their remedies; and Part IV treats discovery and demonstration (holding that discovery always precedes demonstration). The *Logic* went through several editions in Arnauld's lifetime, the last one being the sixth (Amsterdam, 1685). The largest part of the selection presented here is from Part II, specifically those sections dealing with words in general: verbs; simple, compound, and complex prepositions; and compound sentences. Several sections here were not part of the 1662 *Logic*, appearing first in the Paris, 1683, edition. The *Port Royal Grammar* and the *Port Royal Logic* are works that form the immediate transition from classical and medieval grammatical thought to modern speculations and investigations. The Aristotelian categories and Priscian's classification were for the most part rejected (save in school grammars), and a new freedom was enjoyed by the subsequent investigators.

Here and there in Locke's *Essay concerning Human Understanding* (1690; fifteenth edition, 1760), we find mention of language and speculations concerning the problems of mind and naming. Locke felt that language operates through abbreviation:

> Though these complex *Ideas* be not always copied from Nature, yet they are always suited to the end for which abstract *Ideas* are made: And though they be Combinations made or *Ideas,* that are loose enough, and have as little union in themselves, as several other, to which the Mind never gives a connexion that combines them into one *Idea;* yet they are always made for the convenience of Communication, which is the chief end of Language. The use of Language is, by short Sounds to signify with ease and dispatch general Conceptions.
>
> ESSAY, III, V, 7

and that "Though therefore it is the Mind that makes the Collection, so 'tis the Name which is, as it were the Knot, that ties them fast together" (III, v, 10). Locke goes on to say "But Men, in making their general *Ideas,* seeking more the convenience of Language and quick dispatch, by short and comprehensive signs, than the true and precise Nature of Things. . . ." (III, vi, 32).

Locke's notion of language as a means of communication that is both simple and explicit is something which he held in common with Gottfried Wilhelm Leibniz (1646–1716), one of the great German Rationalists. Leibniz's interest in both the calculus and logic were the result of his attempt at finding and proliferating a uniform, unambiguous scientific language (= symbolism). Outside of this, Leibniz encouraged the writing of grammars and dictionaries of as many languages as possible and advocated a standard romanized alphabet for transliteration of languages written in non-Roman scripts. By and large, however, he had little influence on grammatical theory or analysis.

Locke's French disciple, Condillac (1715–1780) made the next contribution to the study of language with his *Traité des sensations* (1754). Condillac added the notion of the passing of time to the static picture of universal grammar, and thereby ushered in the empirical study of word history: pseudoetymologizing was now at an end, and "scientific" etymologies were now possible. Strangely enough, Condillac does not even devote a chapter to etymology; yet, without him, the study of word origins and of the origin of language over the next eighty years would never have developed. In his *Essai sur l'origine des conoissances* [sic] *humaines* (1746), Condillac states that language is not merely the means of communication and aid to memory Locke had made it, but also the necessary prerequisite for thought to occur at all. The origin of language thus becomes the crux of Condillac's whole structure.

The only treatise on the origin of languages of the mid-eighteenth century (that of Rousseau) seems to have been written between 1749 and 1755; but it was only published posthumously in 1782. However, the seeds of this treatise are already visible in Rousseau's essay of 1755 on equality among men. In this essay, Rousseau more than once makes favorable mention of Condillac; their theories of the origin of language were, in fact, quite similar. Both felt that language originated from imitative gestures and natural cries, but that the gestures were more liable to misinterpretation than were the sounds, and so the cries became the dominant aspect of language. Condillac believed that there was an intermediate phase in which spoken verb forms took their time indications from accompanying gestures. Rousseau seems to consider that the gesture-sound transition was made by some sort of agreement, so that it fits better with his idea of a social contract. Such items as the survival of tonal contrast in Chinese were considered as reflexes of primitive features.

The question of the origin of language took on ever greater importance in the middle of the eighteenth century, and in 1769 the Prussian Academy offered a prize for the best essay on how man developed language. The essay submitted by Herder in 1772 won him the prize.

Herder believed that language and thought were inseparable, that language was the content and the form of human thought. Aristotle had assumed that language was dependent upon thought, but Herder's assumption of parallel development was almost revolutionary, as was his notion that the literature and thought of a culture were only accessible through its own language. Edward Sapir [6] has traced much of von Humboldt's speculations on language to Herder's essay, and thus we can link Herder to such mid-twentieth century linguists as Benjamin Lee Whorf and Noam Chomsky. Herder retained the notion that all languages descended from one common source, but he suffered from a restricted temporal perspective, which forced him to search for primitive stages of language within a short span of recorded history.

Within two years of Herder's essay, Friedrich Gottlieb Klopstock (1724–1803), a German poet of the "Sturm und Drang" period, published a number of linguistic theories in his *Die deutsche Gelehrtenrepublik* (1774). The main influence on this work was Leibniz. Klopstock was primarily a prescriptivist, and so he concerned himself with the distressing use of loanwords and technical terms and the importance of orthographic reform. Klopstock also advocated the writing of a history of the German language and the compilation of a German dictionary. Despite his prescriptivist bias, Klopstock seems to have had a modern view of the job of the grammarian, for he emphasizes that the grammarian must present the rules of the language as it is actually used, and not as he wishes it were used. It is the usage which must guide the grammarian, Klopstock continues, "and if he does not do this, he is merely a chatterbox, not a grammarian."

The two "linguistic" essays of Johann Georg Hamann (1730–1788), *Rosenkreuz* (1772) and *Prolegomena* (1774), were written in response to Herder's prize piece, and are largely derivative.

It was in England however, influenced by the work of Locke and Condillac, that the course of linguistics for the next century and a half was shaped. In the same year, 1786, two works appeared that redirected and channeled the study of language. The authors of these works were John Horne Tooke (1736–1812) and Sir William Jones (1746–1794); the essays were *The Diversions of Purley* and the "Third Anniversary Discourse (On the Hindus)" to the Royal Asiatick Society of Bengal.

Horne Tooke's *Epea Pteroenta or the Diversions of Purley*, an unfortunately desultory attempt at the scientific study of language, appeared in two volumes in 1786 and 1805. The *Diversions* is in dialogue form; Horne Tooke opens by explaining just "how traditional grammar has gone astray . . . Words being the signs of things, grammar rightly began by admitting only as many parts of speech as there were sorts of things," but this proved unsatisfactory. Grammarians then "reversed the process

[6] *Modern Philology*, V (1907–1908), 109–142.

and . . . postulated as many differences of things as of signs," but this did not help much, and the attempt at philosophically solving the problems of language did not get much further.[7] Tooke's theories are dependent upon those of Locke and Condillac, but he differs from the latter in doing away with the dependency of thought on language: for Horne Tooke "all the operations of thought reside in language alone. He does not need the doctrine that language makes thought possible, because language is thought." (p. 53) The strangest thing about Horne Tooke's *Diversions*, however, was that it blocked the Continental philological researches founded on Jones' work from getting to England for nearly forty years. Jones' influence was on the Continent, not on England. In the first volume of the *Diversions* Horne Tooke had written that "all future etymologists, and perhaps some philosophers, will acknowledge their obligation to me" (p. 146), and for one generation of Englishmen, at least, he was right.

It was the work of Sir William Jones which founded the entire school of historical linguistics, and which, more than the work of any other single person, gave impetus to the study of language till a decade ago. Even American descriptivism, the dominant school of the first half of the twentieth century, could not have grown up without Jones' ground-breaking efforts, and it is only within the last decade that linguists have looked back to the philosophic and universal grammarians from Vaugelas through von Humboldt for points of view that had been swamped by the sudden rush of enthusiasm for the historical-comparative method.

Jones' influence is not only seen in his historical and comparative work, nor merely in his descriptive grammatical studies, nor in these plus his many translations from Persian and Sanskrit; for it was Jones' work on transliterating Sanskrit and Persian and his "Dissertation on the Orthography of Asiatick Words in Roman Letters" (*Works*, vol. III, 253–318) which, a half-century later, spurred Ellis and Pitman to work on English spelling reform, led to Lepsius' *Standard Alphabet* (1855), and to Sweet's "Broad Romic" (1877), and the International Phonetic Alphabet (1889).

Perhaps we can best illustrate Jones' theories of transcription by giving his version of a poem by Addison:

> Sò hwen sm énjel, bai divain camánd,
> i
> Widh rais n tempests shécs a gilti land,
> Sch az ah lét ór pél Britanya pást,
> i
> Cálm and s rín hi draivz dhi fyúryas blást,
> i
> And, pl z'd dh'ālmaitiz ārderz tu perfórm,
> Raids in dhi hwerlwind and dairects dhi stārm.

---

[7] H. Aarsleff, *The Study of Language in England: 1780–1860* (Princeton, N.J., 1967), 45 ff.

The first selection by Jones in this anthology is his epochal discourse "On the Hindus"; it requires no further comment. The second selection, however, from the "Preface" to *The Persian Language*, is included here because it illustrates Jones' great interest in other cultures and other languages—something he shares with many figures of the Enlightenment in Europe—and his attempt at making these languages and cultures accessible to the educated Westerner. Not only are these writings of tremendous influence, they are interesting in themselves; they are the product of a great mind breaking new land.

The immediate effect of Jones' work can be seen in the various essays of Friedrich Schlegel (1772–1829) and his brother August (1767–1845), Franz Bopp (1791–1867), A. F. Pott (1802–1887), Rasmus Christian Rask (1787–1832), and Jacob and Wilhelm Grimm (1785–1863 and 1786–1859). In fact, the opening of Friedrich Schlegel's *Über die Sprache und Weisheit der Indier* (1808) was nearly a verbatim translation of Jones' "On the Hindus."

Despite the fame of the Schlegel brothers, the first really important contributions to historical-comparative linguistics came with Rasmus Christian Rask's Icelandic grammar (1811), Bopp's *Über das Conjugationssystem der Sanskritsprache in Vergleichung mit jenem der griechischen, lateinischen, persischen, und germanischen Sprache* (Concerning the Conjugation System of Sanskrit in Comparison with that of Greek, Latin, Persian, and Germanic, 1816), the first edition of volume one of Grimm's *Deutsche Grammatik* (1819), and Rask's "Dissertation Respecting the Best Method of Expressing the Sounds of the Indian Languages in European Characters" (*Transactions of the Literary and Agricultural Society of Colombo*, 1822). These were the works which launched the flood of compendia in the nineteenth and early twentieth centuries, and thus shaped most of modern linguistics. However, before universal or philosophical grammar lapsed into its century-long coma, overwhelmed by compendia like Bopp's *Vergleichende Grammatik des Sanskrit, Zend, Griechischen, Lateinischen, Littauischen, Altslavischen, und Deutschen* (Comparative Grammar of Sanskrit, Avestan, Greek, Latin, Lithuanian, Old Church Slavic, and German; six vols., 1833–1852; 2d ed., 3 vols., 1856–1861), and Pott's *Etymologische Forschungen auf dem Gebiete der indogermanischen Sprachen* (Etymological Researches into the Indo-European Languages, 2 vols., 1833–1836), it reached the heights of expression in the work of Wilhelm von Humboldt (1767–1835).

Von Humboldt's first philosophical work was his *Über den Dualis* (Concerning the Dual, 1828), which was largely metaphysical. His magnum opus was to be his work on the language of the Kawis of Java. Unfortunately, he never finished this work and the fragments were posthumously edited, and the introduction *Über die Verschiedenheit des menschlichen Sprachbaus und ihren Einfluss auf die geistige Entwicklung des Menschengeschlechts* (Concerning the Variety of Human Language and its Influence on the Intellectual Development of Mankind, 1830–1835, published in 1836) was the first work to state that the character and structure of a language expresses the inner life and knowledge of its speakers, and that languages differ from one another as their speakers differ. Von Humboldt's "inner structure" is not precisely what we would call word order, but still falls within the range of syntax. According to von Humboldt it is the job of the morphological analysis of speech to clarify the ways in which lanuages differ as regards this "inner form" and to classify and arrange them accordingly.

This inner form producer, then, is much like the syntactic component of a transformational-generative grammar, and the *grammaire raisonnée* of the Cartesians is very similar to the semantic component. Had linguistics not turned from the universal grammarians' hypotheses of the period from 1660 to 1835, the "state of the art" today would be very different from what it is. But the empirical data and the methodology necessary to confirm these hypotheses were not available in the 1830s, and it was only after many decades of historical-comparative and descriptive data collection and data analysis that linguists were able to turn back to the Port Royal grammar and von Humboldt for insights into the nature of language, rather than into individual languages or language families.

PLATO

Cratylus

PERSONS OF THE DIALOGUE

Socrates, Hermogenes, Cratylus

Hermogenes   Suppose that we make Socrates a party to the argument?

Cratylus   If you please.

Her   I should explain to you, Socrates, that our friend Cratylus has been arguing about names; he says that they are natural and not conventional; not a portion of the human voice which men agree to use; but that there is a truth or correctness in them, which is the same for Hellenes as for barbarians. Whereupon I ask him, whether his own name of Cratylus is a true name or not, and he answers "Yes." And Socrates? "Yes." Then every man's name, as I tell him, is that which he is called. To this he replies—"If all the world were to call you Hermogenes, that would not be your name." And when I am anxious to have a further explanation he is ironical and mysterious, and seems to imply that he has a notion of his own about the matter, if he would only tell, and

Plato, *Cratylus*, in *The Dialogues of Plato* (trans. B. Jowett), 3d ed., vol. I (Oxford, 1892), 323–371. Some footnotes omitted.

could entirely convince me, if he chose to be intelligible. Tell me, Socrates, what this oracle means; or rather tell me, if you will be so good, what is your own view of the truth or correctness of names, which I would far sooner hear.

Socrates   Son of Hipponicus, there is an ancient saying, that "hard is the knowledge of the good." And the knowledge of names is a great part of knowledge. If I had not been poor, I might have heard the fifty-drachma course of the great Prodicus, which is a complete education in grammar and language—these are his own words—and then I should have been at once able to answer your question about the correctness of names. But, indeed, I have only heard the single-drachma course, and therefore, I do not know the truth about such matters; I will, however, gladly assist you and Cratylus in the investigation of them. When he declares that your name is not really Hermogenes, I suspect that he is only making fun of you;—he means to say that you are no true son of Hermes, because you are always looking after a fortune and never in luck. But, as I was saying, there is a good deal of difficulty in this sort of knowledge, and therefore we had better leave the question open until we have heard both sides.

Her   I have often talked over this matter, both with Cratylus and others, and cannot convince myself that there is any principle of correctness in names other than convention and agreement; any name which you give, in my opinion, is the right one, and if you change that and give another, the new name is as correct as the old—we frequently change the names of our slaves, and the newly-imposed name is as good as the old: for there is no name given to anything by nature; all is convention and habit of the users;—such is my view. But if I am mistaken I shall be happy to hear and learn of Cratylus, or of any one else.

Soc   I dare say that you may be right, Hermogenes: let us see;—Your meaning is, that the name of each thing is only that which anybody agrees to call it?

Her   That is my notion.

Soc   Whether the giver of the name be an individual or a city?

Her   Yes.

Soc   Well, now, let me take an instance;—suppose that I call a man a horse or a horse a man, you mean to say that a man will be rightly called a horse by me individually, and rightly called a man by the rest of the world; and a horse again would be rightly called a man by me and a horse by the world:—that is your meaning?

Her   He would, according to my view.

Soc   But how about truth, then? you would acknowledge that there is in words a true and a false?

Her   Certainly.

Soc   And there are true and false propositions?

Her   To be sure.

Soc   And a true proposition says that which is, and a false proposition says that which is not?

Her   Yes; what other answer is possible?

Soc   Then in a proposition there is a true and false?

Her   Certainly.

Soc   But is a proposition true as a whole only, and are the parts untrue?

Her   No; the parts are true as well as the whole.

Soc   Would you say the large parts and not the smaller ones, or every part?

Her   I should say that every part is true.

Soc   Is a proposition resolvable into any part smaller than a name?

Her   No; that is the smallest.

Soc   Then the name is a part of the true proposition?

Her   Yes.

Soc   Yes, and a true part, as you say.

Her   Yes.

Soc   And is not the part of a falsehood also a falsehood?

Her   Yes.

Soc   Then, if propositions may be true and false, names may be true and false?

Her   So we must infer.

Soc   And the name of anything is that which any one affirms to be the name?

Her   Yes.

Soc   And will there be so many names of each thing as everybody says that there are? and will they be true names at the time of uttering them?

Her   Yes, Socrates, I can conceive no correctness of names other than this; you give one name, and I another; and in different cities and countries there are different names for the same things; Hellenes differ from barbarians in their use of names, and the several Hellenic tribes from one another.

Soc   But would you say, Hermogenes, that the things differ as the names differ? and are they relative to individuals, as Protagoras tells us? For he says that man is the measure of all things, and that things are to me as they appear to me, and that they are to you as they appear to you. Do you agree with him, or would you say that things have a permanent essence of their own?

Her   There have been times, Socrates, when I have been driven in my perplexity to take refuge with Protagoras; not that I agree with him at all.

Soc   What! have you even been driven to admit that there was no such thing as a bad man?

Her   No, indeed; but I have often had reason to think that there are very bad men, and a good many of them.

Soc   Well, and have you ever found any very good ones?

Her   Not many.

Soc   Still you have found them?

Her   Yes.

Soc   And would you hold that the very good were the very wise, and the very evil very foolish? Would that be your view?

Her   It would.

Soc   But if Protagoras is right, and the truth is that things are as they appear to any one, how can some of us be wise and some of us foolish?

Her   Impossible.

Soc   And if, on the other hand, wisdom and folly are really distinguishable, you will allow, I think, that the assertion of Protagoras can hardly be correct. For if what appears to each man is true to him, one man cannot in reality be wiser than another.

Her   He cannot.

Soc   Nor will you be disposed to say with Euthydemus, that all things equally belong to all men at the same moment and always; for neither on his view can there be some good and others bad, if virtue and vice are always equally to be attributed to all.

Her   There cannot.

Soc   But if neither is right, and things are not relative to individuals, and all things do not equally belong to all at the same moment and always, they must be supposed to have their own proper and permanent essence; they are not in relation to us, or influenced by us, fluctuating according to our fancy, but they are independent, and maintain to their own essence the relation prescribed by nature.

Her   I think, Socrates, that you have said the truth.

Soc   Does what I am saying apply only to the things themselves, or equally to the actions which proceed from them? Are not actions also a class of being?

Her   Yes, the actions are real as well as the things.

Soc   Then the actions also are done according to their proper nature, and not according to our opinion of them? In cutting, for example, we do not cut as we please, and with any chance instrument; but we cut with the proper instrument only, and according to the natural process of cutting; and the natural process is right and will succeed, but any other will fail and be of no use at all.

Her   I should say that the natural way is the right way.

Soc   Again, in burning, not every way is the right way; but the right way is the natural way, and the right instrument the natural instrument.

Her   True.

Soc   And this holds good of all actions?

Her   Yes.

Soc   And speech is a kind of action?

Her   True.

Soc   And will a man speak correctly who speaks as he pleases? Will not the successful speaker rather be he who speaks in the natural way of speaking, and as things ought to be spoken, and with the natural instrument? Any other mode of speaking will result in error and failure.

Her   I quite agree with you.

Soc   And is not naming a part of speaking? for in giving names men speak.

Her   That is true.

Soc   And if speaking is a sort of action and has a relation to acts, is not naming also a sort of action?

Her   True.

Soc   And we saw that actions were not relative to ourselves, but had a special nature of their own?

Her   Precisely.

Soc   Then the argument would lead us to infer that names ought to be given according to a natural process, and with a proper instrument, and not at our pleasure: in this and no other way shall we name with success.

Her   I agree.

Soc   But again, that which has to be cut has to be cut with something?

Her   Yes.

Soc   And that which has to be woven or pierced has to be woven or pierced with something?

Her   Certainly.

Soc   And that which has to be named has to be named with something?

Her   True.

Soc   What is that with which we pierce?

Her   An awl.

Soc   And with which we weave?

Her   A shuttle.

Soc   And with which we name?

Her   A name.

Soc   Very good: then a name is an instrument?

Her   Certainly.

Soc   Suppose that I ask, "What sort of instrument is a shuttle?" And you answer, "A weaving instrument."

Her   Well.

Soc   And I ask again, "What do we do when we weave?"— The answer is, that we separate or disengage the warp from the woof.

Her   Very true.

Soc   And may not a similar description be given of an awl, and of instruments in general?

Her   To be sure.

Soc   And now suppose that I ask a similar question about names: will you answer me? Regarding the name as an instrument, what do we do when we name?

Her   I cannot say.

Soc   Do we not give information to one another, and distinguish things according to their natures?

Her   Certainly we do.

Soc   Then a name is an instrument of teaching and of distinguishing natures, as the shuttle is of distinguishing the threads of the web.

Her   Yes.

Soc   And the shuttle is the instrument of the weaver?

Her   Assuredly.

Soc   Then the weaver will use the shuttle well—and well means like a weaver? and the teacher will use the name well—and well means like a teacher?

Her   Yes.

Soc   And when the weaver uses the shuttle, whose work will he be using well?

Her   That of the carpenter.

Soc   And is every man a carpenter, or the skilled only?

Her   Only the skilled.

Soc   And when the piercer uses the awl, whose work will he be using well?

Her   That of the smith.

Soc   And is every man a smith, or only the skilled?

Her   The skilled only.

Soc   And when the teacher uses the name, whose work will he be using?

Her   There again I am puzzled.

Soc   Cannot you at least say who gives us the names which we use?

Her   Indeed I cannot.

Soc   Does not the law seem to you to give us them?

Her   Yes, I suppose so.

Soc   Then the teacher, when he gives us a name, uses the work of the legislator?

Her   I agree.

Soc   And is every man a legislator, or the skilled only?

Her   The skilled only.

Soc   Then, Hermogenes, not every man is able to give a name, but only a maker of names; and this is the legislator, who of all skilled artisans in the world is the rarest.

Her   True.

Soc   And how does the legislator make names? and to what does he look? Consider this in the light of the previous instances: to what does the carpenter look in making the shuttle? Does he not look to that which is naturally fitted to act as a shuttle?

Her   Certainly.

Soc   And suppose the shuttle to be broken in making, will he make another, looking to the broken one? or will he look to the form according to which he made the other?

Her   To the latter, I should imagine.

Soc   Might not that he justly called the true or ideal shuttle?

Her   I think so.

Soc   And whatever shuttles are wanted, for the manufacture of garments, thin or thick, of flaxen, woollen, or other material, ought all of them to have the true form of the shuttle; and whatever is the shuttle best adapted to each kind of work, that ought to be the form which the maker produces in each case.

Her   Yes.

Soc   And the same holds of other instruments: when a man has discovered the instrument which is naturally adapted to each work, he must express this natural form, and not others which he fancies, in the material, whatever it may be, which he employs; for example, he ought to know how to put into iron the forms of awls adapted by nature to their several uses?

Her   Certainly.

Soc   And how to put into wood forms of shuttles adapted by nature to their uses?

Her   True.

Soc   For the several forms of shuttles naturally answer to the several kinds of webs; and this is true of instruments in general.

Her   Yes.

Soc   Then, as to names: ought not our legislator also to know how to put the true natural name of each thing into sounds and syllables, and to make and give all names with a view to the ideal name, if he is to be a namer in any true sense? And we must remember that different legislators will not use the same syllables. For neither does every smith, although he may be making the same instrument for the same purpose, make them all of the same iron. The form must be the same, but the material may vary, and still the instrument may be equally good of whatever iron made, whether in Hellas or in a foreign country;—there is no difference.

Her   Very true.

Soc   And the legislator, whether he be Hellene or barbarian, is not therefore to be deemed by you a worse legislator, provided he gives the true and proper form of the name in whatever syllables; this or that country makes no matter.

Her   Quite true.

Soc   But who then is to determine whether the proper form is given to the shuttle, whatever sort of wood may be used? the carpenter who makes, or the weaver who is to use them?

Her   I should say, he who is to use them, Socrates.

Soc   And who uses the work of the lyre-maker? Will not he be the man who knows how to direct what is being done, and who will know also whether the work is being well done or not?

Her   Certainly.

Soc   And who is he?

Her   The player of the lyre.

Soc   And who will direct the shipwright?

Her   The pilot.

Soc   And who will be best able to direct the legislator in his work, and will know whether the work is well done, in this or any other country? Will not the user be the man?

Her   Yes.

Soc   And this is he who knows how to ask questions?

Her   Yes.

Soc   And how to answer them?

Her   Yes.

Soc   And him who knows how to ask and answer you would call a dialectician?

Her   Yes; that would be his name.

Soc   Then the work of the carpenter is to make a rudder, and the pilot has to direct him, if the rudder is to be well made.

Her   True.

Soc   And the work of the legislator is to give names, and the dialectician must be his director if the names are to be rightly given?

Her   That is true.

Soc   Then, Hermogenes, I should say that this giving of names can be no such light matter as you fancy, or the work of light or chance persons; and Cratylus is right in saying that things have names by nature, and that not every man is an artificer of names, but he only who looks to the name which each thing by nature has, and is able to express the true forms of things in letters and syllables.

Her   I cannot answer you, Socrates; but I find a difficulty in changing my opinion all in a moment, and I think that I should be more readily persuaded, if you would show me what this is which you term the natural fitness of names.

Soc   My good Hermogenes, I have none to show. Was I not telling you just now (but you have forgotten), that I knew nothing, and proposing to share the enquiry with you? But now that you and I have talked over the matter, a step has been gained; for we have discovered that names have by nature a truth, and that not every man knows how to give a thing a name.

Her   Very good.

Soc   And what is the nature of this truth or correctness of names? That, if you care to know, is the next question.

Her   Certainly, I care to know.

Soc   Then reflect.

Her   How shall I reflect?

Soc   The true way is to have the assistance of those who know, and you must pay them well both in money and in thanks; these are the Sophists, of whom your brother, Callias, has—rather dearly—bought the reputation of wisdom. But you have not yet come into your inheritance, and therefore you had better go to him, and beg and entreat him to tell you what he has learnt from Protagoras about the fitness of names.

Her   But how inconsistent should I be, if, whilst repudiating Protagoras and his truth,[1] I were to attach any value to what he and his book affirm!

Soc   Then if you despise him, you must learn of Homer and the poets.

Her   And where does Homer say anything about names, and what does he say?

[1] "Truth" was the title of the book of Protagoras; cp. Theaet. 161 E.

Soc   He often speaks of them; notably and nobly in the places where he distinguishes the different names which Gods and men give to the same things. Does he not in these passages make a remarkable statement about the correctness of names? For the Gods must clearly be supposed to call things by their right and natural names; do you not think so?

Her   Why, of course they call them rightly, if they call them at all. But to what are you referring?

Soc   Do you not know what he says about the river in Troy who had a single combat with Hephaestus?

"Whom," as he says, "the Gods call Xanthus, and men call Scamander."

Her   I remember.

Soc   Well, and about this river—to know that he ought to be called Xanthus and not Scamander—is not that a solemn lesson? Or about the bird which, as he says,

"The Gods call Chalcis, and men Cymindis:"

to be taught how much more correct the name Chalcis is than the name Cymindis,—do you deem that a light matter? Or about Batieia and Myrina? [2] And there are many other observations of the same kind in Homer and other poets. Now, I think that this is beyond the understanding of you and me; but the names of Scamandrius and Astyanax, which he affirms to have been the names of Hector's son, are more within the range of human faculties, as I am disposed to think; and what the poet means by correctness may be more readily apprehended in that instance: you will remember I dare say the lines to which I refer.[3]

Her   I do.

Soc   Let me ask you, then, which did Homer think the more correct of the names given to Hector's son—Astyanax or Scamandrius?

Her   I do not know.

Soc   How would you answer, if you were asked whether the wise or the unwise are more likely to give correct names?

Her   I should say the wise, of course.

Soc   And are the men or the women of a city, taken as a class, the wiser?

Her   I should say, the men.

[2] Cp. Il. ii. 813, 814:—
"The hill which men call Batieia and the immortals the tomb of the sportive Myrina."

[3] Il. vi. 402.

Soc   And Homer, as you know, says that the Trojan men called him Astyanax (king of the city); but if the men called him Astyanax, the other name of Scamandrius could only have been given to him by the women.

Her   That may be inferred.

Soc   And must not Homer have imagined the Trojans to be wiser than their wives?

Her   To be sure.

Soc   Then he must have thought Astyanax to be a more correct name for the boy than Scamandrius?

Her   Clearly.

Soc   And what is the reason of this? Let us consider:—does he not himself suggest a very good reason, when he says,

"For he alone defended their city and long walls"?

This appears to be a good reason for calling the son of the saviour king of the city which his father was saving, as Homer observes.

Her   I see.

Soc   Why, Hermogenes, I do not as yet see myself; and do you?

Her   No, indeed; not I.

Soc   But tell me, friend, did not Homer himself also give Hector his name?

Her   What of that?

Soc   The name appears to me to be very nearly the same as the name of Astyanax—both are Hellenic; and a king (ἄναξ) and a holder (ἕκτωρ) have nearly the same meaning, and are both descriptive of a king; for a man is clearly the holder of that of which he is king; he rules, and owns, and holds it. But, perhaps, you may think that I am talking nonsense; and indeed I believe that I myself did not know what I meant when I imagined that I had found some indication of the opinion of Homer about the correctness of names.

Her   I assure you that I think otherwise, and I believe you to be on the right track.

Soc   There is reason, I think, in calling the lion's whelp a lion, and the foal of a horse a horse; I am speaking only of the ordinary course of nature, when an animal produces after his kind,[4] and not of extraordinary births;—if contrary to nature a horse have a calf, then I should not call that a foal but a calf; nor do I call any inhuman birth a man, but only a natural birth. And the same may be said of trees and other things. Do you agree with me?

---

[4] Reading οὖ ἄν.

Her   Yes, I agree.

Soc   Very good. But you had better watch me and see that I do not play tricks with you. For on the same principle the son of a king is to be called a king. And whether the syllables of the name are the same or not the same, makes no difference, provided the meaning is retained; nor does the addition or subtraction of a letter make any difference so long as the essence of the thing remains in possession of the name and appears in it.

Her   What do you mean?

Soc   A very simple matter. I may illustrate my meaning by the names of letters, which you know are not the same as the letters themselves with the exception of the four, ϵ, υ, o, ω; the names of the rest, whether vowels or consonants, are made up of other letters which we add to them; but so long as we introduce the meaning, and there can be no mistake, the name of the letter is quite correct. Take, for example, the letter *beta*—the addition of η, τ, a, gives no offence, and does not prevent the whole name from having the value which the legislator intended—so well did he know how to give the letters names.

Her   I believe you are right.

Soc   And may not the same be said of a king? a king will often be the son of a king, the good son or the noble son of a good or noble sire; and similarly the offspring of every kind, in the regular course of nature, is like the parent, and therefore has the same name. Yet the syllables may be disguised until they appear different to the ignorant person, and he may not recognize them, although they are the same, just as any one of us would not recognize the same drugs under different disguises of colour and smell, although to the physician, who regards the power of them, they are the same, and he is not put out by the addition; and in like manner the etymologist is not put out by the addition or transposition or subtraction of a letter or two, or indeed by the change of all the letters, for this need not interfere with the meaning. As was just now said, the names of Hector and Astyanax have only one letter alike, which is the τ, and yet they have the same meaning. And how little in common with the letters of their names has Archepolis (ruler of the city)—and yet the meaning is the same. And there are many other names which just mean "king." Again, there are several names for a general, as, for example, Agis (leader) and Polemarchus (chief in war) and Eupolemus (good warrior); and others which denote a physician, as Iatrocles (famous healer) and Acesimbrotus (curer of mortals); and there are many others which might be cited, differing in their syllables and letters, but having the same meaning. Would you not say so?

Her   Yes.

Soc   The same names, then, ought to be assigned to those who follow in the course of nature?

Her   Yes.

Soc   And what of those who follow out of the course of nature, and are prodigies? for example, when a good and religious man has an irreligious son, he ought to bear the name not of his father, but of the class to which he belongs, just as in the case which was before supposed of a horse foaling a calf.

Her   Quite true.

Soc   Then the irreligious son of a religious father should be called irreligious?

Her   Certainly.

Soc   He should not be called Theophilus (beloved of God) or Mnesitheus (mindful of God), or any of these names: if names are correctly given, his should have an opposite meaning.

Her   Certainly, Socrates.

Soc   Again, Hermogenes, there is Orestes (the man of the mountains) who appears to be rightly called; whether chance gave the name, or perhaps some poet who meant to express the brutality and fierceness and mountain wildness of his hero's nature.

Her   That is very likely, Socrates.

Soc   And his father's name is also according to nature.

Her   Clearly.

Soc   Yes, for as his name, so also is his nature; Agamemnon (admirable for remaining) is one who is patient and persevering in the accomplishment of his resolves, and by his virtue crowns them; and his continuance at Troy with all the vast army is a proof of that admirable endurance in him which is signified by the name Agamemnon.[5] I also think that Atreus is rightly called; for his murder of Chrysippus and his exceeding cruelty to Thyestes are damaging and destructive to his reputation—the name is a little altered and disguised so as not to be intelligible to every one, but to the etymologist there is no difficulty in seeing the meaning, for whether you think of him as ἀτειρὴς the stubborn, or as ἄτρεστος the fearless, or as ἀτηρὸς the destructive one, the name is perfectly correct in every point of view. And I think that Pelops is also named appropriately; for, as the name implies, he is rightly called Pelops who sees what is near only (ὁ τὰ πέλας ὁρῶν).

Her   How so?

Soc   Because, according to the tradition, he had no forethought or foresight of all the evil which the murder of Myrtilus would entail upon his whole race in remote ages; he saw only what was at hand and immediate,—or in other words, πέλας (near), in his eagerness to win

---

[5] Ἀγαμέμνων = ἀγαστὸς μένων.

Hippodamia by all means for his bride. Every one would agree that the name of Tantalus is rightly given and in accordance with nature, if the traditions about him are true.

Her   And what are the traditions?

Soc   Many terrible misfortunes are said to have happened to him in his life—last of all, came the utter ruin of his country; and after his death he had the stone suspended (ταλαντεία) over his head in the world below—all this agrees wonderfully well with his name. You might imagine that some person who wanted to call him ταλάντατος (the most weighed down by misfortune), disguised the name by altering it into Tantalus; and into this form, by some accident of tradition, it has actually been transmuted. The name of Zeus, who is his alleged father, has also an excellent meaning, although hard to be understood, because really like a sentence, which is divided into two parts, for some call him Zena (Ζῆνα), and use the one half, and others who use the other half call him Dia (Δία); the two together signify the nature of the God, and the business of a name, as we were saying, is to express the nature. For there is none who is more the author of life to us and to all, than the lord and king of all. Wherefore we are right in calling him Zena and Dia, which are one name, although divided, meaning the God through whom all creatures always have life (δι᾽ ὃν ζῆν ἀεὶ πᾶσι τοῖς ζῶσιν ὑπάρχει). There is an irreverence, at first sight, in calling him son of Cronos (who is a proverb for stupidity), and we might rather expect Zeus to be the child of a mighty intellect. Which is the fact; for this is the meaning of his father's name: Κρόνος quasi Κόρος (κορέω, to sweep), not in the sense of a youth, but signifying τὸ καθαρὸν καὶ ἀκήρατον τοῦ νοῦ, the pure and garnished mind (sc. ἀπὸ τοῦ κορεῖν). He, as we are informed by tradition, was begotten of Uranus, rightly so called (ἀπὸ τοῦ ὁρᾶν τὰ ἄνω) from looking upwards; which, as philosophers tell us, is the way to have a pure mind, and the name Uranus is therefore correct. If I could remember the genealogy of Hesiod, I would have gone on and tried more conclusions of the same sort on the remoter ancestors of the Gods,—then I might have seen whether this wisdom which has come to me all in an instant, I know not whence, will or will not hold good to the end.

Her   You seem to me, Socrates, to be quite like a prophet newly inspired, and to be uttering oracles.

Soc   Yes, Hermogenes, and I believe that I caught the inspiration from the great Euthyphro of the Prospaltian deme, who gave me a long lecture which commenced at dawn: he talked and I listened, and his wisdom and enchanting ravishment has not only filled my ears but taken possession of my soul, and to-day I shall let his superhuman power work and finish the investigation of names—that will be the way; but to-morrow, if you are so disposed, we will conjure him away, and make a purgation of him, if we can only find some priest or sophist who is skilled in purifications of this sort.

Her   With all my heart; for I am very curious to hear the rest of the enquiry about names.

Soc   Then let us proceed; and where would you have us begin, now that we have got a sort of outline of the enquiry? Are there any names which witness of themselves that they are not given arbitrarily, but have a natural fitness? The names of heroes and of men in general are apt to be deceptive because they are often called after ancestors with whose names, as we were saying, they may have no business; or they are the expression of a wish like Eutychides (the son of good fortune), or Sosias (the Saviour), or Theophilus (the beloved of God), and others. But I think that we had better leave these, for there will be more chance of finding correctness in the names of immutable essences;—there ought to have been more care taken about them when they were named, and perhaps there may have been some more than human power at work occasionally in giving them names.

Her   I think so, Socrates.

Soc   Ought we not to begin with the consideration of the Gods, and show that they are rightly named Gods?

Her   Yes, that will be well.

Soc   My notion would be something of this sort:—I suspect that the sun, moon, earth, stars, and heaven, which are still the Gods of many barbarians, were the only Gods known to the aboriginal Hellenes. Seeing that they were always moving and running, from their running nature they were called Gods or runners (θεούς, θέοντας); and when men became acquainted with the other Gods, they proceeded to apply the same name to them all. Do you think that likely?

Her   I think it very likely indeed.

Soc   What shall follow the Gods?

Her   Must not demons and heroes and men come next?

Soc   Demons! And what do you consider to be the meaning of this word? Tell me if my view is right.

Her   Let me hear.

Soc   You know how Hesiod uses the word?

Her   I do not.

Soc   Do you not remember that he speaks of a golden race of men who came first?

Her   Yes, I do.

Soc   He says of them—

"But now that fate has closed over this race
They are holy demons upon the earth,
Beneficent, averters of ills, guardians of mortal men." [6]

[6] Hesiod. Works and Days, 120ff.

Her   What is the inference?

Soc   What is the inference! Why, I suppose that he means by the golden men, not men literally made of gold, but good and noble; and I am convinced of this, because he further says that we are the iron race.

Her   That is true.

Soc   And do you not suppose that good men of our own day would by him be said to be of golden race?

Her   Very likely.

Soc   And are not the good wise?

Her   Yes, they are wise.

Soc   And therefore I have the most entire conviction that he called them demons, because they were δαήμονες (knowing or wise), and in our older Attic dialect the word itself occurs. Now he and other poets say truly, that when a good man dies he has honour and a mighty portion among the dead, and becomes a demon; which is a name given to him signifying wisdom. And I say too, that every wise man who happens to be a good man is more than human (δαιμόνιον) both in life and death, and is rightly called a demon.

Her   Then I rather think that I am of one mind with you; but what is the meaning of the word "hero"? (ἥρως, in the old writing ἔρως.)

Soc   I think that there is no difficulty in explaining, for the name is not much altered, and signifies that they were born of love.

Her   What do you mean?

Soc   Do you not know that the heroes are demigods?

Her   What then?

Soc   All of them sprang either from the love of a God for a mortal woman, or of a mortal man for a Goddess; think of the word in the old Attic, and you will see better that the name heros is only a slight alteration of Eros, from whom the heroes sprang: either this is the meaning, or, if not this, then they must have been skillful as rhetoricians and dialecticians, and able to put the question (ἐρωτᾶν), for εἴρειν is equivalent to λέγειν. And therefore, as I was saying, in the Attic dialect the heroes turn out to be rhetoricians and questioners. All this is easy enough; the noble breed of heroes are a tribe of sophists and rhetors. But can you tell me why men are called ἄνθρωποι?—that is more difficult.

Her   No, I cannot; and I would not try even if I could, because I think that you are the more likely to succeed.

Soc   That is to say, you trust to the inspiration of Euthyphro.

Her   Of course.

Soc   Your faith is not vain; for at this very moment a new and ingenious thought strikes me, and, if I am not careful, before to-morrow's dawn I shall be wiser than I ought to be. Now, attend to me;

and first, remember that we often put in and pull out letters in words, and give names as we please and change the accents. Take, for example, the word Διὶ φίλος; in order to convert this from a sentence into a noun, we omit one of the iotas and sound the middle syllable grave instead of acute; as, on the other hand, letters are sometimes inserted in words instead of being omitted, and the acute takes the place of the grave.

Her   That is true.

Soc   The name ἄνθρωπος, which was once a sentence, and is now a noun, appears to be a case just of this sort, for one letter, which is the a, has been omitted, and the acute on the last syllable has been changed to a grave.

Her   What do you mean?

Soc   I mean to say that the word "man" implies that other animals never examine, or consider, or look up at what they see, but that man not only sees (ὄπωπε) but considers and looks up at that which he sees, and hence he alone of all animals is rightly called ἄνθρωπος, meaning ἀναθρῶν ἃ ὄπωπεν.

Her   May I ask you to examine another word about which I am curious?

Soc   Certainly.

Her   I will take that which appears to me to follow next in order. You know the distinction of soul and body?

Soc   Of course.

Her   Let us endeavour to analyze them like the previous words.

Soc   You want me first of all to examine the natural fitness of the word ψυχὴ (soul), and then of the word σῶμα (body)?

Her   Yes.

Soc   If I am to say what occurs to me at the moment, I should imagine that those who first used the name ψυχὴ meant to express that the soul when in the body is the source of life, and gives the power of breath and revival (ἀναψῦχον), and when this reviving power fails then the body perishes and dies, and this, if I am not mistaken, they called psyche. But please stay a moment; I fancy that I can discover something which will be more acceptable to the disciples of Euthyphro, for I am afraid that they will scorn this explanation. What do you say to another?

Her   Let me hear.

Soc   What is that which holds and carries and gives life and motion to the entire nature of the body? What else but the soul?

Her   Just that.

Soc   And do you not believe with Anaxagoras, that mind or soul is the ordering and containing principle of all things?

Her   Yes; I do.

Soc   Then you may well call that power φυσέχη which carries and holds nature (ἤ φύσιν ὀχεῖ καὶ ἔχει), and this may be refined away into ψυχή.

Her   Certainly; and this derivation is, I think, more scientific than the other.

Soc   It is so; but I cannot help laughing, if I am to suppose that this was the true meaning of the name.

Her   But what shall we say of the next word?

Soc   You mean σῶμα (the body).

Her   Yes.

Soc   That may be variously interpreted; and yet more variously if a little permutation is allowed. For some say that the body is the grave (σῆμα) of the soul which may be thought to be buried in our present life; or again the index of the soul, because the soul gives indications to (σημαίνει) the body; probably the Orphic poets were the inventors of the name, and they were under the impression that the soul is suffering the punishment of sin, and that the body is an enclosure or prison in which the soul is incarcerated, kept safe (σῶμα, σώζηται), as the name σῶμα implies, until the penalty is paid; according to this view, not even a letter of the word need be changed.

Her   I think, Socrates, that we have said enough of this class of words. But have we any more explanations of the names of the Gods, like that which you were giving to Zeus? I should like to know whether any similar principle of correctness is to be applied to them.

Soc   Yes, indeed, Hermogenes; and there is one excellent principle which, as men of sense, we must acknowledge,—that of the Gods we know nothing, either of their natures or of the names which they give themselves; but we are sure that the names by which they call themselves, whatever they may be, are true. And this is the best of all principles; and the next best is to say, as in prayers, that we will call them by any sort or kind of names or patronymics which they like, because we do not know of any other. That also, I think, is a very good custom, and one which I should much wish to observe. Let us, then, if you please, in the first place announce to them that we are not enquiring about them; we do not presume that we are able to do so; but we are enquiring about the meaning of men in giving them these names,—in this there can be small blame.

Her   I think, Socrates, that you are quite right, and I would like to do as you say.

Soc   Shall we begin, then, with Hestia, according to custom?

Her   Yes, that will be very proper.

Soc   What may we suppose him to have meant who gave the name Hestia?

Her   That is another and certainly a most difficult question.

Soc   My dear Hermogenes, the first imposers of names must surely have been considerable persons; they were philosophers, and had a good deal to say.

Her   Well, and what of them?

Soc   They are the men to whom I should attribute the imposition of names. Even in foreign names, if you analyze them, a meaning is still discernible. For example, that which we term οὐσία is by some called ἐσία, and by others again ὠσία. Now that the essence of things should be called ἐστία, which is akin to the first of these (ἐσία = ἐστία), is rational enough. And there is reason in the Athenians calling that ἐστία which participates in οὐσία. For in ancient times we too seem to have said ἐσία for οὐσία, and this you may note to have been the idea of those who appointed that sacrifices should be first offered to ἐστία, which was natural enough if they meant that ἐστία was the essence of things. Those again who read ὠσία seem to have inclined to the opinion of Heracleitus, that all things flow and nothing stands; with them the pushing principle (ὠθοῦν) is the cause and ruling power of all things, and is therefore rightly called ὠσία. Enough of this, which is all that we who know nothing can affirm. Next in order after Hestia we ought to consider Rhea and Cronos, although the name of Cronos has been already discussed. But I dare say that I am talking great nonsense.

Her   Why, Socrates?

Soc   My good friend, I have discovered a hive of wisdom.

Her   Of what nature?

Soc   Well, rather ridiculous, and yet plausible.

Her   How plausible?

Soc   I fancy to myself Heracleitus repeating wise traditions of antiquity as old as the days of Cronos and Rhea, and of which Homer also spoke.

Her   How do you mean?

Soc   Heracleitus is supposed to say that all things are in motion and nothing at rest; he compares them to the stream of a river, and says that you cannot go into the same water twice.

Her   That is true.

Soc   Well, then, how can we avoid inferring that he who gave the names of Cronos and Rhea to the ancestors of the Gods, agreed pretty much in the doctrine of Heracleitus? Is the giving of the names of streams to both of them purely accidental? Compare the line in which Homer, and, as I believe, Hesiod also, tells of

"Ocean, the origin of Gods, and mother Tethys."

And again, Orpheus says, that

"The fair river of Ocean was the first to marry, and he espoused his sister Tethys, who was his mother's daughter." [7]

You see that this is a remarkable coincidence, and all in the direction of Heracleitus.

Her I think that there is something in what you say, Socrates; but I do not understand the meaning of the name Tethys.

Soc Well, that is almost self-explained, being only the name of a spring, a little disguised; for that which is strained and filtered (διαττώμενον, ἠθούμενον) may be likened to a spring, and the name Tethys is made up of these two words.

Her The idea is ingenious, Socrates.

Soc To be sure. But what comes next?—of Zeus we have spoken.

Her Yes.

Soc Then let us next take his two brothers, Poseidon and Pluto, whether the latter is called by that or by his other name.

Her By all means.

Soc Poseidon is ποσίδεσμος, the chain of the feet; the original inventor of the name had been stopped by the watery element in his walks, and not allowed to go on, and therefore he called the ruler of this element Poseidon; the ε was probably inserted as an ornament. Yet, perhaps, not so; but the name may have been originally written with a double λ and not with a σ, meaning that the God knew many things (πολλὰ εἰδώς). And perhaps also he being the shaker of the earth, has been named from shaking (σείειν), and then π and δ have been added. Pluto gives wealth (πλοῦτος), and his name means the giver of wealth, which comes out of the earth beneath. People in general appear to imagine that the term Hades is connected with the invisible (ἀειδὲς); and so they are led by their fears to call the God Pluto instead.

Her And what is the true derivation?

Soc In spite of the mistakes which are made about the power of this deity, and the foolish fears which people have of him, such as the fear of always being with him after death, and of the soul denuded of the body going to him,[8] my belief is that all is quite consistent, and that the office and name of the God really correspond.

Her Why, how is that?

Soc I will tell you my own opinion; but first, I should like to ask you which chain does any animal feel to be the stronger? and which confines him more to the same spot,—desire or necessity?

Her Desire, Socrates, is stronger far.

---

[7] Il. xiv. 201, 302:—the line is not found in the extant works of Hesiod.

[8] Cp. Rep. 3. 386, 387.

Soc   And do you not think that many a one would escape from Hades, if he did not bind those who depart to him by the strongest of chains?

Her   Assuredly they would.

Soc   And if by the greatest of chains, then by some desire, as I should certainly infer, and not by necessity?

Her   That is clear.

Soc   And there are many desires?

Her   Yes.

Soc   And therefore by the greatest desire, if the chain is to be the greatest?

Her   Yes.

Soc   And is any desire stronger than the thought that you will be made better by associating with another?

Her   Certainly not.

Soc   And is not that the reason, Hermogenes, why no one, who has been to him, is willing to come back to us? Even the Sirens, like all the rest of the world, have been laid under his spells. Such a charm, as I imagine, is the God able to infuse into his words. And, according to this view, he is the perfect and accomplished Sophist, and the great benefactor of the inhabitants of the other world; and even to us who are upon earth he sends from below exceeding blessings. For he has much more than he wants down there; wherefore he is called Pluto (or the rich). Note also, that he will have nothing to do with men while they are in the body, but only when the soul is liberated from the desires and evils of the body. Now there is a great deal of philosophy and reflection in that; for in their liberated state he can bind them with the desire of virtue, but while they are flustered and maddened by the body, not even father Cronos himself would suffice to keep them with him in his own far-famed chains.

Her   There is a deal of truth in what you say.

Soc   Yes, Hermogenes, and the legislator called him Hades, not from the unseen (ἀειδὲς)—far otherwise, but from his knowledge (εἰδέναι) of all noble things.

Her   Very good; and what do we say of Demeter, and Herè, and Apollo, and Athene, and Hephaestus, and Ares, and the other deities?

Soc   Demeter is ἡ διδοῦσα μήτηρ, who gives food like a mother; Herè is the lovely one (ἐρατὴ)—for Zeus, according to tradition, loved and married her; possibly also the name may have been given when the legislator was thinking of the heavens, and may be only a disguise of the air (ἀὴρ), putting the end in the place of the beginning. You will recognize the truth of this if you repeat the letters of Herè several times over. People dread the name of Pherephatta as they dread the name of Apollo,

—and with as little reason; the fear, if I am not mistaken, only arises from their ignorance of the nature of names. But they go changing the name into Phersephone, and they are terrified at this; whereas the new name means only that the Goddess is wise (σοφή); for seeing that all things in the world are in motion (φερομένων), that principle which embraces and touches and is able to follow them, is wisdom. And therefore the Goddess may be truly called Pherepaphe (Φερεπάφα), or some name like it, because she touches that which is in motion (τοῦ Φερομένου ἐφαπτομένη), herein showing her wisdom. And Hades, who is wise, consorts with her, because she is wise. They alter her name into Pherephatta now-a-days, because the present generation care for euphony more than truth. There is the other name, Apollo, which, as I was saying, is generally supposed to have some terrible significance. Have you remarked this fact?

Her   To be sure I have, and what you say is true.

Soc   But the name, in my opinion, is really most expressive of the power of the God.

Her   How so?

Soc   I will endeavor to explain, for I do not believe that any single name could have been better adapted to express the attributes of the God, embracing and in a manner signifying all four of them,—music, and prophecy, and medicine, and archery.

Her   That must be a strange name, and I should like to hear the explanation.

Soc   Say rather an harmonious name, as beseems the God of Harmony. In the first place, the purgations and purifications which doctors and diviners use, and their fumigations with drugs magical or medicinal, as well as their washings and lustral sprinklings, have all one and the same object, which is to make a man pure both in body and soul.

Her   Very true.

Soc   And is not Apollo the purifier, and the washer, and the absolver from all impurities?

Her   Very true.

Soc   Then in reference to his ablutions and absolutions, as being the physician who orders them, he may be rightly called Ἀπολούων (purifier); or in respect of his powers of divination, and his truth and sincerity, which is the same as truth, he may be most fitly called Ἀπλῶς, from ἁπλοῦς (sincere), as in the Thessalian dialect, for all the Thessalians call him Ἀπλός; also he is ἀεὶ βάλλων (always shooting), because he is a master archer who never misses; or again, the name may refer to his musical attributes, and then, as in ἀκόλουθος, and ἄκοιτις, and in many other words the a is supposed to mean "together," so the meaning of the name Apollo will be "moving together," whether in the poles of heaven as they are called, or in the harmony of song, which is termed concord, because he moves all together by an harmonious power, as astronomers and musicians ingeniously declare. And he is the God who presides over harmony, and makes all things move together, both among Gods and among men. And as in the words ἀκόλουθος and ἄκοιτις the α is substituted for an ο, so the name 'Απόλλων is equivalent to ὁμοπολῶν; only the second λ is added in order to avoid the ill-omened sound of destruction (ἀπολῶν). Now the suspicion of this destructive power still haunts the minds of some who do not consider the true value of the name, which, as I was saying just now,[9] has reference to all the powers of the God, who is the single one, the everdarting, the purifier, the mover together (ἁπλοῦς, ἀεὶ βάλλων, ἀπολούων, ὁμοπολῶν). The name of the Muses and of music would seem to be derived from their making philosophical enquiries (μῶσθαι); and Leto is called by this name, because she is such a gentle Goddess, and so willing (ἐθελήμων) to grant our requests; or her name may be Letho, as she is often called by strangers—they seem to imply by it her amiability, and her smooth and easy-going way of behaving. Artemis is named from her healthy (ἀρτεμὴς), well-ordered nature, and because of her love of virginity, perhaps because she is a proficient in virtue (ἀρετὴ), and perhaps also as hating intercourse of the sexes (τὸν ἄροτον μισήσασα). He who gave the Goddess her name may have had any or all of these reasons.

Her   What is the meaning of Dionysus and Aphrodite?

Soc   Son of Hipponicus, you ask a solemn question; there is a serious and also a facetious explanation of both these names; the serious explanation is not to be had from me, but there is no objection to your hearing the facetious one; for the Gods too love a joke. Διόνυσος is simply διδοὺς οἶνον (giver of wine), Διδοίννσος, as he might be called in fun,— and οἶνος is properly οἰόνους, because wine makes those who drink, think (οἴεσθαι) that they have a mind (νοῦν) when they have none. The derivation of Aphrodite, born of the foam (ἀφρὸς), may be fairly accepted on the authority of Hesiod.

Her   Still there remains Athene, whom you, Socrates, as an Athenian, will surely not forget; there are also Hephaestus and Ares.

Soc   I am not likely to forget them.

Her   No, indeed.

Soc   There is no difficulty in explaining the other appellation of Athene.

Her   What other appellation?

Soc   We call her Pallas.

----

[9] Omitting πολύ.

Her　　To be sure.

Soc　　And we cannot be wrong in supposing that this is derived from armed dances. For the elevation of oneself or anything else
above the earth, or by the use of the hands, we call shaking (πάλλειν),
or dancing.

Her　　That is quite true.

Soc　　Then that is the explanation of the name Pallas?

Her　　Yes; but what do you say of the other name?

Soc　　Athene?

Her　　Yes.

Soc　　That is a graver matter, and there, my friend, the modern
interpreters of Homer may, I think, assist in explaining the view of the
ancients. For most of these in their explanations of the poet, assert that
he meant by Athene "mind" (νοῦς) and "intelligence" (διάνοια), and the
maker of names appears to have had a singular notion about her; and
indeed calls her by a still higher title, "divine intelligence" (θεοῦ νόησις),
as though he would say: This is she who has the mind of God (θεονόα);—
using α as a dialectical variety for η, and taking away ι and σ. Perhaps,
however, the name θεονόη may mean "she who knows divine things"
(θεῖα νοοῦσα) better than others. Nor shall we be far wrong in supposing
that the author of it wished to identify this Goddess with moral intelligence (ἐν ἤθει νόησιν), and therefore gave her the name ἠθονόη; which,
however, either he or his successors have altered into what they thought
a nicer form, and called her Athene.

Her　　But what do you say of Hephaestus?

Soc　　Speak you of the princely lord of light (φάεος ἵστορα)?

Her　　Surely.

Soc　　Ἥφαιστος is Φαῖστος, and has added the η by attraction;
that is obvious to anybody.

Her　　That is very probable, until some more probable notion
gets into your head.

Soc　　To prevent that, you had better ask what is the derivation of Ares.

Her　　What is Ares?

Soc　　Ares may be called, if you will, from his manhood (ἄρρεν)
and manliness, or if you please, from his hard and unchangeable nature,
which is the meaning of ἄρρατος: the latter is a derivation in every way
appropriate to the God of war.

Her　　Very true.

Soc　　And now, by the Gods, let us have no more of the Gods,
for I am afraid of them; ask about anything but them, and thou shalt see
how the steeds of Euthyphro can prance.

Her   Only one more God! I should like to know about Hermes, of whom I am said not to be a true son. Let us make him out, and then I shall know whether there is any meaning in what Cratylus says.

Soc   I should imagine that the name Hermes has to do with speech, and signifies that he is the interpreter (ἑρμηνεὺς), or messenger, or thief, or liar, or bargainer; all that sort of thing has a great deal to do with language; as I was telling you, the word εἴρειν is expressive of the use of speech, and there is an often-recurring Homeric word ἐμήσατο, which means "he contrived"—out of these two words, εἴρειν and μήσασθαι, the legislator formed the name of the God who invented language and speech; and we may imagine him dictating to us the use of this name: "O my friends," says he to us, "seeing that he is the contriver of tales or speeches, you may rightly call him Εἰρέμης." And this has been improved by us, as we think, into Hermes. Iris also appears to have been called from the verb "to tell" (εἴρειν), because she was a messenger.

Her   Then I am very sure that Cratylus was quite right in saying that I was no true son of Hermes (Ἑρμογένης), for I am not a good hand at speeches.

Soc   There is also reason, my friend, in Pan being the double-formed son of Hermes.

Her   How do you make that out?

Soc   You are aware that speech signifies all things (πᾶν), and is always turning them round and round, and has two forms, true and false?

Her   Certainly.

Soc   Is not the truth that is in him the smooth or sacred form which dwells above among the Gods, whereas falsehood dwells among men below, and is rough like the goat of tragedy; for tales and falsehoods have generally to do with the tragic or goatish life, and tragedy is the place of them?

Her   Very true.

Soc   Then surely Pan, who is the declarer of all things (πᾶν) and the perpetual mover (ἀεὶ πολῶν) of all things, is rightly called αἰπόλος (goat-herd), he being the two-formed son of Hermes, smooth in his upper part, and rough and goatlike in his lower regions. And, as the son of Hermes, he is speech or the brother of speech, and that brother should be like brother is no marvel. But, as I was saying, my dear Hermogenes, let us get away from the Gods.

Her   From these sort of Gods, by all means, Socrates. But why should we not discuss another kind of Gods—the sun, moon, stars, earth, aether, air, fire, water, the seasons, and the year?

Soc   You impose a great many tasks upon me. Still, if you wish, I will not refuse.

Her   You will oblige me.

Soc   How would you have me begin? Shall I take first of all him whom you mentioned first—the sun?

Her   Very good.

Soc   The origin of the sun will probably be clearer in the Doric form, for the Dorians call him ἅλιος, and this name is given to him because when he rises he gathers (ἁλίζοι) men together or because he is always rolling in his course (ἀεὶ εἰλεῖν ἰὼν) about the earth; or from αἰσλεῖν, of which the meaning is the same as ποικίλλειν (to variegate), because he variegates the productions of the earth.

Her   But what is σελήνη (the moon)?

Soc   That name is rather unfortunate for Anaxagoras.

Her   How so?

Soc   The word seems to forestall his recent discovery, that the moon receives her light from the sun.

Her   Why do you say so?

Soc   The two words σέλας (brightness) and φῶς (light) have much the same meaning?

Her   Yes.

Soc   This light about the moon is always new (νέον) and always old (ἔνον), if the disciples of Anaxagoras say truly. For the sun in his revolution always adds new light, and there is the old light of the previous month.

Her   Very true.

Soc   The moon is not unfrequently called σελαναία.

Her   True.

Soc   And as she has a light which is always old and always new (ἔνον νέον ἀεὶ), she may very properly have the name σελαενονεοάεια; and this when hammered into shape becomes σελαναία.

Her   A real dithyrambic sort of name that, Socrates. But what do you say of the month and the stars?

Soc   Μεὶς (month) is called from μειοῦσθαι (to lessen), because suffering diminution; the name of ἄστρα (stars) seems to be derived from ἀστραπή, which is an improvement on ἀναστρωπή, signifying the upsetting of the eyes (ἀναστρέφειν ὦπα).

Her   What do you say of πῦρ (fire) and ὕδωρ (water)?

Soc   I am at a loss how to explain πῦρ; either the muse of Euthyphro has deserted me, or there is some very great difficulty in the word. Please, however, to note the contrivance which I adopt whenever I am in a difficulty of this sort.

Her   What is it?

Soc   I will tell you; but I should like to know first whether you can tell me what is the meaning of the word πῦρ?

Her   Indeed I cannot.

Soc   Shall I tell you what I suspect to be the true explanation of this and several other words?—My belief is that they are of foreign origin. For the Hellenes, especially those who were under the dominion of the barbarians, often borrowed from them.

Her   What is the inference?

Soc   Why, you know that any one who seeks to demonstrate the fitness of these names according to the Hellenic language, and not according to the language from which the words are derived, is rather likely to be at fault.

Her   Yes, certainly.

Soc   Well then, consider whether this πῦρ is not foreign; for the word is not easily brought into relation with the Hellenic tongue, and the Phrygians may be observed to have the same word slightly changed, just as they have ὕδωρ (water) and κύνες (dogs), and many other words.

Her   That is true.

Soc   Any violent interpretations of the words should be avoided; for something to say about them may easily be found. And thus I get rid of πῦρ and ὕδωρ. Ἀήρ (air), Hermogenes, may be explained as the element which raises (αἴρει) things from the earth, or as ever flowing (ἀεὶ ῥεῖ), or because the flux of the air is wind, and the poets call the winds "air-blasts," (ἀῆται); he who uses the term may mean, so to speak, air-flux (ἀητόρρουν), in the sense of wind-flux (πνευματόρρουν); and because this moving wind may be expressed by either term he employs the word air (ἀήρ = ἀήτης ῥέω). Αἰθήρ (aether) I should interpret as ἀειθεήρ; this may be correctly said, because this element is always running in a flux about the air (ἀεὶ θεῖ περὶ τὸν ἀέρα ῥέων). The meaning of the word γῆ (earth) comes out better when in the form of γαῖα, for the earth may be truly called "mother" (γαῖα, γεννήτειρα), as in the language of Homer (Od. ix. 118; xiii. 160) γεγάασι means γεγεννῆσθαι.

Her   Good.

Soc   What shall we take next?

Her   There are ὧραι (the seasons), and the two names of the year, ἐνιαυτὸς and ἔτος.

Soc   The ὧραι should be spelt in the old Attic way, if you desire to know the probable truth about them; they are rightly called the ὅραι because they divide (ὁρίζουσιν) the summers and winters and winds and the fruits of the earth. The words ἐνιαυτὸς and ἔτος appear to be the same,—"that which brings to light the plants and growths of the earth in their turn, and passes them in review within itself (ἐν ἑαυτῷ ἐξετάζει):" this is broken up into two words, ἐνιαυτὸς from ἐν ἑαυτῷ, and ἔτος from ἐτάζει, just as the original name of Ζεὺς was divided into Ζῆνα and Δία; and the whole proposition means that this power of reviewing from within is one, but has two names, two words ἔτος and ἐνιαυτὸς being thus formed out of a single proposition.

Her   Indeed, Socrates, you make surprising progress.

Soc   I am run away with.

Her   Very true.

Soc   But am not yet at my utmost speed.

Her   I should like very much to know, in the next place, how you would explain the virtues. What principle of correctness is there in those charming words—wisdom, understanding, justice, and the rest of them?

Soc   That is a tremendous class of names which you are dis-interring; still, as I have put on the lion's skin, I must not be faint of heart; and I suppose that I must consider the meaning of wisdom (φρόνησις) and understanding (σύνεσις), and judgment (γνώμη), and knowledge (ἐπιστήμη), and all those other charming words, as you call them?

Her   Surely, we must not leave off until we find out their meaning.

Soc   By the dog of Egypt I have not a bad notion which came into my head only this moment: I believe that the primeval givers of names were undoubtedly like too many of our modern philosophers, who, in their search after the nature of things, are always getting dizzy from constantly going round and round, and then they imagine that the world is going round and round and moving in all directions; and this appearance, which arises out of their own internal condition, they suppose to be a reality of nature; they think that there is nothing stable or permanent, but only flux and motion, and that the world is always full of every sort of motion and change. The consideration of the names which I mentioned has led me into making this reflection.

Her   How is that, Socrates?

Soc   Perhaps you did not observe that in the names which have been just cited, the motion or flux or generation of things is most surely indicated.

Her   No, indeed, I never thought of it.

Soc   Take the first of those which you mentioned; clearly that is a name indicative of motion.

Her   What was the name?

Soc   Φρόνησις (wisdom), which may signify φορᾶς καὶ ῥοῦ νόησις (perception of motion and flux), or perhaps φορᾶς ὄνησις (the blessing of motion), but is at any rate connected with φέρεσθαι (motion);

γνώμη (judgment), again, certainly implies the ponderation or consideration (νώμησις) of generation, for to ponder is the same as to consider; or, if you would rather, here is νόησις, the very word just now mentioned, which is νέου ἕσις (the desire of the new); the word νέος implies that the world is always in process of creation. The giver of the name wanted to express this longing of the soul, for the original name was νεόεσις, and not νόησις; but η took the place of a double ε. The word σωφροσύνη is the salvation (σωτηρία) of that wisdom (φρόνησις) which we were just now considering. Ἐπιστήμη (knowledge) is akin to this, and indicates that the soul which is good for anything follows (ἕπεται) the motion of things, neither anticipating them nor falling behind them; wherefore the word should rather be read as ἐπιστημένη, inserting ἐν. Σύνεσις (understanding) may be regarded in like manner as a kind of conclusion; the word is derived from συνιέναι (to go along with) and, like ἐπίστασθαι (to know), implies the progression of the soul in company with the nature of things. Σοφία (wisdom) is very dark, and appears not to be of native growth; the meaning is, touching the motion or stream of things. You must remember that the poets, when they speak of the commencement of any rapid motion, often use the word ἐσύθη (he rushed); and there was a famous Lacedaemonian who was named Σοῦς (Rush), for by this word the Lacedaemonians signify rapid motion, and the touching (ἐπαφή) of motion is expressed by σοφία, for all things are supposed to be in motion. Good (ἀγαθὸν) is the name which is given to the admirable (ἀγαστῷ) in nature; for, although all things move, still there are degrees of motion; some are swifter, some slower; but there are some things which are admirable for their swiftness, and this admirable part of nature is called ἀγαθόν. Δικαιοσύνη (justice) is clearly δικαίου σύνεσις (understanding of the just); but the actual word δίκαιον is more difficult; men are only agreed to a certain extent about justice, and then they begin to disagree. For those who suppose all things to be in motion conceive the greater part of nature to be a mere receptacle; and they say that there is a penetrating power which passes through all this, and is the instrument of creation in all, and is the subtlest and swiftest element; for if it were not the subtlest, and a power which none can keep out, and also the swiftest, passing by other things as if they were standing still, it could not penetrate through the moving universe. And this element, which superintends all things and pierces (διαϊὸν) all, is rightly called δίκαιον; the letter κ is only added for the sake of euphony. Thus far, as I was saying, there is a general agreement about the nature of justice; but I, Hermogenes, being an enthusiastic disciple, have been told in a mystery that the justice of which I am speaking is also the cause of the world: now a cause is that because of which anything is created; and some one comes and whispers in my ear that justice is rightly so called because partaking of the nature of the cause, and I begin, after hearing what he has said, to interrogate him gently: "Well, my excellent friend," say I, "but if all this be true, I still want to know what is justice." Thereupon they think that I ask tiresome questions, and am leaping over the barriers, and have been already sufficiently answered, and they try to satisfy me with one derivation after another, and at length they quarrel. For one of them says that justice is the sun, and that he only is the piercing (διαϊόντα) and burning (κάοντα) element which is the guardian of nature. And when I joyfully repeat this beautiful notion, I am answered by the satirical remark, "What, is there no justice in the world when the sun is down?" And when I earnestly beg my questioner to tell me his own honest opinion, he says, "Fire in the abstract;" but this is not very intelligible. Another says, "No, not fire in the abstract, but the abstraction of heat in the fire." Another man professes to laugh at all this, and says, as Anaxagoras says, that justice is mind, for mind, as they say, has absolute power, and mixes with nothing, and orders all things, and passes through all things. At last, my friend, I find myself in far greater perplexity about the nature of justice than I was before I began to learn. But still I am of opinion that the name, which has led me into this digression, was given to justice for the reasons which I have mentioned.

> *Her*   I think, Socrates, that you are not improvising now; you must have heard this from some one else.

> *Soc*   And not the rest?

> *Her*   Hardly.

> *Soc*   Well, then, let me go on in the hope of making you believe in the originality of the rest. What remains after justice? I do not think that we have as yet discussed courage (ἀνδρεία),—injustice (ἀδικία), which is obviously nothing more than a hindrance to the penetrating principle (διαϊόντος), need not be considered. Well, then, the name of ἀνδρεία seems to imply a battle;—this battle is in the world of existence, and according to the doctrine of flux is only the counterflux (ἐναντία ῥοή): if you extract the δ from ἀνδρεία, the name at once signifies the thing, and you may clearly understand that ἀνδρεία is not the stream opposed to every stream, but only to that which is contrary to justice, for otherwise courage would not have been praised. The words ἄρρην (male) and ἀνήρ (man) also contain a similar allusion to the same principle of the upward flux (τῇ ἄνω ῥοῇ). Γυνή (woman) I suspect to be the same word as γονή (birth): θῆλυ (female) appears to be partly derived from θηλή (the teat), because the teat is like rain, and makes things flourish (τεθηλέναι).

> *Her*   That is surely probable.

> *Soc*   Yes; and the very word θάλλειν (to flourish) seems to fig-

ure the growth of youth, which is swift and sudden ever. And this is expressed by the legislator in the name, which is a compound of θεῖν (running), and ἄλλεσθαι (leaping). Pray observe how I gallop away when I
get on smooth ground. There are a good many names generally thought
to be of importance, which have still to be explained.

Her   True.

Soc   There is the meaning of the word τέχνη (art), for
example.

Her   Very true.

Soc   That may be identified with ἐχονόη, and expresses the
possession of mind: you have only to take away the τ and insert two
o's, one between the χ and ν, and another between the ν and η.

Her   That is very shabby etymology.

Soc   Yes, my dear friend; but then you know that the original
names have been long ago buried and disguised by people sticking on
and stripping off letters for the sake of euphony, and twisting and be-
dizening them in all sorts of ways: and time too may have had a share
in the change. Take, for example, the word κάτοπτρον; why is the letter
ρ inserted? This must surely be the addition of some one who cares nothing about the truth, but thinks only of putting the mouth into shape.
'And the additions are often such that at last no human being can possibly
make out the original meaning of the word. Another example is the word
σφὶγξ, σφιγγὸς, which ought properly to be φὶγξ, φιγγὸς, and there are
other examples.

Her   That is quite true, Socrates.

Soc   And yet, if you are permitted to put in and pull out any
letters which you please, names will be too easily made, and any name
may be adapted to any object.

Her   True.

Soc   Yes, that is true. And therefore a wise dictator, like
yourself, should observe the laws of moderation and probability.

Her   Such is my desire.

Soc   And mine, too, Hermogenes. But do not be too much of
a precisian, or "you will unnerve me of my strength." When you have
allowed me to add μηχανή (contrivance) to τέχνη (art) I shall be at the
top of my bent, for I conceive μηχανή to be a sign of great accomplishment—ἄνειν; for μῆκος has the meaning of greatness, and these two, μῆκος
and ἄνειν, make up the word μηχανή. But, as I was saying, being now at
the top of my bent, I should like to consider the meaning of the two
words ἀρετὴ (virtue) and κακία (vice); ἀρετὴ I do not as yet understand,
but κακία is transparent, and agrees with the principles which preceded,
for all things being in a flux (ἰόντων), κακία is κακῶς ἰὸν (going badly);
and this evil motion when existing in the soul has the general name of

κακία, or vice, specially appropriated to it. The meaning of κακῶς ἰέναι may be further illustrated by the use of δειλία (cowardice), which ought to have come after ἀνδρεία, but was forgotten, and, as I fear, is not the only word which has been passed over. Δειλία signifies that the soul is bound with a strong chain (δεσμὸς), for λίαν means strength, and therefore δειλία expresses the greatest and strongest bond of the soul; and ἀπορία (difficulty) is an evil of the same nature (from α not, and πορεύεσθαι to go), like anything else which is an impediment to motion and movement. Then the word κακία appears to mean κακῶς ἰέναι, or going badly, or limping and halting; of which the consequence is, that the soul becomes filled with vice. And if κακία is the name of this sort of thing, ἀρετή will be the opposite of it, signifying in the first place ease of motion, then that the stream of the good soul is unimpeded, and has therefore the attribute of ever flowing without let or hindrance, and is therefore called ἀρετή, or, more correctly, ἀειρειτή (ever-flowing), and may perhaps have had another form, αἱρετή (eligible), indicating that nothing is more eligible than virtue, and this has been hammered into ἀρετή. I daresay that you will deem this to be another invention of mine, but I think that if the previous word κακία was right, then ἀρετή is also right.

Her　But what is the meaning of κακὸν, which has played so great a part in your previous discourse?

Soc　That is a very singular word about which I can hardly form an opinion, and therefore I must have recourse to my ingenious device.

Her　What device?

Soc　The device of a foreign origin, which I shall give to this word also.

Her　Very likely you are right; but suppose that we leave these words, and endeavour to see the rationale of καλὸν and αἰσχρόν.

Soc　The meaning of αἰσχρὸν is evident, being only ἀεὶ ἴσχον ῥοῆς (always preventing from flowing), and this is in accordance with our former derivations. For the name-giver was a great enemy to stagnation of all sorts, and hence he gave the name ἀεισχοροῦν to that which hindered the flux (ἀεὶ ἴσχον ῥοῦν), and this is now beaten together into αἰσχρόν.

Her　But what do you say of καλόν?

Soc　That is more obscure; yet the form is only due to the quantity, and has been changed by altering ου into ο.

Her　What do you mean?

Soc　This name appears to denote mind.

Her　How so?

Soc　Let me ask you what is the cause why anything has a name; is not the principle which imposes the name the cause?

Her   Certainly.

Soc   And must not this be the mind of Gods, or of men, or of both?

Her   Yes.

Soc   Is not mind that which called (καλέσαν) things by their names, and is not mind the beautiful (καλόν)?

Her   That is evident.

Soc   And are not the works of intelligence and mind worthy of praise, and are not other works worthy of blame?

Her   Certainly.

Soc   Physic does the work of a physician, and carpentering does the works of a carpenter?

Her   Exactly.

Soc   And the principle of beauty does the works of beauty?

Her   Of course.

Soc   And that principle we affirm to be mind?

Her   Very true.

Soc   Then mind is rightly called beauty because she does the works which we recognize and speak of as the beautiful?

Her   That is evident.

Soc   What more names remain to us?

Her   There are the words which are connected with ἀγαθὸν and καλὸν, such as συμφέρον and λυσιτελοῦν, ὠφέλιμον, κερδαλέον, and their opposites.

Soc   The meaning of συμφέρον (expedient) I think that you may discover for yourself by the light of the previous examples,—for it is a sister word to ἐπιστήμη, meaning just the motion (φορὰ) of the soul accompanying the world, and things which are done upon this principle are called σύμφορα or συμφέροντα, because they are carried round with the world.

Her   That is probable.

Soc   Again, κερδαλέον (gainful) is called from κέρδος (gain), but you must alter the δ into ν if you want to get at the meaning; for this word also signifies good, but in another way; he who gave the name intended to express the power of admixture (κεραννύμενον) and universal penetration in the good; in forming the word, however, he inserted a δ instead of an ν, and so made κέρδος.

Her   Well, but what is λυσιτελοῦν (profitable)?

Soc   I suppose, Hermogenes, that people do not mean by the profitable the gainful or that which pays (λύει) the retailer, but they use the word in the sense of swift. You regard the profitable (λυσιτελοῦν), as that which being the swiftest thing in existence, allows of no stay in things and no pause or end of motion, but always, if there begins to be any end, lets things go again (λύει), and makes motion immortal and unceasing: and in this point of view, as appears to me, the good is happily denominated λυσιτλοῦν—being that which looses (λύον) the end (τέλος) of motion. Ὠφέλιμον (the advantageous) is derived from ὀφέλλειν, meaning that which creates and increases; this latter is a common Homeric word, and has a foreign character.

Her And what do you say of their opposites?

Soc Of such as are mere negatives I hardly think that I need speak.

Her Which are they?

Soc The words ἀξύμφορον (inexpedient), ἀνωφελὲς (unprofitable), ἀλυσιτελὲς (unadvantageous), ἀκερδὲς (ungainful).

Her True.

Soc I would rather take the words βλαβερὸν (harmful), ζημιῶδες (hurtful).

Her Good.

Soc The word βλαβερὸν is that which is said to hinder or harm (βλάπτειν) the stream (ῥοῦν); βλάπτον is βουλόμενον ἅπτειν (seeking to hold or bind); for ἅπτειν is the same as δεῖν, and δεῖν is always a term of censure; βουλόμενον ἅπτειν ῥοῦν (wanting to bind the stream) would properly be βουλαπτεροῦν, and this, as I imagine, is improved into βλαβερόν.

Her You bring out curious results, Socrates, in the use of names; and when I hear the word βουλαπτεροῦν I cannot help imagining that you are making your mouth into a flute, and puffing away at some prelude to Athene.

Soc That is the fault of the makers of the name, Hermogenes; not mine.

Her Very true; but what is the derivation of ζημιῶδες?

Soc What is the meaning of ζημιῶδες?—let me remark, Hermogenes, how right I was in saying that great changes are made in the meaning of words by putting in and pulling out letters; even a very slight permutation will sometimes give an entirely opposite sense; I may instance the word δέον, which occurs to me at the moment, and reminds me of what I was going to say to you, that the fine fashionable language of modern times has twisted and disguised and entirely altered the original meaning both of δέον, and also of ζημιῶδες, which in the old language is clearly indicated.

Her What do you mean?

Soc I will try to explain. You are aware that our forefathers loved the sounds ι and δ, especially the women, who are most conservative of the ancient language, but now they change ι into η or ε, and δ into ζ; this is supposed to increase the grandeur of the sound.

Her How do you mean?

Soc   For example, in very ancient times they called the day either ἱμέρα or ἑμέρα, which is called by us ἡμέρα.

Her   That is true.

Soc   Do you observe that only the ancient form shows the intention of the giver of the name? of which the reason is, that men long for (ἱμείρουσι) and love the light which comes after the darkness, and is therefore called ἱμέρα, from ἵμερος, desire.

Her   Clearly.

Soc   But now the name is so travestied that you cannot tell the meaning, although there are some who imagine the day to be called ἡμέρα because it makes things gentle (ἥμερα).

Her   Such is my view.

Soc   And do you know that the ancients said δυογὸν and not ζυγόν?

Her   They did so.

Soc   And ζυγὸν (yoke) has no meaning—it ought to be δυογὸν, which word expresses the binding of two together (δυεῖν ἀγωγὴ) for the purpose of drawing;—this has been changed into ζυγὸν, and there are many other examples of similar changes.

Her   There are.

Soc   Proceeding in the same train of thought I may remark that the word δέον (obligation) has a meaning which is the opposite of all the other appellations of good; for δέον is here a species of good, and is, nevertheless, the chain (δεσμὸς) or hinderer of motion, and therefore own brother of βλαβερόν.

Her   Yes, Socrates; that is quite plain.

Soc   Not if you restore the ancient form, which is more likely to be the correct one, and read διὸν instead of δέον; if you convert the ε into an ι after the old fashion, this word will then agree with other words meaning good; for διὸν, not δέον, signifies the good, and is a term of praise; and the author of names has not contradicted himself, but in all these various appellations, δέον (obligatory), ὠφέλιμον (advantageous), λυσιτελοῦν (profitable), κερδαλέον (gainful), ἀγαθὸν (good), συμφέρον (expedient), εὔπορον (plenteous), the same conception is implied of the ordering or all-pervading principle which is praised, and the restraining and binding principle which is censured. And this is further illustrated by the word ζημιώδης (hurtful), which if the ζ is only changed into δ as in the ancient language, becomes δημιώδης; and this name, as you will perceive, is given to that which binds motion (δοῦντι ἰόν).

Her   What do you say of ἡδονὴ (pleasure), λύπη (pain), ἐπιθυμία (desire), and the like, Socrates?

Soc   I do not think, Hermogenes, that there is any great difficulty about them—ἡδονὴ is ἡ ὄνησις, the action which tends to advantage; and the original form may be supposed to have been ἡονὴ, but this has been altered by the insertion of the δ. Λύπη appears to be derived from the relaxation (λύειν) which the body feels when in sorrow; ἀνία (trouble) is the hindrance of motion (a and ἰέναι); ἀλγηδὼν (distress), if I am not mistaken, is a foreign word, which is derived from ἀλγεινὸς (grievous); ὀδύνη (grief) is called from the putting on (ἔνδυσις) sorrow; in ἀχθηδὼν (vexation) "the word too labours," as any one may see; χαρὰ (joy) is the very expression of the fluency and diffusion of the soul (χέω); τέρψις (delight) is so called from the pleasure creeping (ἕρπον) through the soul, which may be likened to a breath (πνοή) and is properly ἑρπνοῦν, but has been altered by time into τερπνόν; εὐφροσύνη (cheerfulness) and ἐπιθυμία explain themselves; the former, which ought to be εὐφεροσύνη and has been changed into εὐφροσύνη, is named, as every one may see, from the soul moving (φέρεσθαι) in harmony with nature; ἐπιθυμία is really ἡ ἐπὶ τὸν θυμὸν ἰοῦσα δύναμις, the power which enters into the soul; θυμὸς (passion) is called from the rushing (θύσεως) and boiling of the soul; ἵμερος (desire) denotes the stream (ῥοῦς) which most draws the soul διὰ τὴν ἔσιν τῆς ῥοῆς—because flowing with desire (ἱέμενος), and expresses a longing after things and violent attraction of the soul to them, and is termed ἵμερος from possessing this power; πόθος (longing) is expressive of the desire of that which is not present but absent, and in another place (που); this is the reason why the name πόθος is applied to things absent, as ἵμερος is to things present; ἔρως (love) is so called because flowing in (ἐσρῶν) from without; the stream is not inherent, but is an influence introduced through the eyes, and from flowing in was called ἔσρος (influx) in the old time when they used ο for ω, and is called ἔρως, now that ω is substituted for ο. But why do you not give me another word?

Her What do you think of δόξα (opinion), and that class of words?

Soc Δόξα is either derived from δίωξις (pursuit), and expresses the march of the soul in the pursuit of knowledge, or from the shooting of a bow (τόξον); the latter is more likely, and is confirmed by οἴησις (thinking), which is only οἶσις (moving), and implies the movement of the soul to the essential nature of each thing—just as βουλὴ (counsel) has to do with shooting (βολή); and βούλεσθαι (to wish) combines the notion of aiming and deliberating—all these words seem to follow δόξα, and all involve the idea of shooting, just as ἀβουλία, absence of counsel, on the other hand, is a mishap, or missing, or mistaking of the mark, or aim, or proposal, or object.

Her You are quickening your pace now, Socrates.

Soc   Why yes, the end I now dedicate to God, not, however, until I have explained ἀνάγκη (necessity), which ought to come next, and ἑκούσιον (the voluntary). Ἑκούσιον is certainly the yielding (εἶκον) and unresisting—the notion implied is yielding and not opposing, yielding, as I was just now saying, to that motion which is in accordance with our will; but the necessary and resistant being contrary to our will, implies error and ignorance; the idea is taken from walking through a ravine which is impassable, and rugged, and overgrown, and impedes motion—and this is the derivation of the word ἀναγκαῖον (necessary) ἀν' ἄγκη ἰὸν, going through a ravine. But while my strength lasts let us persevere, and I hope that you will persevere with your questions.

Her   Well, then, let me ask about the greatest and noblest, such as ἀλήθεια (truth) and ψεῦδος (falsehood) and ὂν (being), not forgetting to enquire why the word ὄνομα (name), which is the theme of our discussion, has this name of ὄνομα.

Soc   You know the word μαίεσθαι (to seek)?

Her   Yes;—meaning the same as ζητεῖν (to enquire).

Soc   The word ὄνομα seems to be a compressed sentence, signifying ὂν οὗ ζήτημα (being for which there is a search); as is still more obvious in ὀνομαστὸν (notable), which states in so many words that real existence is that for which there is a seeking (ὂν οὗ μάσμα); ἀλήθεια is also an agglomeration of θεία ἄλη (divine wandering), implying the divine motion of existence; Ψεῦδος (falsehood) is the opposite of motion; here is another ill name given by the legislator to stagnation and forced inaction, which he compares to sleep (εὕδειν); but the original meaning of the word is disguised by the addition of Ψ; ὂν and οὐσία are ἰὸν with an ι broken off; this agrees with the true principle, for being (ὂν) is also moving (ἰὸν), and the same may be said of not being, which is likewise called not going (οὐκίον or σὐκὶ ὂν = οὐκ ἰόν).

Her   You have hammered away at them manfully; but suppose that some one were to say to you, what is the word ἰὸν, and what are ῥέον and δοῦν?—show me their fitness.

Soc   You mean to say, how should I answer him?

Her   Yes.

Soc   One way of giving the appearance of an answer has been already suggested.

Her   What way?

Soc   To say that names which we do not understand are of foreign origin; and this is very likely the right answer, and something of this kind may be true of them; but also the original forms of words may have been lost in the lapse of ages; names have been so twisted in all manner of ways, that I should not be surprised if the old language when compared with that now in use would appear to us to be a barbarous tongue.

Her   Very likely.

Soc   Yes, very likely. But still the enquiry demands our earnest attention and we must not flinch. For we should remember, that if a person go on analysing names into words, and enquiring also into the elements out of which the words are formed, and keeps on always repeating this process, he who has to answer him must at last give up the enquiry in despair.

Her   Very true.

Soc   And at what point ought he to lose heart and give up the enquiry? Must he not stop when he comes to the names which are the elements of all other names and sentences; for these cannot be supposed to be made up of other names? The word ἀγαθὸν (good), for example, is, as we were saying, a compound of ἀγαστὸς (admirable) and θοός (swift). And probably θοός is made up of other elements, and these again of others. But if we take a word which is incapable of further resolution, then we shall be right in saying that we have at last reached a primary element, which need not be resolved any further.

Her   I believe you to be in the right.

Soc   And suppose the names about which you are now asking should turn out to be primary elements, must not their truth or law be examined according to some new method?

Her   Very likely.

Soc   Quite so, Hermogenes; all that has preceded would lead to this conclusion. And if, as I think, the conclusion is true, then I shall again say to you, come and help me, that I may not fall into some absurdity in stating the principle of primary names.

Her   Let me hear, and I will do my best to assist you.

Soc   I think that you will acknowledge with me, that one principle is applicable to all names, primary as well as secondary—when they are regarded simply as names, there is no difference in them.

Her   Certainly not.

Soc   All the names that we have been explaining were intended to indicate the nature of things.

Her   Of course.

Soc   And that this is true of the primary quite as much as of the secondary names, is implied in their being names.

Her   Surely.

Soc   But the secondary, as I conceive, derive their significance from the primary.

Her   That is evident.

Soc   Very good; but then how do the primary names which precede analysis show the natures of things, as far as they can be shown; which they must do, if they are to be real names? And here I will ask you a question: Suppose that we had no voice or tongue, and wanted to communicate with one another, should we not, like the deaf and dumb, make signs with the hands and head and the rest of the body?

Her   There would be no choice, Socrates.

Soc   We should imitate the nature of the thing; the elevation of our hands to heaven would mean lightness and upwardness; heaviness and downwardness would be expressed by letting them drop to the ground; if we were describing the running of a horse, or any other animal, we should make our bodies and their gestures as like as we could to them.

Her   I do not see that we could do anything else.

Soc   We could not; for by bodily imitation only can the body ever express anything.

Her   Very true.

Soc   And when we want to express ourselves, either with the voice, or tongue, or mouth, the expression is simply their imitation of that which we want to express.

Her   It must be so, I think.

Soc   Then a name is a vocal imitation of that which the vocal imitator names or imitates?

Her   I think so.

Soc   Nay, my friend, I am disposed to think that we have not reached the truth as yet.

Her   Why not?

Soc   Because if we have we shall be obliged to admit that the people who imitate sheep, or cocks, or other animals, name that which they imitate.

Her   Quite true.

Soc   Then could I have been right in what I was saying?

Her   In my opinion, no. But I wish that you would tell me, Socrates, what sort of an imitation is a name?

Soc   In the first place, I should reply, not a musical imitation, although that is also vocal; nor, again, an imitation of what music imitates; these, in my judgment, would not be naming. Let me put the matter as follows: All objects have sound and figure, and many have colour?

Her   Certainly.

Soc   But the art of naming appears not to be concerned with imitations of this kind; the arts which have to do with them are music and drawing?

Her True.

Soc Again, is there not an essence of each thing, just as there is a colour, or sound? And is there not an essence of colour and sound as well as of anything else which may be said to have an essence?

Her I should think so.

Soc Well, and if any one could express the essence of each thing in letters and syllables, would he not express the nature of each thing?

Her Quite so.

Soc The musician and the painter were the two names which you gave to the two other imitators. What will this imitator be called?

Her I imagine, Socrates, that he must be the namer, or name-giver, of whom we are in search.

Soc If this is true, then I think that we are in a condition to consider the names ῥοή (stream), ἰέναι (to go), σχέσις (retention), about which you were asking; and we may see whether the namer has grasped the nature of them in letters and syllables in such a manner as to imitate the essence or not.

Her Very good.

Soc But are these the only primary names, or are there others?

Her There must be others.

Soc So I should expect. But how shall we further analyse them, and where does the imitator begin? Imitation of the essence is made by syllables and letters; ought we not, therefore, first to separate the letters, just as those who are beginning rhythm first distinguish the powers of elementary, and then of compound sounds, and when they have done so, but not before, they proceed to the consideration of rhythms?

Her Yes.

Soc Must we not begin in the same way with letters; first separating the vowels, and then the consonants and mutes, into classes, according to the received distinctions of the learned; also the semi-vowels, which are neither vowels, nor yet mutes; and distinguishing into classes the vowels themselves? And when we have perfected the classification of things, we shall give them names, and see whether, as in the case of letters, there are any classes to which they may be all referred; and hence we shall see their natures, and see, too, whether they have in them classes as there are in the letters; and when we have well considered all this, we shall know how to apply them to what they resemble—whether one letter is used to denote one thing, or whether there is to be an admixture of several of them; just, as in painting, the painter who wants to depict anything sometimes uses purple only, or any other colour, and sometimes mixes up several colours, as his method is when he has to paint flesh colour or anything of that kind—he uses his colours as his figures appear to require them; and so, too, we shall apply letters to the expression of objects, either single letters when required, or several letters; and so we shall form syllables, as they are called, and from syllables make nouns and verbs; and thus, at last, from the combinations of nouns and verbs arrive at language, large and fair and whole; and as the painter made a figure, even so shall we make speech by the art of the namer or the rhetorician, or by some other art. Not that I am literally speaking of ourselves, but I was carried away—meaning to say that this was the way in which (not we but) the ancients formed language, and what they put together we must take to pieces in like manner, if we are to attain a scientific view of the whole subject; and we must see whether the primary, and also whether the secondary elements are rightly given or not, for if they are not, the composition of them, my dear Hermogenes, will be a sorry piece of work, and in the wrong direction.

  Her That, Socrates, I can quite believe.

  Soc Well, but do you suppose that you will be able to analyse them in this way? for I am certain that I should not.

  Her Much less am I likely to be able.

  Soc Shall we leave them, then? or shall we seek to discover, if we can, something about them, according to the measure of our ability, saying by way of preface, as I said before of the Gods, that of the truth about them we know nothing, and do but entertain human notions of them. And in this present enquiry, let us say to ourselves, before we proceed, that the higher method is the one which we or others' who would analyse language to any good purpose must follow; but under the circumstances, as men say, we must do as well as we can. What do you think?

  Her I very much approve.

  Soc That objects should be imitated in letters and syllables, and so find expression, may appear ridiculous, Hermogenes, but it cannot be avoided—there is no better principle to which we can look for the truth of first names. Deprived of this, we must have recourse to divine help, like the tragic poets, who in any perplexity have their gods waiting in the air; and must get out of our difficulty in like fashion, by saying that "the Gods gave the first names, and therefore they are right." This will be the best contrivance, or perhaps that other notion may be even better still, of deriving them from some barbarous people, for the barbarians are older than we are; or we may say that antiquity has cast a veil over them, which is the same sort of excuse as the last; for all these are not reasons but only ingenious excuses for having no reasons concerning the truth of words. And yet any sort of ignorance of first or primitive names involves an ignorance of secondary words; for they can only be explained by the primary. Clearly then the professor of languages should be able to give a very lucid explanation of first names, or let him be assured he will only talk nonsense about the rest. . . .

ARISTOTLE

Poetics

ANALYSIS OF DICTION
OR LANGUAGE IN GENERAL

To all Diction belong the following parts. —The letter, the syllable, the conjunction, the noun, the verb, the article, the case, the discourse or speech.

1. A Letter is an indivisible sound; yet not all such sounds are letters, but those only that are capable of forming an intelligible sound. For there are indivisible sounds of brute creatures; but no such sounds are called letters. Letters are of three kinds: vowels, semi-vowels, and mutes. The vowel is that which has a distinct sound without articulation, as *a* or *o*. The semi-vowel, that which has a distinct sound with articulation, as *s* and *r*. The mute, that which, with articulation, has yet no sound by itself; but, joined with one of those letters that have some sound, becomes audible, as *g* and *d*. These all differ from each other, as they are produced by different configurations, and in different parts, of the mouth; as they are aspirated or smooth, long or short; as their tone is acute, grave, or intermediate: the detail of all which is the business of the metrical treatises.

Aristotle, *Poetics* (trans. Thomas Twining, Oxford, 1789; reprinted, London: Cassell & Co., Ltd., 1901), 59–65.

2. A Syllable is a sound without signification, composed of a mute and a vowel; for *g r*, without *a*, is not a syllable; with *a*, as *g r a*, it is. But these differences also are the subject of the metrical art.

3. A Conjunction is a sound without signification,. . . . of such a nature as, out of several sounds, each of them significant, to form one significant sound.

4. An Article is a sound without signification, which marks the beginning or the end of a sentence, or distinguishes, as when we say, Τὸ φημὶ, or Τὸ περὶ, etc.

5. A Noun is a sound composed of other sounds; significant, without expression of time, and of which no part is by itself significant; for even in double words the parts are not taken in the sense that separately belongs to them. Thus, in the word Theodorus, dorus is not significant.

6. A Verb is a sound composed of other sounds; significant—with expression of time—and of which, as of the noun, no part is by itself significant. Thus, in the words, man, white, indication of time is not included; in the words, he walks, he walked, etc., it is included; the one expressing the present time, the other the past.

7. Cases belong to nouns and verbs. Some cases express relation, as, of, to, and the like; others number, as man, or men, etc. Others relate to action or pronunciation, as those of interrogation, of command, etc.; for ἐβαδισεν (did he go?) and (go) are verbal cases of that kind.

8. Discourse, or speech, is a sound significant composed of other sounds, some of which are significant by themselves; for all discourse is not composed of verbs and nouns—the definition of man, for instance. Discourse, or speech, may subsist without a verb; some significant part, however, it must contain: significant as the word, Cleon, is in "Cleon walks."

A discourse or speech is one in two senses, either as it signifies one thing or several things made one by conjunction. Thus, the "Iliad" is one by conjunction, the definition of man by signifying one thing.

DIFFERENT KINDS OF WORDS

Of words, some are single—by which I mean composed of parts not significant—and some double; of which last some have one part significant, and some both parts significant. A word may also be triple, quadruple, etc., like many of those used by the Megaliotae, as HERMOCAÏCOXANTHUS. Every word is either common, or foreign, or metaphorical, or ornamental, or invented, or extended, or contracted, or altered.

By common words I mean such as are in general and established use; by foreign, such as belong to a different language: so that the same word may evidently be both common and foreign, though not to the same people. The word Σιγόνον to the Cyprians is common, to us foreign.

A metaphorical word is a word transferred from its proper sense; either from genus to species, or from species to genus, or from one species to another, or in the way of analogy.

1. From genus to species, as:

"Secure in yonder port my vessel stands."

For to be at anchor is one species of standing or being fixed.

2. From species to genus, as:

"to Ulysses,
A thousand generous deeds we owe."

For a thousand is a certain definite many, which is here used for many in general.

3. From one species to another, as:

Χαλκῷ απὸ ψνχὴν ἐρύσυς

(The brazen falchion drew away his life.)

And,

Τάμ ἄρτειρέϊ Χαλκῷ

(Cut by the ruthless sword.)

For here the poet uses Ταμεῖν, to cut off, instead of ἐρυσαι, to draw forth, ἐρυσαι instead of Ταμεῖν: each being a species of taking away.

4. In the way of analogy—when, of four terms, the second bears the same relation to the first, as the fourth to the third; in which case, the fourth may be substituted for the second, and the second for the fourth. And sometimes the proper term is also introduced besides its relative term.

Thus, a cup bears the same relation to Bacchus as a shield to Mars. A shield, therefore, may be called the cup of Mars, and a cup the shield of Bacchus. Again, evening being to day, what old age is to life, the evening may be called the old age of the day, and old age, the evening of life; or, as Empedocles has expressed it, "Life's setting sun." It sometimes happens, that there is no proper analogous term, answering to the term borrowed; which yet may be used in the same manner, as if there were. For instance: to sow, is the term appropriated to the action of dispersing seed upon the earth; but the dispersion of rays from the sun is expressed by no appropriated term; it is, however, with respect to the sun's light, what sowing is with respect to seed. Hence the poet's expression of the sun—

>"—sowing abroad
>His heaven-created flame."

There is, also another way of using this kind of metaphor, by adding to the borrowed word a negation of some of those qualities which belong to it in its proper sense: as if, instead of calling a shield the cup of Mars, we should call it the wineless cup.

An invented word is a word never before used by any one, but coined by the poet himself; for such, it appears, there are: as ἐούνтας for κέρατα, horns, or ἀρητήρ for ἱερεύς, a priest.

A word is extended, when for the proper vowel a longer is substituted, or a syllable is inserted. A word is contracted when some part of it is retrenched. Thus, πόληος, for πόλεως, and Πηληιάδεω for Πηλείδου, are extended words, contracted, such as κρι, and δω, and οψ, e.g.—μία γίγνεται ἀμφοτέρων ὄψ.

An altered word is a word of which part remains in its usual state, and part is of the poet's making: as in, δεξιτερὸν κατὰ μαζόν δεξιτερὸν is for δεξιόν.

Further, nouns are divided into masculine, feminine, and neuter. The masculine are those which end in ν, ρ, σ, or in some letter compounded of σ and a mute; these are two, Ψ and ξ. The feminine are those which end in the vowels always long, as η, or ω; or, in α, of the doubtful vowels: so that the masculine and the feminine terminations are equal in number; for as to Ψ and ξ, they are the same with terminations in σ. No noun ends in a mute, or a short vowel. There are but three ending in ι: μέλι, κόμμι, πέπερι: five ending in υ: πῶϋ, νάπυ, γόνυ, δόρυ, ἄστυ.

The neuter terminate in these two last-mentioned vowels, and in ν and σ.

M. T. VARRO

On the Latin Language

BOOK V

. . . 2. Inasmuch as each and every word has two innate features, from what thing and to what thing the name is applied (therefore, when the question is raised from what thing *pertinacia* "obstinacy" is, it is shown to be from *pertendere* "to persist": to what thing it is applied, is told when it is explained that it is *pertinacia* "obstinacy" in a matter in which there ought not to be persistence but there is, because it is *perseverantia* "steadfastness" if a person persists in that in which he ought to hold firm), that former part, where they examine why and whence words are, the Greeks call Etymology, that other part they call Semantics. Of these two matters I shall speak in the following books, not keeping them apart, but giving less attention to the second.

3. These relations are often rather obscure for the following reasons: Not every word that has been applied, still exists, because lapse of time has blotted out some. Not every word that is in use, has been applied without inaccuracy of some kind, nor does every word which has been applied correctly remain as it originally was; for many words are dis-

Reprinted by permission of the publishers and The Loeb Classical Library from Roland G. Kent, translator of Varro, *De Lingua Latina*. Cambridge, Mass.: Harvard University Press. Footnotes omitted.

guised by change of the letters. There are some whose origin is not from native words of our own language. Many words indicate one thing now, but formerly meant something else, as in the case with *hostis* "enemy": for in olden times by this word they meant a foreigner from a country independent of Roman laws, but now they give the name to him whom they then called *perduellis* "enemy."

4. I shall take as starting-point of my discussion that derivative or case-form of the words in which the origin can be more clearly seen. It is evident that we ought to operate in this way, because when we say *inpos* "lacking power" in the nominative, it is less clear that it is from *potentia* "power" than when we say *inpotem* in the accusative; and it becomes the more obscure, if you say *pos* "having power" rather than *inpos*; for *pos* seems to mean rather *pons* "bridge" than *potens* "powerful."

5. There are few things which lapse of time does not distort, there are many which it removes. Whom you saw beautiful as a boy, him you see unsightly in his old age. The third generation does not see a person such as the first generation saw him. Therefore those things that oblivion has taken away even from our ancestors, the painstaking of Mucius and Brutus, though it has pursued the runaways, cannot bring back. As for me, even if I cannot track them down, I shall not be the slower for this, but even for this I shall be the swifter in the chase, if I can. For there is no slight darkness in the wood where these things are to be caught, and there are no trodden paths to the place which we wish to attain, nor do there fail to be obstacles in the paths, which could hold back the hunter on his way.

6. Now he who has observed in how many ways the changing has taken place in those words, new and old, in which there is any and every manner of variation in popular usage, will find the examination of the origin of the words an easier task; for he will find that words have been changed, as I have shown in the preceding books, essentially on account of two sets of four causes. For the alterations come about by the loss or the addition of single letters and on account of the transposition or the change of them, and likewise by the lengthening or the shortening of syllables, and their addition or loss: since I have adequately shown by examples, in the preceding books, of what sort these phenomena are, I have thought that here I need only set a reminder of that previous discussion.

7. Now I shall set forth the origins of the individual words, of which there are four levels of explanation. The lowest is that to which even the common folk has come; who does not see the sources of *argentifodinae* "silver-mines" and of *viocurus* "road-overseer"? The second is that to which old-time grammar has mounted, which shows how the poet has

made each word which he has fashioned and derived. Here belongs
Pacuvius's

> The whistling of the ropes,

here his

> Incurvate-neckèd flock,

here his

> With his mantle he beshields his arm.

8. The third level is that to which philosophy ascended, and on arrival
began to reveal the nature of those words which are in common use, as,
for example, from what *oppidum* "town" was named, and *vicus* "row of
houses," and *via* "street." The fourth is that where the sanctuary is, and
the mysteries of the high priest: if I shall not arrive at full knowledge
there, at any rate I shall cast about for a conjecture, which even in matters
of our health the physician sometimes does when we are ill.

9. But if I have not reached the hghest level, I shall none the less go
farther up than the second, because I have studied not only by the lamp
of Aristophanes, but also by that of Cleanthes. I have desired to go
farther than those who expound only how the words of the poets are
made up. For it did not seem meet that I seek the source in the case of
the word which Ennius had made, and neglect that which long before
King Latinus had made, in view of the fact that I get pleasure rather
than utility from many words of the poets, and more utility than
pleasure from the ancient words. And in fact are not those words mine
which have come to me by inheritance from King Romulus, rather than
those which were left behind by the poet Livius?

10. Therefore since words are divided into these three groups, those
which are our own, those which are of foreign origin, and those which
are obsolete and of forgotten sources, I shall set forth about our own
why they are, about those of foreign origin whence they are, and as to
the obsolete I shall let them alone: except that concerning some of them
I shall none the less write what I have found or myself conjecture.
In this book I shall tell about the words denoting places and those things
which are in them; in the following book I shall tell of the words denoting times and those things which take place in them; in the third I
shall tell of both these as expressed by the poets.

11. Pythagoras the Samian says that the primal elements of all things
are in pairs, as finite and infinite, good and bad, life and death, day and
night. Therefore likewise there are the two fundamentals, station and

motion, each divided into four kinds: what is stationary or is in motion, is body; where it is in motion, is place; while it is in motion, is time; what is inherent in the motion, is action. The fourfold division will be clearer in this way: body is, so to speak, the runner, place is the race-course where he runs, time is the period during which he runs, action is the running.

12. Therefore it comes about that for this reason all things, in general, are divided into four phases, and these universal; because there is never time without there being motion—for even an intermission of motion is time—; nor is there motion where there is not place and body, because the latter is that which is moved, and the former is where; nor where this motion is, does there fail to be action. Therefore place and body, time and action are the four-horse team of the elements.

13. Therefore because the primal classes of things are four in number, so many are the primal classes of words. From among these, concerning places and those things which are seen in them, I shall put a summary account in this book; but we shall follow them up wherever the kin of the word under discussion is, even if it has driven its roots beyond its own territory. For often the roots of a tree which is close to the line of the property have gone out under the neighbour's cornfield. Wherefore, when I speak of places, I shall not have gone astray, if from *ager* "field" I pass to an *agrarius* "agrarian" man, and to an *agricola* "farmer." The partnership of words is one of many members: the Wine Festival cannot be set on its way without wine, nor can the *Curia Calabra* "Announcement Hall" be opened without the *calatio* "proclamation."

II. 14. Among places, I shall begin with the origin of the word *locus* "place" itself. *Locus* is where something can be *locatum* "placed," or as they say nowadays, *collocatum* "established." That the ancients were wont to use the word in this meaning, is clear in Plautus:

> I have a grown-up daughter, lacking dower, unplaceable,
> Nor can I place her now with anyone.

In Ennius we find:

> O Thracian Land, where Bacchus' fane renowned
> Did Maro place.

15. Where anything comes to a standstill, is a *locus* "place." From this the auctioneer is said *locare* "to place" because he is all the time likewise going on until the price comes to a standstill on someone. Thence also is *locarium* "place-rent," which is given for a lodging or a shop, where the payers take their stand. So also *loci muliebres* "woman's places," where the beginnings of birth are situated.

III. 16. The primal places of the universe, according to the ancient division, are two, *terra* "earth" and *caelum* "sky," and then, according to the division into items, there are many places in each. The places of the sky are called *loca supera* "upper places," and these belong to the gods; the places of the earth are *loca infera* "lower places," and these belong to mankind. *Caelum* "sky" is used in two ways, just as is Asia. For Asia means the Asia, which is not Europe, wherein is even Syria; and Asia means also that part of the aforementioned Asia, in which is Ionia and our province.

17. So *caelum* "sky" is both a part of itself, the top where the stars are, and that which Pacuvius means when he points it out:

> See this around and above, which holds in its embrace
> The earth.

To which he adds:

> That which the men of our days call the sky.

From this division into two, Lucilius set this as the start of his twenty-one books:

> Seeking the time when the ether above and the earth were created.

18. *Caelum*, Aelius writes, was so called because it is *caelatum* "raised above the surface," or from the opposite of its idea, *celatum* "hidden" because it is exposed; not ill the remark, that the one who applied the term took *caelare* "to raise" much rather from *caelum* than *caelum* from *caelare*. But that second origin, from *celare* "to hide," could be said from this fact, that by day it *celatur* "is hidden," no less than that by night it is not hidden.

19. On the whole I rather think that from *chaos* came *choum* and then *cavum* "hollow," and from this *caelum* "sky," since, as I have said, "this around and above, which holds in its embrace the earth," is the *cavum caelum* "hollow sky." And so Andromeda says to Night,

> You who traverse the hollows of sky
> With your chariot marked by the stars.

And Agamemnon says,

> In the shield of the sky, that soundeth on high,

for a shield is a hollow thing. And Ennius likewise, with reference to a cavern,

> Enormous arches of the sky.

20. Wherefore as from *cavum* "hollow" come *cavea* "cavity," and *caullae* "hole or passage," and *convallis* "enclosed valley" as being a *cavata vallis* "hollowed valley," and *cavernae* "caverns" from the *cavatio* "hollowing," as a *cavum* "hollow thing," so developed *caelum* "sky" from *cavum*, which itself was from *chaos*, from which, in Hesiod, come all things.

IV. 21. *Terra* "earth" is—as Aelius writes—named from this fact, that it *teritur* "is trodden"; therefore it is written *tera* in the Books of the Augurs, with one R. From this, the place which is left near a town as common property for the farmers, is the *territorium* "territory," because it *teritur* "is trodden" most. From this, the linen garment which *teritur* "is rubbed" by the body, is an *extermentarium*. From this, in the harvest, is the *tritura* "threshing," because then the grain *teritur* "is rubbed out," and the *tribulum* "threshing-sledge," with which it *teritur* "is rubbed out." From this the boundaries of the fields are called *termini*, because those parts *teruntur* "are trodden" most, on account of the boundary-lane. Therefore this word is pronounced with I in some places in Latium, not *terminus*, but *terimen*, and this form is found in Accius: it is the same word which the Greeks call τέρμων. Perhaps the Latin word comes from the Greek; for Evander, who came to the Palatine, was an Arcadian from Greece.

22. A *via* "road" is indeed an *iter* "way," because it *teritur* "is worn down" by *vehendo* "carrying in wagons"; an *actus* "driving-passage" is likewise an *iter*, because it is worn down by *agendo* "driving of cattle." Moreover an *ambitus* "edge-road" is an *iter* "way," because it *teritur* "is worn" by the going around: for an edge-road is a circuit; from this the interpreters of the *Twelve Tables* define the *ambitus* of the wall as its circuit. Therefore *tera, terra*; and from this the poets have called the surface of the earth, which *sola* "alone" can be trod, the *sola* "soil" of the earth.

23. *Humus* "soil" is, as they think, the same as *terra* "earth"; therefore, they say, Ennius meant men falling to the earth when he said,

> With their elbows the soil they were smiting.

And because *humus* "soil" is *terra* "earth," therefore he who is dead and covered with *terra* is *humatus* "inhumed." From this fact, if on the burial-mound of a Roman who has been burned on the pyre clods are not thrown, or if a bone of the dead man has been kept out for the ceremony of purifying the household, the household remains in mourning; in the latter case, until in the purification the bone is covered with *humus*—as the pontifices say, as long as he is *in-humatus* "not inhumed." Also he is called *humilior* "more humble," who is more downcast toward the *humus*;

the lowest is said to be *humillimus* "most humble," because the *humus* is the lowest thing in the world.

24. From this comes also *humor* "moisture." So therefore Lucilius says:

> Gone is the earth, disappeared into clouds and moisture.

Pacuvius says:

> The land exhales a breeze and dawning damp;

humida, the same as *humecta* "damp." From this, a marshy field is *humidissimus* "most damp"; from this, *udus* and *uvidus* "damp"; from this, *sudor* "sweat" and *udor* "dampness."

25. If this moisture is in the ground no matter how far down, in a place from which it *pote* "can" be taken, it is a *puteus* "well"; unless rather because the Aeolians used to say, like πύταμος for ποταμός "river," so also πύτεος "well" for ποτέος "drinkable," from *potus* "act of drinking," and not φρέαρ "well" as they do now. From *putei* "wells" comes the town-name, such as *Puteoli*, because around this place there are many hot and cold spring-waters; unless rather from *putor* "stench," because the place is often *putidus* "stinking" with smells of sulphur and alum. Outside the towns there are *puticuli* "little pits," named from *putei* "pits," because there the people used to be buried in *putei* "pits"; unless rather, as Aelius writes, the *puticuli* are so called because the corpses which had been thrown out *putescebant* "used to rot" there, in the public burial-place which is beyond the Esquiline. This place Afranius in a comedy of Roman life calls the *Putiluci* "pit-lights," for the reason that from it they look up through *putei* "pits" to the *lumen* "light."

26. A *lacus* "lake" is a large *lacuna* "hollow," where water can be confined. A *palus* "swamp" is a *paululum* "small amount" of water as to depth, but spread quite widely *palam* "in plain sight." A *stagnum* "pool" is from Greek, because they gave the name στεγνός "waterproof" to that which has no fissure. From this, at farmhouses the *stagna* "pools" are round, because a round shape most easily holds water in, but corners are extremely troublesome.

27. *Fluvius* "river" is so named because it *fluit* "flows," and likewise *flumen* "river": from which is written, according to the law of city estates,

> *Stillicidia* "rain-waters" and *flumina* "rivers" shall be allowed to fall and to flow without interference.

Between these there is this difference, that *stillicidium* "rain-water" is so named because it *cadit* "falls" *stillatim* "drop by drop," and *flumen* "river" because it *fluit* "flows" uninterruptedly.

28. An *amnis* is that river which goes around something; for *amnis* is named from *ambitus* "circuit." From this, those who dwell around the Aternus are called *Amiternini* "men of Amiternum." From this, he who *circum it* "goes around" the people as a candidate, *ambit* "canvasses," and he who does otherwise than he should, pleads his case in court as a result of his investigable *ambitus* "canvassing." Therefore the Tiber is called an *amnis*, because it *ambit* "goes around" the Campus Martius and the City; the town Interamna gets its name from its position *inter amnis* "between rivers"; likewise Antemnae because it lies *ante amnis* "in front of the rivers," where the Anio flows into the Tiber—a town which suffered in war and wasted away until it perished.

29. The Tiber, because its source is outside Latium, if the name as well flows forth from there into our language, does not concern the Latin etymologist; just as the Volturnus, because it starts from Samnium, has nothing to do with the Latin language; but because the nearest town to it along the sea is Volturnum, it has come to us and is now a Latin name, as also the name Tiberinus. For we have both a colony named Volturnum and a god named Tiberinus.

30. But about the name of the Tiber there are two accounts. For Etruria believes it is hers, and so does Latium, because there have been those who said that at first, from Thebris, the near-by chieftain of the Veians, it was called the Thebris. There are also those who in their writings have handed down the story that the Tiber was called Albula as its early Latin name, and that later it was changed on account of Tiberinus king of the Latins, because he died there; for, as they relate, it was his burial-place.

V. 31. As all *natura* is divided into sky and earth, so with reference to the regions of the sky the earth is divided into Asia and Europe. For Asia is that part which lies toward the noonday sun and the south wind, Europe that which lies toward the Wain and the north wind. Asia was named from the nymph who, according to tradition, bore Prometheus to Iapetus. Europe was named from Europa the daughter of Agenor, who, Manlius writes, was carried off from Phoenicia by the Bull; a remarkable bronze group of the two was made by Pythagoras at Tarentum.

32. The various localities of Europe are inhabited by many different nations. They are in general denominated by names transferred from the men, like *Sabini* "the Sabine country," and *Lucani* "the country of the Lucanians," or derived from the names of the men, like Apulia and Latium, or both, like Etruria and *Tusci*. Where Latinus once had his kingdom, the field-lands as a whole are called Latian; but when taken piecemeal, they are named after the towns, as Praenestine from Praeneste, and Arician from Aricia.

33. As our State Augurs set forth, there are five kinds of fields: Roman,

Gabine, peregrine, hostic, uncertain. "Roman" field-land is so called from Romulus, from whom Rome got its name. "Gabine" is named from the town Gabii. The "peregrine" is field-land won in war and reduced to peace, which is apart from the Roman and the Gabine, because in these latter the auspices are observed in one uniform manner: "peregrine" is named from *pergere* "to go ahead," that is, from *progredi* "to advance"; for into it their first advance was made out of the Roman field-land. By the same reasoning, the Gabine also is peregrine, but because it has auspices of its own special sort it is held separate from the rest. "Hostic" is named from the *hostes* "enemies." "Uncertain" field-land is that of which it is not known to which of these four classes it belongs.

VI. 34. *Ager* "field" is the name given to land into which they used *agere* "to drive" something, or from which they used to drive something, for the sake of the produce; but others say that it is because the Greeks call it ἀγρός. As an *ager* "field" is that to which driving can be done, so that whereby driving can be done is an *actus* "driveway." Its least limit is set at four feet in width—four perhaps from the fact that by it a four-footed animal is driven—and one hundred and twenty feet in length. For a square actus, both in breadth and in length, the limit would be one hundred and twenty feet. There are many things which the ancients delimited with a multiple of twelve, like the *actus* of twelve ten-foot measures.

35. A *iugerum* is the name given to two square *actus*, *iuncti* "joined" together. A *centuria* "century" was named originally from *centum* "one hundred" *iugera*, and later, when doubled, kept its name, just as the *tribus* "tribes," which got their name from the three parts into which the people were divided, still keep the same name though their number has been multiplied. As where they *agebant* "drove" were *actus* "driveways," so where they *vehebant* "transported" were *viae* "highways"; whither they *convehebant* "transported" their produce were *villae* "farmhouses." Whereby they went, they called an *iter* "road" from *itus* "going"; where the going was narrow, was a *semita* "by-path," as though it were called a *semiter* "half-road."

36. *Ager cultus* "cultivated field-land" is so named from the fact that there the seeds *coalescebant* "united" with the land, and where it is not *consitus* "sown" it is called *incultus* "uncultivated." Because they first used *capere* "to take" the products from the level field-land, it was called *campus* "plain"; after they began to till the adjacent higher places, they called them *colles* "hills" from *colere* "to till." The fields which they did not till on account of woods or that kind where flocks can be grazed, but still they took them for private use, they called *saltus* "woodland-pastures" from the fact that their use was *salvus* "saved." These moreover the Greeks call νέμη "glades" and we call *nemora* "groves."

37. Field-land, because it seemed to be the *fundamentum* "foundation" of animal flocks and of money, was called *fundus* "estate," or else because it *fundit* "pours out" many things every year. *Vineta* and *vineae* "vineyards," from the many *vites* "grape-vines." *Vitis* "grapevine" from *vinum* "wine," this from *vis* "strength"; from this, *vindemia* "vintage," because it is *vinidemia* "wine-removal" or *vitidemia* "vine-removal." *Seges* "standing grain" from *satus* "sowing," that is, *semen* "seed." *Semen* "seed," because it is not completely that which comes from it; from this, *seminaria* "nursery-gardens," *sementes* "sowings," and likewise other words. What the *segetes* "fields of grain" *ferunt* "bear," are *fruges* "field-produce"; from *frui* "to enjoy" comes *fructus* "fruits"; from *spes* "hope" comes *spicae* "ears of grain," where are also the *culmi* "grain-stalks," because they grow on the top of the plain, and a top is a *culmen*.

38. Where the cut grain-sheaves *arescunt* "dry out" for threshing, is an *area* "threshing-floor." On account of the likeness to these, clean places in the city are called *areae;* from which may be also the Gods' *ıra* "altar," because it is clean—unless rather from *ardor* "fire"; for the intention of using it for an *ardor* makes it an *ara*; and from this the *area* itself is not far away, because it is the *ardor* of the sun which *arefacit* "does the drying."

39. *Ager restibilis* "land that withstands use" is that which *restituitur* "is restored" and replanted yearly; on the other hand, that which receives an intermission is called *novalis ager* "renewable field-land," from *novare* "to renew." *Arvus* "ploughable" and *arationes* "ploughings," from *arare* "to plough"; from this, what the ploughshare *sustulit* "has removed" is a *sulcus* "furrow"; whither that earth is thrown, that is, *proiecta* "thrown forth," is the *porca* "ridge."

40. *Prata* "meadows" are named from this, that they are *parata* "prepared" without labour. *Rura* "country-lands" are so called because in the fields the same operations must be done every year *rursum* "again," that you may again get their fruits. Sulpicius writes, however, that it is a just right for the country-lands of the populace to be divided for lavish distribution as bonus to discharged soldiers. *Praedia* "estates" are named, as also *praedes* "bondsmen," from *praestare* "to offer as security," because these, when given as pledge to the official authorities, *praestent* "guarantee" the good faith of the party in the case. . . .

63. The poets, in that they say that the fiery seed fell from the Sky into the sea and Venus was born "from the foam-masses," through the conjunction of fire and moisture, are indicating that the *vis* "force" which they have is that of Venus. Those born of this *vis* have what is called *vita* "life," and that was meant by Lucilius:

Life is force, you see; to do everything force doth compel us.

64. Wherefore because the Sky is the beginning, Saturn was named from *satus* "sowing"; and because fire is a beginning, waxlights are presented to patrons at the Saturnalia. *Ops* is the Earth, because in it is every *opus* "work" and there is *opus* "need" of it for living, and therefore Ops is called mother, because the Earth is the mother. For she

> All men hath produced in all the lands, and takes them back again,

she who

> Gives the rations,

as Ennius says, who

> Is Ceres, since she brings (*gerit*) the fruits.

For with the ancients, what is now G, was written C.

65. These same gods Sky and Earth are Jupiter and Juno, because, as Ennius says,

> That one is the Jupiter of whom I speak, whom Grecians call
> Air; who is the windy blast and cloud, and afterwards the rain;
> After rain, the cold: he then becomes again the wind and air.
> This is why those things of which I speak to you are Jupiter:
> Help he gives to men, to fields and cities, and to beasties all.

Because all come from him and are under him, he addresses him with the words:

> O father and king of the gods and the mortals.

Pater "father" because he *patefacit* "makes evident" the seed; for then it *patet* "is evident" that conception has taken place, when that which is born comes out from it.

66. This same thing the more ancient name of Jupiter shows even better: for of old he was called *Diovis* and *Diespiter*, that is, *dies pater* "Father Day"; from which they who come from him are called *dei* "deities," and *dius* "god" and *divum* "sky," whence *sub divo* "under the sky," and *Dius Fidius* "god of faith." Thus from this reason the roof of his temple is pierced with holes, that in this way the *divum*, which is the *caelum* "sky," may be seen. Some say that it is improper to take an oath by his name, when you are under a roof. Aelius said that *Dius Fidius* was a son of *Diovis*, just as the Greeks call Castor the son of Zeus, and he thought that he was *Sancus* in the Sabine tongue, and *Hercules* in

Greek. He is likewise called *Dispater* in his lowest capacity, when he is joined to the earth, where all things vanish away even as they originate; and because he is the end of these *ortus* "creations," he is called *Orcus.*

67. Because Juno is Jupiter's wife, and he is Sky, she *Terra* "Earth," the same as *Tellus* "Earth," she also, because she *iuvat* "helps" *una* "along" with Jupiter, is called Juno, and *Regina* "Queen," because all earthly things are hers.

68. *Sol* "Sun" is so named either because the Sabines called him thus, or because he *solus* "alone" shines in such a way that from this god there is the daylight. *Luna* "Moon" is so named certainly because she alone *"lucet"* shines at night. Therefore she is called *Noctiluca* "Night-Shiner" on the Palatine; for there her temple *noctu lucet* "shines by night." Certain persons call her Diana, just as they call the Sun Apollo (the one name, that of Apollo, is Greek, the other Latin); and from the fact that the Moon goes both high and widely, she is called *Diviana.* From the fact that the Moon is wont to be under the lands as well as over them, Ennius's *Epicharmus* calls her *Proserpina.* Proserpina received her name because she, like a *serpens* "creeper," moves widely now to the right, now to the left. *Serpere* "to creep" and *proserpere* "to creep forward" meant the same thing, as Plautus means in what he writes:

Like a forward-creeping beast.

69. She appears therefore to be called by the Latins also Juno Lucina, either because she is also the Earth, as the natural scientists say, and *lucet* "shines"; or because from that light of hers in which a conception takes place until that one in which there is a birth into the light, the Moon continues to help, until she has brought it forth into the light when the months are past, the name Juno Lucina was made from *iuvare* "to help" and *lux* "light." From this fact women in child-birth invoke her; for the Moon is the guide of those that are born, since the months belong to her. It is clear that the women of olden times observed this, because women have given this goddess credit notably for their eyebrows. For Juno Lucina ought especially to be established in places where the gods give light to our eyes.

70. *Ignis* "fire" is named from *gnasci* "to be born," because from it there is birth, and everything which is born the fire enkindles; therefore it is hot, just as he who dies loses the fire and becomes cold. From the fire's *vis ac violentia* "force and violence," now in greater measure, Vulcan was named. From the fact that fire on account of its brightness *fulget* "flashes," come *fulgur* "lightning-flash" and *fulmen* "thunderbolt," is called *fulguritum.* . . .

BOOK VI

I. 1. The sources of the words which are names of places and are names of those things which are in these places, I have written in the preceding book. In the present book I shall speak about the names of times and of those things which in the performance take place or are said with some time-factor, such as sitting, walking, talking: and if there are any words of a different sort attached to these, I shall give heed rather to the kinship of the words than to the rebukes of my listener. . . .

II. 3. First we shall speak of the time-names, then of those things which take place through them, but in such a way that first we shall speak of their essential nature: for nature was man's guide to the imposition of names. Time, they say, is an interval in the motion of the world. This is divided into a number of parts, especially from the course of the sun and the moon. Therefore from their *temperatus* "moderated" career, *tempus* "time" is named, and from this comes *tempestiva* "timely things"; and from their *motus* "motion," the *mundus* "world," which is joined with the sky as a whole.

4. There are two motions of the sun: one with the sky, in that the moving is impelled by Jupiter as ruler, who in Greek is called Δία, when it comes from east to west; wherefore this time is from this god called a *dies* "day." *Meridies* "noon," from the fact that it is the *medius* "middle" of the *dies* "day." The ancients said D in this word, and not R, as I have seen at Praeneste, cut on a sun-dial. *Solarium* "sun-dial" was the name used for that on which the hours were seen in the *sol* "sunlight"; or also there is the water-clock, which Cornelius set up in the shade in the Basilica of Aemilius and Fulvius. The beginning of the day is *mane* "early morning," because then the day *manat* "trickles" from the east, unless rather because the ancients called the good *manum*: from a superstitious belief of the same kind as influences the Greeks, who, when a light is brought, make a practice of saying, "Goodly light!"

5. *Suprema* means the last part of the day; it is from *superrimum*. This time, the *Twelve Tables* say, is sunset; but afterwards the Plaetorian Law declares that this time also should be "last" at which the praetor in the Comitium has announced to the people the *suprema* "end of the session." In line with this, *crepusculum* "dusk" is said from *creperum* "obscure"; this word they took from the Sabines, from whom come those who were named *Crepusci*, from Amiternum, who had been born at that time of day, just like the *Lucii*, who were those born at dawn (*prima luce*) in the Reatine country. *Crepusculum* means doubtful: from this doubtful matters are called *creperae* "obscure," because dusk is a time

when to many it is doubtful whether it is even yet day or is already night.

6. *Nox* "night" is called *nox*, because, as Pacuvius says,

> All will be stiff with frost unless the sun break in,

because it *nocet* "harms"; unless it is because in Greek night is νύξ. When the first star has come out (the Greeks call it Hesperus, and our people call it *Vesperugo*, as Plautus does:

> The evening star sets not, nor yet the Pleiades),

this time is by the Greeks called ἑσπέρα, and *vesper* "evening" in Latin; just as, because the same star before sunrise is called *iubar* "dawn-star," because it is *iubata* "maned," Pacuvius's herdsman says:

> When morning-star appears and night has run her course.

And Ennius's Ajax says:

> I see light in the sky—can it be dawn?

7. The time between dusk and dawn is called the *nox intempesta* "dead of night," as in the *Brutus* of Cassius, in the speech of Lucretia:

> By dead of night he came unto our home.

Aelius used to say that *intempesta* means the period when it is not a time for activity, which others have called the *concubium* "general rest," because practically all persons then *cubabant* "were lying down"; others, from the fact that *silebatur* "silence was observed," have called it the *silentium* "still" of the night, the time which Plautus likewise calls the *conticinium* "general silence": for he writes:

> We'll see, I want it done. At general-silence time come back.

QUINTILIAN

Institutes of Oratory

BOOK ONE

Chapter Four

In regard to the boy who has attained facility in reading and writing, the next object is instruction from the grammarians. Nor is it of importance whether I speak of the Greek or Latin grammarian, though I am inclined to think that the Greek should take the precedence. Both have the same method. This profession, then, distinguished as it is, most fittingly, into two parts, the art of speaking correctly, and the interpretation of the poets, carries more beneath than it shows on its surface. For not only is the art of writing combined with that of speaking, but correct reading also precedes illustration, and with all these is joined the exercise of judgment, which the old grammarians, indeed, used with such severity that they not only allowed themselves to distinguish certain verses with a particular mark of censure, and to remove from their sets, as spurious, certain books which had been inscribed with false titles, but even brought some authors within their canon, and excluded others altogether from classification. Nor is it sufficient to have read the poets only; every class of writers must be studied, not simply for matter, but for words, which often receive their authority from writers. Nor can grammar be complete without a knowledge of music, since the grammarian has to speak of meter and rhythm; nor, if he is ignorant of astronomy, can he understand the poets, who, to say nothing of other matters, so often allude to the rising and setting of the stars in marking the seasons; nor must he be unacquainted with philosophy, both on account of numbers of passages, in almost all poems, drawn from the most abstruse subtleties of physical investigation, and also on account of Empedocles among the Greeks, and Varro and Lucretius among the Latins, who have committed the precepts of philosophy to verse. The grammarian has also need of no small portion of eloquence, that he may speak aptly and fluently on each of those subjects which are here mentioned. Those, therefore, are not to be heeded who deride this science as trifling and empty; for unless it lays a sure foundation for the future orator, whatever superstructure you raise will surely fall. It is an art which is necessary to the young, pleasing to the old, and an agreeable companion in retirement. Alone, of all departments of learning, it has in it more service than show.

Let no man, therefore, look down on the elements of grammar as small matters; not because it requires great labor to distinguish consonants from vowels, and to divide them into the proper number of semivowels and mutes, but because, to those entering the recesses, as it were, of this temple, there will appear much subtlety on points, which may not only sharpen the wits of boys, but may exercise even the deepest erudition and knowledge. Is it in the power of every ear to distinguish accurately the sounds of letters? No more, assuredly, than to distinguish the sounds of musical strings. But all grammarians will at least descend to the discussion of such curious points as these: whether any necessary letters be wanting to us, not indeed when we write Greek, for then we borrow two letters from the Greeks, but, properly, in Latin: as in these words, *seruus* and *uulgus*, the Aeolic digamma is required; and there is a certain sound of a letter between *u* and *i*, for we do not pronounce *optumum* like *optimum;* in *here*, too, neither *e* nor *i* is distinctly heard: whether, again, other letters are redundant (besides the mark of aspiration, which, if it be necessary, requires also a contrary mark), as *k*, which is itself used to designate certain names, and *q* (similar to *k* in sound and shape, except that *q* is slightly slanted by our writers; *koppa* now remains among the Greeks, though only in the list of numbers), as well as *x*, the last of our letters, which indeed we might have done without, if we had not sought it. With regard to vowels, too, it is the business of the grammarian to see whether custom has taken any for consonants, since *iam* is written as *ettam*, and *quos* as *tuos*. But vowels which are joined, as vowels, make either one long vowel, as the ancients wrote, who used the doubling of them instead of the circumflex accent, or two; though perhaps someone may suppose that a syllable may be formed even of three vowels; but this cannot be the case, unless some of them do the duty of consonants. The grammarian will also inquire how two vowels only have the power of uniting with each other, when none of the consonants can break any letter but another consonant. But the letter *i* unites with itself, for *coniicit* is from *iacit;* and so does *u*, as *uulgus* and *seruus* are now written. Let the grammarian also know that Cicero was inclined to write *aiio* and *Maiia* with a double *i;* and, if this be done, the one *i* will be joined to the other as a consonant. Let the boy, therefore, learn what is peculiar in letters, what is common, and what relationship each has to each, and let him wonder why *scabillum* is formed from *scamnum*, or why *bipennis*, an axe with an edge each way, is formed from *pinna*, which means something sharp, that he may not follow the error of those, who, because they think that this word is from two wings, would have the wings of birds called *pinnae*.

Nor let him know only those changes which declension and prepositions introduce, as *secat secuit, cadit excīdit, caedit excīdit, calcat exculcat;* (so *lotus* from *lavare*, whence also *inlotus;* and there are a thousand other similar derivations); but also what alterations have taken place, even in nominative cases, through lapse of time; for, as *Valesii* and *Fusii* have passed into *Valerii* and *Furii*, so *arbos, labos, vapos*, as well as *clamos* and *lases*, have had their day. This very letter *s*, too, which has been excluded from these words, has itself, in some other words, succeeded to the place of another letter; for instead of *mersare* and *pulsare*, they once said *mertare* and *pultare*. They also said *fordeum* and *foedus*, using, instead of the aspiration, a letter similar to *vau;* for the Greeks, on the other hand, are accustomed to aspirate, whence Cicero, in his oration for Fundanius, laughs at a witness who could not sound the first letter of that name. But we have also, at times, admitted *b* into the place of other letters, whence *Burrus, Bruges*, and *Belena*. The same letter moreover has made *bellum* out of *duellum*, whence some have ventured to call the *Duellii, Bellii*. Why need I speak of *stlocus* and *stlites?* Why need I mention that there is a certain relationship of the letter *t* to *d?* Hence, it is far from surprising if, on the old buildings of our city, and well-known temples, is read *Alexanter* and *Cassantra*. Why should I specify that *o* and *u* are interchanged? *Hecoba* and *notrix, Culchides* and *Pulyxena*, were used, and (that this may not be noticed in Greek words only), *dederont* and *probaveront*. So *Odysseus*, whom the Aeolians made *Ulysses*, was turned into *Ulixes*. Was not *e*, too, put in the place of *i*, as

Menerva, leber, magester, and *Diiove* and *Veiove* for *Diiovi* and *Veiovi?* But it is enough for me to point to the subject; for I do not teach but admonish those who are to teach. The attention of the learner will then be transferred to syllables, on which I shall make a few remarks under the head of orthography.

He, whom this matter shall concern, will then understand how many parts of speech there are, and what they are; though as to their number, writers are by no means agreed. For the more ancient, among whom were Aristotle and Theodectes, said that there were only *verbs, nouns,* and *convinctions,* because, that is to say, they judged that the force of language was in verbs, and the matter of it in nouns (since the one is what we speak, and the other that of which we speak), and that the union of words lay in convinctions, which, I know, are by most writers called conjunctions, but the other term seems to be a more exact translation of συνδέσμῳ. By the philosophers, and chiefly the Stoics, the number was gradually increased; to the convinctions were first added articles, then prepositions; to nouns was added the appellation, next the pronoun, and afterward the participle, partaking of the nature of the verb; to verbs themselves were joined adverbs. Our language does not require articles, and they are therefore divided among other parts of speech. To the parts of speech already mentioned was added the interjection. Other writers, however, certainly of competent judgment, have made eight parts of speech, for instance, Aristarchus, and Palaemon in our own day, who have included the vocable, or appellation, under the name or noun as if a species of it. But those who make the noun one, and the vocable another, reckon nine. But there were some, nevertheless, who even distinguished the vocable from the appellation, so that the vocable should signify any substance manifest to the sight and touch, as a house, a bed; the appellation, that to which one or both of these properties should be wanting, as the wind, heaven, God, virtue. They added also the asseveration, as *heu,* "alas!" and the attrectation, as *faceatim,* "in bundles"— distinctions which are not approved by me. Whether προσηγορία should be translated by "vocable" or "appellation," and whether it should be comprehended under the noun or not, are questions on which, as being of little importance, I leave it free to others to form an opinion.

Let boys in the first place learn to decline nouns and conjugate verbs, for otherwise they will never arrive at the understanding of what is to follow. This admonition would be superfluous to give, were it not that most teachers, through ostentatious haste, begin where they ought to end, and, while they wish to show off their pupils in matters of greater display, retard their progress by attempting to shorten the road. But if a teacher has sufficient learning, and (what is often found not less wanting) be willing to teach what he has learned, he will not be content with stating that there are three genders in nouns, and specifying what nouns have two or all three genders. Nor shall I hastily deem that tutor diligent, who shall have shown that there are irregular nouns, called *epicene*, in which both genders are implied under one, or nouns which, under a feminine termination, signify males, or, with a neuter termination, denote females (as *Muraena* and *Glycerium*). A penetrating and acute teacher will search into a thousand origins of names; derivations which have produced the names *Rufus*, "red," and *Longus*, "long," from personal peculiarities (among which will be some of rather obscure etymology, as *Sulla, Burrhus, Galba, Plancus, Pansa, Scaurus*, and others of the same kind); some also from accidents of birth, as *Agrippa, Opiter, Cordus, Posthumus;* some from occurrences after birth, as *Vopiscus;* while others as *Cotta, Scipio, Laenas, Seranus*, spring from various causes. We may also find people, places, and many other things among the origins of names. That sort of name among slaves, which was taken from their masters, whence *Marcipores* and *Publipores*, has fallen into disuse. Let the tutor consider, also, whether there is not among the Greeks ground for a sixth case, and among us even for a seventh; for when I say *hasta percussi*, "I have struck with a spear," I do not express the sense of an ablative case, nor, if I say the same thing in Greek, that of a dative.

As to verbs, who is so ignorant as not to know their kinds, qualities, persons, and numbers? Those things belong to the reading school and to the lower departments of instruction. But such points as are not determined by inflection will puzzle some people; for it may be doubted, as to certain words, whether they are participles, or nouns formed from the verb, as *lectus, sapiens*. Some verbs look like nouns, as *freudator, nutritor*. Is not the verb in *itur in antiquam silvam* of a peculiar nature, for what beginning of it can you find? *Fletur* is similar to it. We understand the passive sometimes in one way, as,

> *panditur interea domus omnipotentis Olympi;*

sometimes in another, as,

> *totis*
> *usque adeo turbatur agris.*

There is also a third way, as *urbs habitatur*, whence likewise *campus curritur, mare navigatur*. *Pransus* also and *potus* have a different signification from that which their form indicates. I need hardly add that many verbs do not go through the whole course of conjugation. Some, too, undergo a change, as *fero* in the perfect; some are expressed only in the form of the third person, as *licet, piget;* and some bear a resemblance to nouns passing into adverbs; for, as we say *noctu* and *diu*, so we say *dictu* and *factu;* since these words are indeed participial, though not like *dicto* and *facto.* . . .

Chapter Six

By speakers, as well as writers, there are certain rules to be observed. Language is based on reason, antiquity, authority, and custom. It is analogy, and sometimes etymology, that affords the chief support to reason. A certain majesty, and, if I may so express myself, religion, graces the antique. Authority is commonly sought in orators or historians. As to the poets, the obligation of the meter excuses their phraseology, except in those cases when the measure of the feet offers no impediment to the choice of either of two expressions, but they fancifully prefer one to the other, as in the following phrases: *imo de stirpe recisum, aeeriae quo congessere palumbos, silice in nuda,* and the like. Since the judgment of men eminent in eloquence stands in place of reason, then even error is without dishonor in following illustrious guides. Custom, however, is the surest preceptor in speaking: we must use phraseology, like money, which has the public stamp.

But all these particulars require great judgment, especially *analogy,* which, translating it closely from Greek into Latin, people have called *proportion.* It requires that a writer or speaker compare whatever is at all doubtful with something similar concerning which there is no doubt, so as to prove the uncertain by the certain. This is done in two ways: by a comparison of similar words, in respect chiefly to their last syllables (for which reason the words that have but one syllable are said not to be accountable to analogy), and by looking to diminutives. Comparison in nouns shows either their gender or their declension; their gender, as, when it is inquired whether *funis* be masculine or feminine, *panis* may be an object of comparison with it; their declension, as, if it should be a subject of doubt whether we should say *hac domu* or *hac domo,* and *domuum* or *domorum,* then *domus, anus, manus* may be compared with each other. The formation of diminutives shows only the gender of words, as (that I may take the same word for an example) *funiculus* proves that *funis* is masculine. There is also similar reason for comparison in verbs; as if any one, following the old writers, should pronounce *fervere* with the middle syllable short, he would be convicted of speaking incorrectly, since all verbs which end with the letters *e* and *o* in the indicative mood, when they have assumed the letter *e* in the middle syllables in the infinitive, have it necessarily long, as *prandeo, pendeo, spondeo, prandēre, pendēre, spondēre.* But those which have *o* only in the indicative, when they end with the same letter *e* in the infinitive, shorten it, as *lego, dico, curro, legĕre, dicĕre, currĕre;* although there occurs in Lucilius,

> *Fervit aqua et fervet; fervit nunc, fervet ad annum*

"The water boils and will boil; it boils now, and will boil for a year." But with all respect to a man of such eminent learning, if he thinks *fervit* similar to *currit* and *legit, fervo* will be a word like *curro* and *lego,* a word which has never been heard by me. But this is not a just comparison; for *servit* is like *fervit,* and he that follows this analogy must say *fervire* as well as *servire.* The present indicative also is sometimes discovered from the other moods and tenses; for I remember that some people who had blamed me for using the word *pepigi,* were convinced by me of their error; they had allowed, indeed, that the best authors had used *pepigi,* but denied that analogy permitted its use, since the present indicative *paciscor,* as it had the form of a passive verb, made in the perfect tense *pactus sum.* But I, besides adducing the authority of orators and historians, maintained that *pepigi* was also supported by analogy; for, as we read in the Twelve Tables, *ni ita pagunt,* I found *cadunt* similar to *pagunt,* whence the present indicative, though it had fallen into disuse through time, was evidently *pago,* like *cado;* and it was therefore certain that we say *pepigi* like *cecidi.* But we must remember that the course of analogy cannot be traced through all the parts of speech, as it is in many cases at variance with itself. Learned men, indeed, endeavor to justify some departures from it, as, when it is remarked how much *lepus* and *lupus,* though of similar terminations in the nominative, differ in their cases and numbers, they reply that they are not of the same sort, since *lepus* is epicene, and *lupus* masculine; although Varro, in the book in which he relates the origin of the city of Rome, uses *lupus* as feminine, following Ennius and Fabius Pictor. But those same grammarians, when they are asked why *aper* makes *apri,* and *pater, patris,* assert that the first is declined absolutely, and the second with reference to something; and, besides, as both are derived from the Greek, they recur to the rule that πατρός gives *patris,* and κάπρου *apri.* But how will they escape from the fact that nouns, which end with the letters *u* and *s* in the nominative singular, never, even though feminine, end with the syllable -*ris* in the genitive, yet that *Venus* makes *Veneris;* and that, though nouns ending in -*es* have various endings in the genitive, yet their genitive never ends in that same syllable -*ris,* when, nevertheless, *Ceres* obliges us to say *Cereris?* And what shall I say of those parts of speech, which, though all of similar commencement, proceed with different inflections, as *Alba* makes *Albani* and *Albenses, volo, volui* and *volavi?* For analogy itself admits that verbs, which end with the letter *o* in the first person singular, are variously formed in the perfect, as *cado* makes *cecidi; spondeo, spopondi; pingo, pinxi; lego, legi; pono, posui; frango, fregi; laudo, laudavi.*

Analogy was not sent down from heaven when men were first made to give them rules for speaking, but was discovered after men had begun to speak, and after it was observed how each word in speaking terminated. It is not therefore founded on reason, but on example; nor is it a law for speaking, but the mere result of observation, so that nothing but custom has been the origin of analogy. Yet some people adhere to it with a most unpleasantly perverse attachment to exactness; so that they will say *audaciter* in preference to *audacter*, though all orators adopt the latter, and *emicavit* instead of *emicuit*, or *conire* instead of *coire*. Such persons we may allow to say *audivisse*, and *scivisse*, *tribunale*, and *faciliter;* let them also have their *frugalis*, instead of *frugi*, for how else can *frugalitas* be formed? Let them also prove that *centum millia nummum* and *fidem deum* are two solecisms, since they err in both case and number; for we were ignorant of this, and were not merely complying with custom and convenience, as in most cases, of which Cicero treats nobly, as of everything else, in his *De oratore*. Augustus, too, in his letters written to Caius Caesar, corrects him for preferring to say *calidum* rather than *caldum*, not because *calidum* is not Latin, but because it is unpleasing, and, as he has himself expressed it by a Greek word, περίεργον.

All this, indeed, they consider as mere ὀρθοέπειαν "orthoepy," which I by no means set aside, for what is so necessary as correctness of speech? I think that we ought to adhere to it as far as possible, and to make persevering resistance against innovators—but to retain words that are obsolete and disused is a species of impertinence, and of puerile ostentation in little things. Let the extremely learned man, who has saluted you without an aspirate, and with the second syllable lengthened (for the verb, he will say, is *avere*), say also *calefacere* and *conservavisse* rather than what we say; and with these let him join *face, dice*, and the like. His way is the right way; who will deny it? But a smoother and more beaten road is close by the side of it. There is nothing, however, with which I am more offended, than that these men, led away by oblique cases, permit themselves, I do not say not to find, but even to alter nominative cases, as when *ebur* and *robur*, so spoken and written by the greatest authors, are made to change the vowel of the second syllable into *o*, because their genitives are *roboris* and *eboris*, and because *sulpur* and *guttur* preserve the vowel *u* in the genitive. For which reason also *jecur* and *femur* have raised disputes. This change of theirs is not less audacious than if they were to substitute the letter *o* for *u* in the genitive case of *sulpur* and *guttur*, because *eboris* and *roboris* are formed with *o*. Note the example of Antonius Gnipho, who acknowledges that *robur* and *ebur* are proper words, and even *marmur*, but would have the plurals of them to be *robura, ebura, marmura*. But if they had paid attention to the affinity of letters, they would have understood that *roboris* is as fairly formed from *robur* as *militis, limitis*, from *miles, limes*, or *judicis, vindicis*, from *judex, vindex*, and would have observed some other forms to which I have adverted above. Do not similar nominative cases, as I remarked, diverge into very dissimilar forms in the oblique cases, as *Virgo, Juno; fusus, lusus; cuspis, puppis;* and a thousand others? It happens, too, that some nouns are not used in the plural, others not in the singular; some are indeclinable; some depart altogether from the form of their nominatives, as *Jupiter*. The same peculiarity happens in verbs, as *fero, tuli*, of which the perfect is found, and nothing more. Nor is it of much importance, whether those unused parts are actually not in existence, or whether they are too harsh to be used; for what, for example, will *progenies* make in the genitive singular, or what will *spes* make in the genitive plural? Or how will *quire* and *ruere*, form themselves in the perfect passive, or in the passive participles? It is needless to advert to other words, when it is even uncertain whether *senatus* makes *senatus senatui* or *senati senato*. It appears to me, therefore, to have been not unhappily remarked that it is one think to speak Latin, and another to speak grammar. Of analogy I have now said enough, and more than enough.

Etymology, which inquires into the origin of words, is called by Cicero notation, because its designation in Aristotle is σύμβολον, that is, *nota;* for to a literal rendering of "word for word," which would be *veriloquium*, Cicero himself, who formed that word, is averse. There are some, who, looking rather to the meaning of the word, call it "origination." This part of grammar is sometimes of the utmost use; as often, indeed, as the matter, concerning which there is any dispute, stands in need of interpretation; as when Marcus Caelius would prove that he was a *homo frugi*, "a frugal man," not because he was temperate (for on that point he could not speak falsely), but because he was profitable to many, that is *fructuosus*, from whence, he said, was derived *frugality*. A place is accordingly assigned to etymology in definitions. Sometimes, also, it endeavors to distinguish barbarous from polite words; as when a question arises whether Sicily should be called *Triquetra* or *Triquedra*, and whether we should say *meridies* or *medidies;* and similar questions concerning other words which yield to custom. But it carries with it much learning, whether we employ it in treating of words sprung from the Greek, which are very numerous (especially those inflected according to the Aeolic dialect to which our language has most similitude), or in inquiring from our knowledge of ancient history, into the names of men, places, nations, cities. Whence come the names of the *Bruti, Publicolae, Pici;* why do we say *Latium, Italia, Beneventum;* what is our reason for using the terms *Capitol, Quirinal* hill, and *Argiletum?*

I would now allude also to those minuter points on which the greatest lovers of etymology weary themselves: men who bring back to their true derivation, by various and manifold arts, words that have become a little distorted, by shortening or lengthening, adding, taking away, or interchanging letters or syllables. In this pursuit, through weakness of judgment, they run into the most contemptible absurdities. Let *consul* be (I make no objection) from "consulting" or from "judging," for the ancients called *consulere* "judicare," whence still remains the phrase *rogat boni consulas,* that is, *bonum judices.* Let it be old age that has given a name to the senate, for the senators are fathers; let *rex, rector,* and abundance of other words, be indisputably from *rego;* nor would I dispute the ordinary derivation of *tegula, regula,* and other words similar to them; let *classis,* also, be from *calare,* "to call together," and let *lepus* be for *levipes,* and *vulpes* for *volipes.* But shall we also allow words to be derived from contraries, as *lucus,* "a grove," from *luceo,* "to shine," because, being thick with shade, *parum lucet,* it does not shine? As *ludus,* "a school," from *ludo,* "to play," because it is as far as possible from play? As *Ditis,* "Pluto," from *dives,* "rich," because he is by no means rich? Or shall we allow *homo,* "man," to be from *humus,* "the ground," because he was sprung from the ground, as if all animals had not the same origin, or as if the first men had given a name to the ground before they gave one to themselves? Shall we allow *verba,* "words," to be from *aer verberatus,* "beaten air"? Let us go on, and we shall get so far that *stella,* "a star," will be believed to be *luminis stilla,* "a drop of light," the author of which derivation, an eminent man in literature, it would be ungenerous for me to name in regard to a point on which he is censured by me. But those who have recorded such etymologies in books have themselves set their names to them; and Caius Granius thought himself extremely clever for saying that *caelibes,* "bachelors," was the same as *caelites,* "inhabitants of heaven," because they are alike free from a most heavy burden, resting his derivation, too, on an argument from the Greek, for he affirmed that ἠίθεους was used in the same sense. Nor does Modestus yield to him in imagination, for he says that because Saturn cut off the genitalia of *Caelus,* men who have no wives are, therefore, called *caelibes.* Lucius Aelius declares that *pituita,* "phlegm," is so called *quia petat vitam,* because "it aims at life." But who may not be pardoned after Varro, who wished to persuade Cicero (for it was to him that he wrote this), that *ager,* "a field," is so called because *in eo agatur aliquid,* "something is done in it," and that *graculos,* "jackdaws," are so named because they fly *gregatim,* "in flocks," though it is evident that the one is derived from the Greek, and the other from the cries of the birds themselves? But of such importance was it to Varro to make derivations that *merula*, "a blackbird," he declared, was so named because it flies alone, as if *mera volans*. Some have not hesitated to apply to etymology for the origin of every name or word; deducing *Longus* and *Rufus*, as I remarked, from personal peculiarities; *strepere* and *murmurare* from particular sounds; with which they join, also, certain derivatives, as *velox*, "swift," deduced from *velocitas*, "swiftness," and the greater number of compounds (as being similar to them), which, doubtless, have their origin from something, but demand no exercise of ingenuity, for which indeed except on doubtful points there is no opportunity in these investigations.

Words derived from *antiquity* have not only illustrious patrons, but also confer on style a certain majesty, not unattended with pleasure; for they have the authority of age, and, as they have been disused for a time, bring with them a charm similar to that of novelty. But there is need of moderation in the use of them, in order that they may not occur too frequently, nor show themselves too manifestly, since nothing is more detestable than affectation; nor should they be taken from a remote and already forgotten age, as are *topper*, "quickly," *antegerio*, "very much," *exanclare*, "to draw out," *prosapia*, "a race," and the verses of the Salii, which are scarcely understood by the priests themselves. Those verses, however, religion forbids to be changed, and we must use what has been consecrated; but how faulty is speech, of which the greatest virtue is perspicuity, if it needs an interpreter! Consequently, as the oldest of new words will be the best, so the newest of old words will be the best.

The case is similar with regard to *authority*, for though he may seem to commit no fault who uses those words which the greatest writers have handed down to him, yet it is of much importance for him to consider, not only what words they used, but how far they gave a sanction to them. No one would now tolerate from us *tuburchinabundus*, "devouring," or *lurchinabundus*, "voracious," though Cato was the father of them; nor would people endure *lodices*, "blankets," in the masculine gender, though that gender pleases Pollio; nor *gladiola* for "little swords," though Messala has used it; nor *parricidatus*, "parricide," which was thought scarcely endurable in Caelius; nor would Calvus induce me to use *collos*, "necks"; all which words, indeed, those authors themselves would not now use.

There remains, therefore, *custom*, for it would be almost ridiculous to prefer the language which men have spoken rather than that which they now speak. What else, indeed, is old language, but the old manner of speaking? But even for following custom, judgment is necessary; we must settle, in the first place, what that is which we call custom; for if custom be merely termed that which the greater number do, it will furnish a most dangerous rule, not only for language, but, what is of greater importance, for life. For where is there so much virtue that what is right can please the majority? Therefore, to pluck out hairs, to cut the hair of the head in a succession of rings, and to drink to excess in the bath—whatever country those practices may have invaded—will not become the proper custom, because no one of them is undeserving of censure. So just as we do bathe and clip our hair, and take our meals together according to custom, so, in speaking, it is not whatever has become a vicious practice with many that is to be received as a rule of language. For, not to mention how the ignorant commonly speak, we know that whole theatres, and all the crowd of the circus, have frequently uttered barbarous exclamations. Custom in speaking, therefore, I shall call the agreement of the educated, just as I call custom in living the agreement of the good.

Chapter Seven

Since we have mentioned what rules are to be followed in speaking, we must now specify what are to be observed by writers. What the Greeks call *orthography*, we may call the art of writing correctly. This art does not consist in knowing of what letters every syllable is composed (for this study is beneath the profession even of the grammarian), but exercises its whole subtlety, in my opinion, on dubious points. As it is the greatest of folly to place a mark on all long syllables, since most of them are apparent from the very nature of the word that is written, yet it is at times necessary to mark them, as when the same letter gives sometimes one sense and sometimes another, according as it is short or long; thus *malus* is distinguished by a mark, to show whether it means "a tree" or "a bad man"; *palus*, too, signifies one thing when its first syllable is long, and another when its second is long; and when the same letter is short in the nominative and long in the ablative, we have generally to be informed by this mark which quantity we are to adopt.

Grammarians have in like manner thought that the following distinction should be observed: namely, that we should write the preposition *ex*, if the word *specto* was compounded with it, with the addition of *s* in the second syllable, *exspecto;* if *pecto*, without the *s*. It has been a distinction, also, observed by many, that *ad*, when it was a preposition, should take the letter *d*, but when a conjunction, the letter *t;* and that *cum*, if it signified time, should be written with a *q* and two *u*'s following, but if it meant accompaniment, with a *c*. Some other things were even more trifling than these, as that *quicquid* should have a *c* for the fourth letter, lest we should seem to ask a double question, and that we should write *quotidie,* not *cotidie,* to show that it was for *quot diebus.* But these notions have already passed away among other puerilities.

It is however a question, in writing prepositions, whether it is proper to observe the sound which they make when joined to another word, or that which they make when separate, as, for instance, when I pronounce the word *obtinuit;* for our method of writing requires that the second letter should be *b,* while the ear catches rather the sound of *p;* or when I say *immunis,* for the letter *n,* which the composition of the word requires, is influenced by the sound of the following syllable, and changed into another *m.* It is also to be observed, in dividing compound words, where you ought to attach the middle consonant to the first or to the second syllable; for *aruspex,* as its latter part is from *spectare,* will assign the letter *s* to the third syllable, while *abstemius,* as it is formed of *abstinentia temeti,* "abstinence from wine," will leave the *s* to the first syllable. As to *k,* I think it should not be used in any words, except those which it denotes of itself, so that it may be put alone. This remark I have not omitted to make, because there are some who think *k* necessary when *a* follows, even though there is the letter *c,* which suits itself to all vowels.

But orthography submits to custom, and has therefore frequently been altered. I say nothing of those ancient times when there were fewer letters, and when their shapes were different from these of ours, and their natures also different, as that of *o* among the Greeks, which was sometimes long and sometimes short, and, as among us, was sometimes put for the syllable which it expresses by its mere name. I say nothing also of *d,* among the ancient Latins, being added as the last letter to a great number of words, as is apparent from the rostral pillar erected to Caius Duellius in the forum; nor do I speak of *g* being used in the same manner, as, on the *pulvinar* of the Sun, which is worshipped near the temple of Romulus, is read *vesperug,* which we take for *vesperugo.* Nor is it necessary to say anything here of the interchange of letters of which I have spoken above, for perhaps as they wrote they also spoke. . . .

For myself, I think that all words (unless custom has ordered otherwise) should be written in conformity with their sound. For this is the use of letters—to preserve words, and to restore them, like a deposit, to readers; and they ought, therefore, to express exactly what we are to say.

These are the most important points as to speaking and writing correctly. The other two departments, those of speaking with significancy and elegance, I do not indeed take away from the grammarians, but, as the duties of the rhetorician remain for me to explain, I will reserve them for a more important part of my work.

Yet the reflection recurs to me, that some will regard those matters of which I have just treated as extremely trifling, and even as impediments to the accomplishment of anything greater. Nor do I myself think that we ought to descend to extreme solicitude and puerile disputations about them; I even consider that the mind may be weakened and contracted by being fixed upon them. But no part of grammar will be hurtful, except what is superfluous. Was Cicero the less of an orator because he was most attentive to the study of grammar, and because, as appears from his letters, he was a rigid exactor, on all occasions, of correct language from his son? Did the writings of Julius Caesar on analogy diminish the vigor of his intellect? Or was Messala less elegant as a writer, because he devoted whole books, not merely to single words, but even to single letters? These studies are injurious, not to those who pass through them, but only to those who dwell immoderately upon them.

DONATUS

The Ars Minor of Donatus

How many parts of speech are there? Eight. What? Noun, pronoun, verb, adverb, participle, conjunction, preposition, interjection.

CONCERNING THE NOUN

What is a noun? A part of speech which signifies with the case a person or a thing specifically or generally. How many attributes has a noun? Six. What? Quality, comparison, gender, number, form, case. In what does the quality of nouns consist? It is twofold, for either it is the name of one and is called proper, or it is the name of many and is called common. How many degrees of comparison are there? Three. What? Positive, as learned; comparative, as more learned; superlative, as most learned. What nouns are compared? Only common nouns signifying quality or quantity. What case is the comparative degree used with? The ablative without a preposition; for we say, "doctior illo." What case with the superlative? Only the genitive plural: for we say, "doctissimus poetarum." What are the genders of nouns? Four. What? Masculine, as hic magister; feminine, as haec musa; neuter, as hoc scamnum; common, as hic et haec

Reprinted with permission of the Regents of the University of Wisconsin, from Wayland Johnson Chase, The "Ars Minor" of Donatus, 1926, the University of Wisconsin. Footnotes omitted.

sacerdos. There is besides the common of three genders, if so be everything is said, as hic et haec et hoc felix. It is epicene, that is, without distinction of gender, as passer, aquila. The numbers of nouns are how many? Two. What? Singular, as hic magister; plural, as hi magistri. The forms of nouns are how many? Two. What? Simple, as decens, potens; compound as indecens, impotens. In what ways are nouns compounded? Four: from two in their original forms, as suburbanus; from two that have been changed, as efficax, municeps; from an original form and a changed form, as insulsus; from a changed form and an unchanged, as nugigerulus; sometimes from several together, as inexpugnabilis, inperterritus. The cases of nouns are how many? Six. What? Nominative, genitive, dative, accusative, vocative, ablative. Through these, nouns, pronouns, and participles of all genders are declined in this way:

Magister is a common noun of masculine gender, singular number, simple form, nominative and vocative case, which will be declined thus: in the nominative, hic magister; in the genitive, huius magistri; in the dative, huic magistro; in the accusative, hunc magistrum; in the ablative, ab hoc magistro; and in the plural in the nominative, hi magistri; in the genitive, horum magistrorum; in the dative, his magistris; in the accusative, hos magistros; in the vocative, O magistri; in the ablative, ab his magistris.

Musa is a common noun of feminine gender, singular number, simple form, nominative and vocative case, which will be declined thus: in the nominative, haec musa; in the genitive, huius musae; in the dative, huic musae; in the accusative, hanc musam; in the vocative, O musa; in the ablative, ab hac musa; and in the plural in the nominative, hae musae; in the genitive, harum musarum; in the dative, his musis; in the accusative, has musas; in the vocative, O musae; in the ablative, ad his musis.

Scamnum is a common noun of neuter gender, singular number, simple form, nominative, accusative, and vocative case, which will be declined thus: in the nominative, hoc scamnum; in the genitive, huius scamni; in the dative, huic scamno; in the accusative, hoc scamnum; in the vocative, O scamnum; in the ablative, ab hoc scamno; and in the plural in the nominative, haec scamna; in the genitive, horum scamnorum; in the dative, his scamnis; in the accusative, haec scamna; in the vocative, O scamna; in the ablative, ab his scamnis.

Sacerdos is a common noun of common gender, singular number, compound form, nominative and vocative case, which will be declined thus: in the nominative, hic and haec sacerdos; in the genitive, huius sacerdotis; in the dative, huic sacerdoti; in the accusative, hunc and hanc sacerdotem; in the vocative, O sacerdos; in the ablative, ab hoc and ab hac sacerdote; and in the plural in the nominative, hi and hae sacerdotes; in the genitive, horum and harum sacerdotum; in the dative, his sacerdotibus; in the accusative, hos and has sacerdotes; in the vocative, O sacerdotes; in the ablative, ab his sacerdotibus.

Felix is a common noun of all genders, singular number, simple form, nominative and vocative case, which will be declined thus: in the nominative, hic and haec and hoc felix; in the genitive, huius felicis; in the dative, huic felici; in the accusative, hunc and hanc felicem, and hoc felix; in the vocative, O felix; in the ablative, ab hoc and ab hac and ab hoc felice or felici; and in the plural in the nominative, hi and hae felices and haec felicia; in the genitive, horum and harum and horum felicium; in the dative, his felicibus; in the accusative, hos and has felices and haec felicia; in the vocative, O felices and O felicia; in the ablative, ab his felicibus.

Those nouns which have formed their endings in the ablative case singular in "a" or "o," change the genitive plural into what? Into "rum," and the dative and ablative, into "is."

Those nouns which have formed their endings in the ablative case singular in "e" or "i" or "u" change the genitive plural into what? If they have been contracted with "e," into "um"; if prolonged, into "rum"; if with "i," into "ium"; if with "u," into "uum," the letter "u" doubled. They change the dative and ablative into what? All of them into "bus."

CONCERNING THE PRONOUN

What is a pronoun? A part of speech that is often used in place of the noun to convey the same meaning and now and then refers to a person previously mentioned. How many attributes belong to the pronoun? Six. What? Quality, gender, number, form, person, case. In what is the quality of pronouns? It is twofold: for pronouns are either definite or indefinite. Which are definite? Those which stand for persons, as ego, tu, ille. What are indefinite? Those that don't stand for persons, as quis, quae, quod. What are the genders of pronouns? Almost the same as of nouns: masculine as quis, feminine as quae, neuter as quod, common as qualis and talis, of three genders as ego, tu. How many numbers of pronouns are there? Two. What? Singular, as hic; plural, as hi. How many numbers of pronouns are there? Two. What? Simple, as quis, compound, as quisquis. How many persons of pronouns are there? Three. What? First, as ego, second, as tu, third, as ille. How many cases also are there? Six, just as of nouns, through which pronouns of all genders are inflected in this way. Ego is a definite pronoun of all genders, singular number, simple form, first person, nominative case, which will be declined thus: Ego, mei, or mis, mihi, me, a me, and plural, nos, nostrum or nostri, nobis, nos, o (and) a nobis; of the second person, every gender, singular number, tu, tui or tis, tibi, te, o (and) a te, and plural vos, vestrum or vestri, vobis, vos, o (and) a vobis; of the third person, masculine gender, singular number, ille, illius, illi, illum, ab illo, and plural illi, illorum, illis, illos, ab illis; of feminine gender, singular number, illa, illius, illi, illam, ab illa, and plural, illae, illarum, illis, illas, ab illis; of neuter gender, singular number, illud, illius, illi, illud, ab illo, and plural, illa, illorum, illis, illa, ab illis.

Somewhat less definite, of masculine gender, singular number, ipse, ipsius, ipsi, ipsum, ab ipso, and plural, ipsi, ipsorum, ipsis, ipsos, ab ipsis; of feminine gender, singular number, ipsa, ipsius, ipsi, ipsam, ab ipsa, and plural, ipsae, ipsarum, ipsis, ipsas, ab ipsis; of neuter gender, singular number, ipsum, ipsius, ipsi, ipsum, ab ipso, and plural, ipsa, ipsorum, ipsis, ipsa, ab ipsis. Also somewhat less definite, of masculine gender, singular number, iste, istius, isti, istum, ab isto, and plural, isti, istorum, istis, istos, ab istis; of feminine gender, singular number, ista, istius, isti, istam, ab ista, and plural, istae, istarum, istis, istas, ab istis; of neuter gender, singular number, istud, istius, isti, istud, ab isto, and plural, ista, istorum, istis, ista, ab istis. Also the article-like prepositive or demonstrative, of masculine gender, singular number, hic, huius, huic, hunc, o (and) ab hoc, and plural, hi, horum, his, hos, o (and) ab his; of feminine gender, singular number, haec, huius, huic, hanc, o (and) ab hac, and plural, haec, harum, his, has, o (and) ab his; of neuter gender, singular number, hoc, huius, huic, hoc, o (and) ab hoc, and plural, haec, horum, his, haec, o (and) ab his. Also the attributive, or relative of masculine gender, singular number, is, eius, ei, eum, ab eo, and plural, ei, eorum, eis, eos, ab eis; of feminine gender, singular number, ea, eius, ei, eam, ab ea, and plural, eae, earum, eis, eas, ab eis; of neuter gender, singular number, il, eius, ei, id, ab eo, and plural, ea, eorum, eis, ea, ab eis. Also the indefinite of masculine gender, singular number, quis, cuius, cui, quem, a quo or a qui, and plural, qui, quorum, quis or quibus, quos, a quis or a quibus; of feminine gender, singular number, quae, cuius, cui, quam, a qua or a qui, and plural, quae quarum quis or quibus quas a quis or a quibus; of neuter gender, singular number, quod cuius cui quod a quo or a qui, and plural, quae quorum quis or quibus quae a quis or a quibus. Also possessive, definite words which are used in relation to something else, and are singular in each of two ways, and of masculine gender, meus, mei, meo, meum, o (and) a meo, and plural in one of the two ways, mei, meorum, meis, meos, o (and) a meis; of feminine gender, singular number, mea, meae, meam, o (and) a mea, and plural, meae, mearum, meis, meas, o (and) a meis; of neuter gender, singular number, meum, mei, meo, meum, o (and) a meo, and plural, mea, meorum, meis, mea, o (and) a meis; of second person, masculine gender, singular number, tuus, tui, tuo, tuum, a tuo, and plural, tui, tuorum, tuis, tuos, a tuis; of feminine gender, singular number, tua, tuae, tuae, tuam, a tua, and plural, tuae, tuarum, tuis, tuas, a tuis; of neuter gender, singular number, tuum, tui, tuo, tuum, a tuo, and plural, tua, tuorum, tuis, tua, a tuis: of third person, masculine gender, singular number, suus, sui, suo, suum, a suo, and plural, sui, suorum, suis, suos, a suis; of feminine gender, singular number, sua, suae, suae, suam, a sua, and plural, suae, suarum, suis, suas, a suis; of neuter gender, singular number, suum, sui, suo, suum, a suo, and plural, sua, suorum, suis, sua, a suis. Also possessive, definite words, used in relation to something else, plural in one of two ways, and of masculine gender, noster, nostri, nostro, nostrum, o (and) a nostro, and plural in each of the two ways, nostri, nostrorum, nostris, nostros, o (and) a nostris; of feminine gender, singular number, nostra, nostrae, nostrae, nostram, o (and) a nostra, and plural, nostrae, nostrarum, nostris, nostras, o (and) a nostris; of neuter gender, singular number, nostrum, nostri, nostro, nostrum, o (and) a nostro, and plural, nostro, nostrorum, nostris, nostra, o (and) a nostris: of second person, masculine gender, singular number, vester, vestri, vestro, vestrum, a vestro, and plural, vestri, vestrorum, vestris, vestros, a vestris; of feminine gender, singular number, vestra, vestrae, vestrae, vestram, a vestra, and plural, vestrae, vestrarum, vestris, vestras, a vestris; of neuter gender, singular number, vestrum, vestri, vestro, vestrum, a vestro, and plural, vestra, vestrorum, vestris, vestra, a vestris. Give the compounds of these. Egomet, tute, illic, istic, idem; in masculine gender lengthened, in neuter shortened, quisquis, quisnam, quispiam, aliquis, and others.

CONCERNING THE VERB

What is a verb? A part of speech with tense and person, without case, signifying "to perform some action," or "to suffer," or neither. How many attributes has the verb? Seven. What? Quality, conjugation, gender, number, inflection, tense, person. In what does the quality of verbs consist? In modes and in forms. What are the modes? Indicative, as lego; imperative, as lege; optative, as utinam legerem; subjunctive, as cum legam; infinitive, as legere; impersonal, as legitur. How many forms of verbs are there? Four. What? Undefined, as lego; desiderative, as lecturio; frequentative, as lectito; inchoative, as fervesco, calesco. How many conjugations of verbs are there? Three. What? First, second, third. What is the first? It has in the indicative mode, present time, singular number, second person in the active and neuter verb, long "a" before the last letter; in the passive, common, and deponent, before the last syllable, as amo, amas, amor, amaris; and the future tense of the same mode, ends the syllable in "bo" and "bor," as amo amabo, amor amabor. What is the second? It has in the indicative mode, present tense, singular number, second person, active and neuter verb, long "e" before the last letter; in the passive, common, and deponent, before the last syllable, as doceo doces, doceor doceris; and the future tense of the same mode, ends the syllable in "bo" and in "bor," as doceo docebo, doceor docebor. What is the third? That which in the indicative mode, present tense, singular number, second person, active and neuter verb, has a short "i" or a long "i" before the last letter; in the passive, common, and deponent, in place of "i," short "e" or long "i" before the last syllable, as lego legis, legor legeris, audio audis, audior audiris; and the future tense of the same mode ends in "am" and in "ar," as lego legam, legor legar, audio audiam, audior audiar. It can be seen immediately in the imperative and in the infinitive whether the letter "i" is short or long. For short "i" is turned into "e"; if it has been made long, it is not changed. When does the third conjugation end the future tense not in "am" only, but also in "bo"? Occasionally when it has had the letter "i" not shortened but lengthened, as eo is ibo: queo quis quibo. How many kinds of verbs are there? Five. What? Active, passive, neuter, deponent, common. What are the active? Those that end in "o," and make the passive by adding the letter "r," as lego legor. What are the passive? Those which end in "r" and, when that has been dropped, return into the active, as legor lego. What are the neuter? Those which end in "o" as active, but are not Latin when the letter "r" has been added, as sto curro: we do not say, "stor curror." Which are the deponent? Those which end in "r" as passive, but are not Latin when that is withdrawn, as luctor loquor. Which are common? Those which end in "r" as deponent, but fall into two forms, of the one undergoing action, and the one acting, as osculor criminor; for we say, "osculor te," and "osculor a te," "criminor te," and "criminor a te." How many numbers of verbs are there? Two. What? Singular, as lego, plural, as legimus. How many forms of verbs are there? Two. What? Simple, as lego; compound, as neglego. How many tenses of verbs are there? Three. What? Present, as lego; preterite, as legi; future, as legam. How many tenses are there in the inflection of verbs? Five. What? Present, as lego; preterite imperfect, as legebam; preterite perfect, as legi; preterite pluperfect, as legeram; future, as legam. How many persons of verbs are there? Three. What? First, as lego; second, as legis; third, as legit.

Give the inflection of the active verb. Lego, an active verb, in the indicative mode, a word of present time, singular number, simple form, first person, third short conjugation, which will be inflected thus: lego, legis, legit, and plural, legimus, legitis, legunt; in the same mode in the preterite imperfect tense, legebam, legebas, legebat, and plural, legebamus, legebatis, legebant; in the same mode in the preterite perfect tense, legi, legisti, legit, and plural, legimus, legistis, legerunt or legere; in the same mode in the preterite pluferfect tense, legeram, legeras, legerat, and plural, legeramus, legeratis, legerant; in the same mode in the future tense, legam, leges, leget, and plural, legemus, legetis, legent. In the imperative mode in the present tense for the second and third person, lege or legas, legat, and plural, legamus, legite, or legatis, legant; in the same mode in the future tense, legito or legas, legito or legat, and plural, legamus, legitote, or legatis, legant or legunto or leguntote. In the optative mode in the present and the preterite imperfect tense, utinam legerem, legeres, legeret, and plural, utinam legeremus, legeretis, legerent; in the same mode in the preterite perfect tense and in the pluperfect, utinam legissem, legisses, legisset, and plural, utinam legissemus, legissetis, legissent; in the same mode in the future tense, utinam legam, legas, legat, and plural, utinam legamus, legatis, legant. In the subjunctive mode in the present tense, cum legam, legas, legat, and plural, cum legamus, legatis, legant; in the same mode in the preterite imperfect, cum legerem, legeres, legeret, and plural, cum legeremus, legeretis, legerent; in the same mode in the perfect preterite tense, cum legerim, legeris, legerit, and plural, cum legerimus, legeritis, legerint; in the same mode in the pluperfect preterite tense, cum legissem, legisses, legisset, and plural, cum legissemus, legissetis, legissent; in the same mode in the future tense, cum legero, legeris, legerit, and plural, cum legerimus, legeritis, legerint. In the infinitive mode in numbers and persons in the present tense and the preterite imperfect, legere; in the perfect preterite and the pluperfect, legisse; in the future, lectum ire or lecturum esse. For the impersonal verb in the present tense, legitur; in the imperfect preterite, legebatur; in the perfect preterite, lectum est or lectum fuit; in the pluperfect preterite, lectum erat or lectum fuerat; in the future, legetur. Gerundives or participial verbs are these: legendi, legendo, legendum, lectum, lectu. Two participles are derived from the active verb, of the present tense and of the future, of the present, legens; of the future, lecturus. Legor, a passive verb in the indicative mode, a word of present tense, singular number, simple form, first person, third short conjugation, which is inflected thus: legor, legeris or legere, legitur, and plural, legimur, legimini, leguntur; in the same mode in the imperfect preterite tense, legebar, legebaris or legebare, legebatur, and plural, legebamur, legebamini, legebantur; in the same mode in the perfect preterite tense, lectus sum, es, est, and plural, lecti sumus, estis, sunt; and in that mode with a sense of remoter time, lectus fui, fuisti, fuit, and plural, lecti fuimus, fuistis, fuerunt or fuere; in the same mode in the pluperfect preterite tense, lectus eram, eras, erat, and plural, lecti eramus, eratis, erant; and in the same mode with a sense of remoter time, lectus fueram, fueras, fuerat, and plural, lecti fueramus, fueratis, fuerant; in the same mode in the future tense, legar, legeris or legere, legetur, and plural, legemur, legemini, legentur; in the imperative mode in the present tense for the second and third person, legere or legaris, legatur, and plural, legamur, legimini or legamini, legantur; in the same mode in the future tense, legitor or legaris, legitor or legatur, and plural, legamur, legimini or legiminor, legantur or leguntor; in the optative mode in the present tense and in the imperfect preterite, utinam legerer, legereris or legerere, legeretur, and plural, utinam legeremur, legeremini, legerentur; in the same mode in the preterite perfect tense and the pluperfect, utinam lectus essem, esses, esset, and plural, utinam lecti essemus, essetis, essent; and in that mode with a sense of remoter time, utinam lectus fuissem, fuisses, fuisset, and plural, utinam lecti fuissemus, fuissetis, fuissent; in the same mode in the future tense, utinam legar, legaris or legare, legatur, and plural, utinam legamur, legamini, legantur; in the subjunctive mode in the present tense, cum legar, legaris or legare, legatur, and plural, cum legamur, legamini, legantur; in the same mode in the imperfect preterite tense, cum legerer, legereris or legerere, legeretur, and plural, cum legeremur, legeremini, legerentur; in the same mode in the perfect preterite tense, cum lectus sim, sis, sit, and plural, cum lecti simus, sitis, sint; and in that mode with a sense of remoter time, cum lectus fuerim, fueris, fuerit, and plural, cum lecti fuerimus, fueritis, fuerint; in the same mode in the pluperfect preterite tense, cum lectus essem, esses, esset, and plural, cum lecti essemus, essetis, essent; and in that mode with a sense of remoter time, cum lectus fuissem, fuisses, fuisset, and plural, cum lecti fuissemus, fuissetis, fuissent; in the same mode in the future tense, cum lectus ero, eris, erit, and plural, cum lecti erimus, eritis, erint; and in that mode with a sense of remoter time, cum lectus fuero, fueris, fuerit, and plural, cum lecti fuerimus, fueritis, fuerint. In the infinitive mode in numbers and persons in the present tense and in the imperfect preterite, legi; in the perfect preterite and the pluperfect, lectum esse or fuisse; in the future, lectum iri. Two participles are derived from the passive verb, of the preterite tense and of the future; of the preterite, lectus; of the future, legendus. The neuter verb follows the rule of the active verb; the common and the deponent, of the passive.

CONCERNING THE ADVERB

What is an adverb? A part of speech which, added to a verb, explains the meaning of it and completes it. What attributes has an adverb? Three. Meaning, comparison, form. In what does the meaning of adverbs consist? Because they are adverbs of place, or of time, or of number, or of denying, or of affirming, or of showing, or of desiring, or of encouraging, or of order, or of enquiry, or of likeness, or of quality, or of quantity, or of doubting, or personal, or of calling, or of replying, or of separating, or of swearing, or of choosing, or of grouping, or of preventing, or of result, or of comparing. Give the adverbs of place. As hic or ibi, intus or foris, illic or inde. Give those of time. As hodie, nuper, aliquando;

those of number, as semel, bis; of negation, as non; of affirmation, as etiam quinni; of demonstration, as eu, ecce; of desire, as utinam; of urging, as eia; of order, as deinde; of interrogation, as cur, quare, quamobrem; of likeness, as quasi, ceu; of quality, as docte, pulchre; of quantity, as multum, parum; of doubt, as forsitan, fortasse; personal, as mecum, tecum, secum, nobiscum, vobiscum; of calling, as heus; of replying, as heu; of separating, as seorsum; of swearing, as edepol, ecastor, hercle, medius fidius; of selecting, as potius, immo; of grouping, as simul, una; of preventing, as ne; of result, as forte, fortuitu; of comparing, as magis or tam. Comparison of adverbs consists in what? In three degrees of comparison: positive, comparative, superlative. Give an adverb of the positive degree. As docte: of the comparative, as doctius; of the superlative, as doctissime. We do not say, "magis doctius" and "tam doctissime" because magis and tam are joined only to the positive degree, although our ancestors said "tam magis" and "quam magis." How many forms of adverbs are there? Two. What? Simple and compound; simple, as docte, prudenter; compound, as indocte, imprudenter. Adverbs of location are concerned with in the place, or from the place, or to the place. But in loco and de loco have the same meaning, as intus sum, intus exeo, foris sum, foris venio. Ad locum has another meaning, as intro eo, foras eo. But we do not say thus, "de intus and de foris," though we say, "in foras" or "ad foras."

CONCERNING THE PARTICIPLE

What is a participle? A part of speech partaking of the nature of the noun, and of the verb; of the noun, the genders and cases; of the verb, the tenses and meanings; of both, the number and form. How many attributes has the participle? Six. What? Gender, case, tense, meaning, number, form. How many genders of participles are there? Four. What? Masculine, as hic lectus; feminine, as haec lecta; neuter, as hoc lectum; common in three genders, as hic and haec and hoc legens. How many cases of participles are there? Six. What? Nominative, as hic legens; genitive, as huius legentis; dative, as huic legenti; accusative, as hunc legentem; vocative, as O legens; ablative, as ab hoc legente. How many tenses of participles are there? Three. What? Present, as legens; preterite, as lectus; future, as lecturus and legendus. In what do the meanings of participles consist? Because two participles come from the active verb, present and future, as legens lecturus; from the passive two, preterite and future, as lectus legendus; from the neuter two, just as from the active, present, and future, as stans, staturus; from the deponent three, present, preterite, and future, as loquens, locutus, locuturus; from the common four, present, preterite, and two futures, as criminans, criminatus, criminaturus, criminandus. How many numbers of participles are there? Two. What? Singular, as hic legens; plural, as hi legentes. How many forms of participles are there? Two. What? Simple, as legens; compound, as neglegens. Give the declension of the participle. Legens is a participle coming from the active verb of present tense, every gender, singular number, simple form, nominative, accusative, and vocative case, which will be declined thus: in the nominative, hic and haec and hoc legens; genitive, huius legentis; dative, huic legenti; accusative, hunc and hanc legentem and hoc legens; vocative, O legens; ablative, ab hoc and ab hac and ab hoc legente or legenti; and plural nominative, hi and hae legentes and haec legentia; genitive, horum and harum and horum legentium; dative, his legentibus; accusative, hos and has legentes and haec legentia; vocative, O legentes and O legentia; ablative, ab his legentibus. Lecturus, lectura, lecturum, participles coming from the active verb of future tense, masculine, feminine and neuter gender, singular number, simple form, nominative and vocative case, which will be declined thus: in the nominative, lecturus, lectura, lecturum; genitive, lecturi, lecturae, lecturi; dative, lecturo, lecturae, lecturo; accusative, lecturum, lecturam, lecturum; vocative, lecture, lectura, lecturum; ablative, ab hoc lecturo, ab hac lectura, ab hoc lecturo; and plural nominative, lecturi, lecturae, lectura; genitive, lecturorum, lecturarum, lecturorum; dative, lecturis; accusative, lecturos, lecturas, lectura; vocative, lecturi, lecturae, lectura; ablative, ab his lecturis. Lectus, lecta, lectum, participles coming from the passive verb of preterite tense, masculine, feminine and neuter gender, singular number, simple form, nominative and vocative case, which will be declined thus: in the nominative, lectus, lecta, lectum; genitive, lecti, lectae, lecti; dative, lecto, lectae, lecto; accusative, lectum, lectam, lectum; vocative, lecte, lecta, lectum, ablative, ab hoc lecto, ab hac lecta, ab hoc lecto; and plural nominative, lecti, lectae, lecta; genitive, lectorum, lectarum, lectorum; dative, lectis; accusative, lectos, lectas, lecta; vocative, lecti, lectae, lecta; ablative, ab his lectis. Legendus, legenda, legendum, participles coming from the passive verb of future tense, masculine, feminine, and neuter gender, singular number, simple form, nominative and vocative case, which will be declined thus: in the nominative, legendus, legenda, legendum; genitive, legendi, legendae, legendi; dative, legendo, legendae, legendo; accusative, legendum, legendam, legendum; vocative, legende, legenda, legendum; ablative, ab hoc legendo, ab hac legenda, ab hoc legendo; and plural nominative, legendi, legendae, legenda; genitive, legendorum, legendarum, legendorum; dative, legendis; accusative, legendos, legendas, legenda; vocative, legendi, legendae, legenda; ablative, ab his legendis.

CONCERNING THE CONJUNCTION

What is a conjunction? The part of speech which binds together the sentence and sets it in order. How many attributes has a conjunction? Three. What? Function, form, order. The function of conjunctions is of how many sorts? Five. What? Copulative, disjunctive, expletive, causal, rational. Give the copulatives. Et, que, at, atque, ac, ast. Give the disjunctives. Aut, ve, vel, ne, nec, neque. Give the expletives. Quidem, equidem, saltim, videlicet, quamquam, quamvis, quoque, autem, porro, porro autem, tamen. Give the causals. Si, etsi, etiamsi, siquidem, quando quidem, quin, quin etiam, quatinus, sin, seu, sive, nam, namque, ni nisi, nisi si, si enim, etenim, ne, sed, interea, licet, quamobrem, praesertim, item, itemque, ceterum, alioquin, praeterea. Give the rationals. Ita, itaque, enim, enimvero, quia, quapropter, quoniam, quoniam quidem, quippe, ergo, ideo, igitur, scilicet, propterea, idcirco. How many forms of conjunctions are there? Two. What? Simple, as nam; compound, as namque. The order of conjunctions depends on what? Accordingly as they are conjunctions which are placed before, as ac, ast; or placed afterward, as que, autem; or general, as et, igitur, ergo.

ABOUT THE PREPOSITION

What is a preposition? A part of speech which, placed before other parts of speech, completes their meaning or alters it or diminishes it. How many attributes has a preposition? One. What? Case alone. How many? Two. What? Accusative and ablative. Give the prepositions of [used with] the accusative case. Ad, apud, ante, adversum, cis, citra, circum, circa, contra, erga, extra, inter, intra, infra, juxta, ob, pone, per, prope, secundum, post, trans, ultra, praeter, propter, supra, usque, penes. How are they used? Namely, we say ad patrem, apud villam, ante aedes, adversum inimicos, cis Renum, citra forum, circum vicinos, circa templum, contra hostem, erga propinquos, extra terminos, inter naves, intra moenia, infra tectum, juxta macellum, ob augurium, pone tribunal, per parietem, prope fenestram, secundum fores, post tergum, trans ripam, ultra fines, praeter officium, propter rem, supra caelum, usque oceanum, penes arbitros. Give the prepositions used with the ablative case. A, ab, abs, cum, coram, clam, de, e, ex, pro, prae, palam, sine, absque, tenus. How are they used? Namely, we say a domo, ab homine, abs quolibet, cum exercitu, coram testibus, clam custodibus, de foro, e iure, ex praefectura, pro clientibus, prae timore, palam omnibus, sine labore, absque iniuria, tenus pube, though we say pube tenus. Give prepositions of both cases. In, sub, super, subter. When are "in" and "sub" used with the accusative case? Whenever we mean that either we or someone else are going, have gone, are about to go *into* a place. When with the ablative? When we mean that either we or someone else are, have been, are about to be, *in* a place. In with the accusative case, "itur in antiquam silvam"; in with the ablative case, "stans celsa in puppe"; sub with the accusative case, "postesque sub ipsos Nituntur gradibus"; sub with the ablative case, "arma sub adversa posuit radiantia quercu." Super has what force? When it means place, it more often governs the accusative case than the ablative; when we make mention of anyone, in the ablative only, as "multa super Priamo rogitans." In has what force? As when it governs the accusative case and signifies against, as in adulterum, in desertorem. Subter has what force? The same as the former, meaning to a place and in a place. Which are the prepositions which govern words and can be used only in compounds? Di, dis, re, se, am, con. How? Thus, we say diduco, distraho, recipio, secubo, amplector, congredior. Which are those which cannot be joined? Apud and penes. Which are joined and are separated? All the rest.

ABOUT THE INTERJECTION

What is an interjection? A part of speech signifying a state of the mind by an unusual tone of the voice. What attribute has an interjection? Only meaning. The meaning of an interjection is in what? Because we signify joy, as evax; or grief, as heu; or wonder, as papae; or fear, as attat; and any others that are like them.

ST. ANSELM

De Grammatico

Tutor . . . When it is asserted that literate is a quality, this assertion is only correct if made in the sense which occurs in Aristotle's treatise *On the Categories*.

Student But doesn't that treatise make the point, "Everything which is, is one or other of either substance or quantity or quality," and so on? So if *man* alone is literate, a substance alone is literate. How comes it then that that treatise accounts *literate* a quality rather than a substance?

T Although the text in question might be interpreted in the way you claim, for everything which is is some one or other of the things you mention, nevertheless Aristotle's main intention in that book was not to show this, but rather to show how every name or verb *signifies* one or other of them.

It was not his aim to show the nature of individual circumstances, nor yet of what circumstances individual words are appellative; rather he wished to show what circumstances they signify.

However, since words only signify circumstances, he had, in order to

St. Anselm, *De Grammatico*, in *The De Grammatico of St. Anselm*, Desmond P. Henry, University of Notre Dame Publications in Mediaeval Studies, vol. XVIII (Notre Dame, Ind., 1964), 70-73.

indicate what words signify, to indicate what those circumstances might be.

For, without going into further detail, the classification which he undertook at the opening of his work *On the Categories* is enough to bear out what I assert. He does not say, "Each item of whatever is is either a substance or a quantity," and so on, nor yet, "Each item of whatever is expressed in an incomplex fashion has "substance" or "quality" as its appellation," but rather, "Each item of whatever is expressed in an incomplex fashion *signifies* a substance or a quality."

    S   Your point is persuasive.

    T   Now when Aristotle says, "Each item of whatever is expressed in an incomplex fashion signifies a substance or a quantity," and so on, to which type of signification does it appear to you that he is referring—to that whereby the utterances as such signify precisively, and which pertains to them essentially, or to that other type which is oblique and only accidental to the utterances?

    S   He can only be referring to that sort of signification whereby they signify precisively, and which he himself imputes to such utterances when defining the noun and the verb.

    T   And do you consider that anywhere in his work he treated the matter otherwise than he did in this classification, or that any of his followers wished to adopt an attitude differing from his on this topic, when writing on logic?

    S   Their writings contain no grounds whatsoever for such an opinion, for at no point does one find any of them proffering an utterance to show something it can signify obliquely; they always proffer an utterance to show what it signifies precisively. Thus, when they want to show a substance, none of them proffers *white* or *literate*; however, *white* and *literate*, and so on, are advanced as examples when they are dealing with quality.

    T   So that if, given the aforementioned classification, I were to ask you what *literate* is in terms of that classification, and in keeping with the opinions of those whose logical writings make appeal to it, what kind of a question would I be asking, and what kind of a reply would you give?

    S   This question must concern either the word or the circumstance it signifies. Hence, since it is agreed that in terms of this distinction *literate* signifies literacy and not man, I would reply immediately:

if your question concerns the word, then it is a word signifying quality;

if, however, your question is about the circumstance, then it *is* a quality.

    T   You realise, do you not, that in this same text Aristotle refers to words by the name of the circumstance which those words signify, and not by the name of those of which they are merely appellative? Thus, when he says, "Every substance seems to signify this particular thing," what he means is, "Every word *signifying* a substance." It is in this way that he names, or rather *shows* circumstances— as you reminded us just now—by recourse to utterances which only signify them, and which frequently are not appellative of them at all.

    S   I can't help realising this. Hence, whether the question is posed in respect of the word or in respect of the circumstance, when one asks what *literate* is according to the treatise of Aristotle, and according to his followers, the correct answer is: a quality.

However, from the point of view of appellation it certainly is a substance.

    T   Quite so: we mustn't be disturbed by the fact that logicians make written assertions about words insofar as they signify, and yet, in speaking, given the appellative function of those words, use them in a fashion which is at variance with those assertions, any more than we are when the grammarians assert one thing about a word considered as an exemplar, but quite another when it is considered in relation to the constitution of circumstances.

After all, they tell us that "stone" is masculine in gender, "rock" feminine, but "property" neuter, and that "to fear" is an active verb, whereas "to be feared" is passive; yet no one asserts that a stone is masculine, a rock feminine, or property neither masculine nor feminine, nor that to fear is to perform an action, whereas to be feared is to undergo an action.

PETER OF SPAIN

Tractatus Suppositionum

Some linguistic expressions are complex, as "The man runs"; others are incomplex, as "man," because it is an incomplex term. A term, as it is taken here, is a word which signifies the universal or the particular, as "man" or "Sortes" and so forth. Moreover, each and every incomplex term either signifies substance, or quality, or quantity, or relation, or action, or passion, or place, or time, or position, or habit. Signification, as it is taken here, is the representation, established by convention, of a thing by an utterance. Wherefore, since every thing is either a universal or a particular, it follows necessarily that words which do not signify a universal or a particular do not signify any thing. And so they would not be terms in the sense in which "term" is taken here, as for example the signs of universality and particularity are not terms.

Of significations, one is that of a substantial thing and is accomplished through a substantive noun, as "man"; another is that of an adjectival thing and is accomplished through an adjective, as "white," or through a verb, as "running." This is not, in the strict sense, substantival or adjectival signification, but is rather the signification of something sub-

Peter of Spain (Pope John XXI), "Tractatus Suppositionum" from the *Summulae Logicales,* in *The Summulae Logicales of Peter of Spain,* Joseph P. Mullally, University of Notre Dame Publications in Mediaeval Studies, vol. VIII (Notre Dame, Ind., 1945), 3 and 5.

stantively or adjectivally, because to signify something substantively or adjectivally are modes of words, while adjectivity and substantivity are modes and differences of the things which are signified and which do not signify.

Substantive nouns are said to stand for or denote (*supponere*), but adjectives or verbs are said to characterize (*copulare*). Supposition (*suppositio*) is the acceptance of a substantive term as denoting something. Supposition and signification differ, however, because signification is accomplished through the imposition of a word to signify a thing, while supposition is the acceptance of a term, already significant, as denoting something; as when one says: "Man runs," the term "man" is taken to denote Sortes, Plato and the rest of men. Thus, signification is prior to supposition. They also differ in that signification belongs to the word, whereas supposition belongs to the term already composed of the word and its signification. Therefore, to denote (*supponere*) and to signify (*significare*) are not the same, but rather are different, as holds by the topic of co-ordinates and inflections.[1] Furthermore, signification is the relation of a sign to the signified, whereas supposition is the relation of that which denotes to that which is denoted. Therefore, supposition is not signification. Characterization (*copulatio*) is the acceptance of an adjectival term for something.

Of suppositions, one type is general; the other, discrete. General supposition is that which is accomplished by means of a general term, such as "man," "animal." Discrete supposition is that which is accomplished by means of a discrete term, such as "Sortes," or by means of a general term taken in conjunction with a demonstrative pronoun, as "this man," which is a discrete term.

[1] Aristotle, *Topica*, II, 9, 114a26–114b5.

ANTOINE ARNAULD

The Art of Thinking

Chapter 13: Nominal Definitions

We must now make a few remarks about the use of nominal definitions, lest they be abused.

Our first observation is that no attempt should be made to define all words; such an attempt would be useless, even impossible, to achieve. To define a word which already expresses a distinct idea unambiguously would be useless; for the goal of definition—to join to a word one clear and distinct idea—has already been attained. Words which express ideas of simple things are understood by all and require no definition. If men occasionally introduce some obscurity into such a simple, clear idea, a writer who uses the word to express the clear idea need not fret; for attention is directed primarily to what is clear in the idea. Examples of words expressing such ideas are the following: "being," "thought," "extension," "equality," "duration," "time," and other similar ones. Although some may obscure the idea of time by the definition they offer—for example, saying that time is the measure of motion according to before and after—men never base their understanding of time upon such a

Abridged from Antoine Arnauld: *The Art of Thinking*, translated by James Dickoff and Patricia James, copyright © 1964 by The Bobbs-Merrill Company, Inc., reprinted by permission of the Liberal Arts Press Division.

definition but rather conceive time in the natural fashion. The learned and the ignorant alike understand the same thing and do so with the same facility when someone says to them that it takes less time for a horse to go a league than it does a tortoise.

Further, it is impossible to define all words. In defining we employ a definition to express the idea which we want to join to the defined word; and if we then wanted to define "the definition," still other words would be needed—and so on to infinity. Hence, it is necessary to stop at some primitive words, which are not defined. To define too much is just as great a failing as to define too little: Either way we would fall into the confusion that we claim to avoid.

Our second observation is that existing definitions should not be changed unless reasonable objection can be taken to them. If our "new" usage is in accord at least with the usage of the educated, the word will be more readily understood than if we first detach the word from the idea customarily joined to the word and then attach the word to a new idea. To change a customary mathematical definition would be a mistake unless the definition were confused and the idea expressed not sufficiently clear, as perhaps may be the case with the definition of "angle" and "proportion" in Euclid.

Thirdly, we observe that in defining a word we should, as far as possible, follow custom, not giving to the word a meaning too far removed from the word's original meaning nor one contrary to the word's etymology. To define "parallelogram," for example, as a figure which is bounded by three straight lines would be a violation of the etymology of the word "parallelogram." In defining, we should for the most part content ourselves with removing from ambiguous words all but one meaning so that we can join the word to that meaning exclusively. For example, in common usage "heat" means the feeling that we have when we draw near the fire as well as a quality that we imagine as in the fire but as completely similar to that which we feel. To avoid this ambiguity we restrict the word "heat" to express only one of the ideas. So, we define "heat" as "that feeling one has when he draws near the fire"; to the cause of that feeling we give a completely different name, say, "potential heat."

This third observation was prompted by the following consideration. Once a word has been joined to an idea, men do not easily separate the two: Whenever the word is used the old idea recurs, making a man forget any different idea given in a definition. So, to define a nonsense word like *"bara"* as a figure bounded by three straight lines would be easier than to attempt to remove from the word "parallelogram" its customary idea and then to join to "parallelogram" the idea of a figure whose sides cannot be parallel.

The alchemist makes a practice of flaunting common usage. He delights in changing for no good reason the names of almost everything of which he speaks. The names he gives things are names which already express ideas that have no true relation to the ideas with which the names are newly joined. This practice gives rise to some outrageous reasonings. A certain man thought the plague to be an affect of a severe case of lead poisoning, that is, a "Saturnian evil." So, he claimed that people would be cured of the pestilence if they wore about their necks a small piece of lead (called by chemists "saturn") upon which was engraved on a Saturday (which derives its name from Saturn) the figure by which astronomers represent the planet Saturn. How absurd to prescribe a cure based on nothing more than similarity between names!

[Still more intolerable is the alchemist's practice of using the language of the sacred mysteries of religion in order to veil his so-called secrets. Some have been impious enough to apply what Scripture says of the true Christians to the chimerical Rosicrucian Brotherhood, declaring the Rosicrucians to be the chosen race, the royal priesthood, the holy nation, the people whom God has chosen and whom he has called out of darkness into his wonderful light. The alchemist describes a Rosicrucian as one who has attained to a glorious immortality made possible by the alchemist's discovery of a way to retain the soul within the body. This method makes use of the philosopher's stone, gold, said by the alchemist to be the most fixed and incorruptible of bodies. Gassendi in his examination of Fludd's philosophy exposes these mad dreams and other similar ones. Gassendi's exposition makes clear that there is scarcely a more reprehensible turn of mind than is exhibited by these enigmatical writers who believe that the most groundless thoughts—not to say the most false and impious ones—will pass for grand mysteries if reclothed in forms unintelligible to the common man.]

PART II: JUDGMENT

Chapter 1: Words as They Function in Sentences [1683]

Our purpose here is to explain the various observations men have made about judgment. Judgments are propositions expressed by sentences. Since sentences themselves are composed of words, we begin our explanation with a discussion of the principal kinds of words—nouns, pronouns, and verbs.

To inquire whether this preliminary explanation belongs to grammar or to logic is of little import. Suffice it to say that whatever is useful in achieving the goal at which a particular art aims belongs to that art, whether such knowledge belongs to one art alone or whether that knowledge is common to several arts and sciences. The goal of logic is to think well. Clearly, then, an understanding of different functions of words—that is, of sounds which are used to express ideas—is useful to logic. An idea is usually closely linked to some sound so that the sound evokes the expressed idea and the idea evokes the expressing sound.

In general we may say that words are distinct and articulate sounds used by men as signs of mental activity. Since all mental activity can be reduced to conceiving, judging, reasoning, and ordering—as we have already remarked—words may be signs of any one of these activities. There are principally three kinds of words—namely, nouns, pronouns, and verbs (which take the place of nouns but in a peculiar way). Each of these three kinds will be treated in some detail.

1. CONCERNING NOUNS   The words set apart to refer to things or modes of things are called nouns.

Nouns which refer to things are called substantive nouns—as "earth" or "sun"; nouns which refer to modes, referring at the same time to the substance of the mode, are called adjectival nouns—as "good," "just," and "round." When the mind conceives a mode by abstraction, without relating the mode to its substance, the mode then subsists by itself in some fashion in the mind. Consequently, the mode is referred to by a substantival noun—as "wisdom," "whiteness," or "color."

Contrariwise, when a substance is conceived in its relation to some thing (that is, when the substance is conceived as a mode of that thing), the word which refers to the substance in this relation is an adjective—as "human" or "carnal." But this mode referred to by the adjective can itself be reified and is then referred to by a substantive noun. Thus, the substantive noun "human" gives rise to the adjective "human" which in turn gives rise to the adjectival noun "humanity."

There are nouns which in grammar pass as substantive nouns but which, since they refer to a manner of being or a mode of a substance, are really adjectival nouns—as "king," "philosopher," or "doctor." The reason such words can pass for substantive nouns is that the mode each refers to belongs to but a single kind of thing so that when the word is spoken we have in mind the idea of the mode as well as the idea of thing of which the mode is a mode.

Similarly, the expressions "the red" and "the white" and others like them are really adjectives because a relation to a substance is indicated. The substance need not be referred to because of its indeterminateness. "The red" refers to all red things; "the white" to all white things; or, using the parlance of geometry, "the red" refers to any red thing whatsoever.

As an adjective then has two referents: One referent, the mode, is distinctly indicated; the other referent, the substance, is confusedly indicated. Although the mode is distinctly referred to, it is nonetheless only indirectly referred to; the substance, however, although it is only confusedly referred to, is referred to directly. The word "white" refers indirectly, though distinctly, to whiteness.

2. CONCERNING PRONOUNS   A pronoun takes the place of a noun and thus enables us to avoid wearisome repetition. But when a pronoun replaces a noun in an expression, the expression no longer has the same effect as before. Not at all. Pronouns remove the displeasure caused by repetition; for a pronoun can represent a noun in a confused manner. Nouns lay things bare to the mind; pronouns present them as veiled— although the mind recognizes that the same thing is referred to by both noun and pronoun. Consequently, there is nothing strange in having the noun and pronoun joined together: Thou, Phaedria; behold, I, John.

3. CONCERNING THE DIFFERENT KINDS OF PRONOUNS   Men, recognizing that it was often vain or in poor taste to name themselves, introduced the first-person pronouns—"I," "me." Then, the second-person pronouns —"thou," "you"—were introduced to facilitate reference to the person being addressed. And finally, the third-person pronouns were introduced to avoid repetition of the names of things or persons other than the auditor or the speaker. One kind of third-person pronouns are demonstrative pronouns—"this," "that," "these," "those"; the demonstratives are so named because they refer by pointing, as with a finger. Another kind of pronouns are the reflexives—as "myself," "yourself," "himself," and so on; the reflexives are so named because they indicate a relation of the thing referred to, to itself.

We have already remarked that although a pronoun has the same referent as the replaced noun, the reference is made only confusedly by the pronoun. But there is something special about a pronoun like "this" when "this" is used without an expressed noun. The pronoun "this" when used alone is always a substitute for a noun which refers very generally or confusedly—in particular, for the noun "thing." Thus, the pronoun "this" refers confusedly, as does any pronoun; but in addition, the noun that a "this" replaces itself refers in a very general and confused way.

4. CONCERNING THE RELATIVE PRONOUN   Still another kind of pronouns are the relative pronouns—"who," "which." The relative pronouns share a common feature with other kinds of pronouns; but relative pronouns also possess a distinctive characteristic. Like other pronouns, a relative pronoun is used in place of a noun and refers confusedly. What is peculiar, however, is that the expression of which the relative is a constituent part can be either the subject or the predicate of a sentence.

The relative pronoun introduces those added or subordinate clauses which we shall subsequently discuss at some length—for instance, "God who is good," "the Word which is visible."

I presume here that the notions of subject and predicate of a sentence are understood even though they have not been explained. Such notions are so common that they are ordinarily understood before any study of logic is undertaken. Any person who does not understand them has only to refer to that part of the text where they are explained.

We are now able to answer this question: What is the precise meaning of the word "that" when it follows the verb and appears to be related to nothing, as in "John answered that he was not the Christ," or as in "Pilate said that he found no guilt in Jesus Christ"? Some people will say that such a "that" functions as an adverb. But the truth is that such a "that" functions as a relative pronoun. So, in the sentence "John answered that he was not the Christ," the "that" is the introductory word of a sentence—namely, "he was not the Christ"—which is part of the predicate of the sentence whose subject is "John"; for we can think of this sentence as the sentence "John was answering that he was not the Christ."

Such a "that" also has the second function of a relative pronoun, namely, that of taking the place of the noun to which "that" is related. Even so, many capable people have been led astray, saying that in sentences like "John answered that he was not the Christ" the "that" lacks this second characteristic of the relative pronoun. But if we think of this sentence as "John gave the response that he was not the Christ," we see that "that" does indeed have the same referent as the noun "response" to which the "that" is related.

"I assume that you will be discreet," "I say that you are wrong" can be analyzed in a similar fashion. We can think of "I assume that you will be discreet" as "I make the assumption that you will be discreet," in which case the antecedent of "that" is "assumption." We can think of "I say that you are wrong" as "I make the assertion that you are wrong," in which case the antecedent of "that" is "assertion."

In Greek an article when placed after a noun functions as a pronoun. But a Greek article used in this fashion, though it takes the place of a noun, never functions as the introductory word of a sentence. Understanding that the Greek article can function as a pronoun, we reject a cleric's contention that Luke's passage (chapter 22), must be translated as "This is my body, my body given for you" or as "This is my body, the body given for you." We hold that the passage is no worse translated as "This is my body which is given for you." When an article functions as a pronoun in a Greek sentence, two ends are achieved: (1) Repetition of a noun is avoided, and (2) the qualifying phrase is not subordinated to but remains a part of the independent clause. If we translate Luke's passage as "This is my body, my body given for you," we have not reflected the use of the Greek article to avoid repetition. If we translate the passage as "This is my body which is given for you," we avoid repetition but we no longer have the qualifying phrase as a part of the main clause. Thus, one translation is as bad as the other, despite the cleric's contrary claim.

Chapter 2: The Verb [1683]

With the exception of a few points, all that we have said in chapter 1 concerning nouns and pronouns was taken from a little book printed quite some time ago under the title *General Grammar*. I simply repeat here what that author says about verbs in his chapter 13, for I believe that nothing need be added to his treatment.

Man, this grammarian observes, has just as great a need for words indicating the activity of assertion as for words expressing ideas, for much of our thinking is in fact asserting. A verb is nothing else but a word whose principal function is to indicate assertion—that is to say, to indicate not only that a man conceives certain things but rather that he judges concerning these things and makes an assertion. A noun like "assertion" expresses the idea of assertion, but only verbe indicate the activity of asserting.

The principal function of the verb, we said, is to indicate assertion. The indicative mood of a verb is used for this principal function. Later we shall show that the verb is used to indicate other activities of the mind —desiring, asking, praying, commanding, and so on. These subordinate functions are indicated by inflections of the verbs and by moods other than the indicative. In this chapter we are restricting ourselves to a discussion of the indicative mood—that is, to a discussion of the verb's principal function. Accordingly, we say a verb's function is to connect the two terms of a sentence so that the sentence indicates a connection between ideas. But the only verb which functions in such a limited way in a sentence is the verb "to be," called the copulative verb. Moreover, the verb "to be" functions in this limited way only in its third-person singular present tense, and even then not always. For since men tend to abbreviate their expressions, one and the same word is used both to indicate the activity of assertion and to express ideas.

1. In addition to using the verb to assert, men have used it to express ideas. For example, the two words "Peter lives" (or in Latin, "*Petrus vivit*") is a sentence simply because the word "lives" serves two functions: It expresses the attribute of being alive as well as indicating the assertion that Peter is alive. Consequently, to say "Peter lives" is the same as to say "Peter is alive." Because men use verbs both to indicate

assertion and to express ideas, each language has many verbs rather than just the one copulative verb.

2. In some languages—Latin, for example—a verb can have three functions: It indicates an assertion, serves as subject or as predicate, or as both subject and predicate of the sentence. For example, *"sum homo"* ("I am a man") is a sentence in which the verb *"sum"* both indicates an assertion and supplies the subject *"ego."* Similarly, a single word—as *"vivo"* ("I live") or *"sedo"* ("I sit")—is a sentence, for the verb (1) indicates an assertion and supplies (2) subject and (3) predicate for the sentence. A Latin verb can supply a subject of a sentence in virtue of being inflected to indicate person and number.

3. In addition to indicating the activity of assertion a verb indicates the time with respect to which an assertion is made. For example, when I say to you "You dined," I assert that you are a diner with respect to the past. Because verbs function as time-indicators, verbs have various tenses.

Because a word may have more than one function, even clever people have difficulty in isolating the essential nature of a verb. The accidental functions of a verb tend to obscure its essential function—that of indicating the activity of assertion.

Aristotle, emphasizing the time-indicating function of the verb, defines a verb as a word which signifies with time. Others, such as Buxtorf, considering the subject-supplying function of the verb, have supplemented Aristotle's definition by defining a verb as a word which may be inflected to indicate both person and time. Still others, focusing upon the idea-expressing function of the verb and noting that the ideas expressed by verbs are commonly actions and passions, claim that the essential nature of the verb is to express the ideas of actions and passions. And finally, Julius Caesar Scaliger thought that he solved a great mystery when in his book on the principles of the Latin language he observed that the distinction between nouns and verbs arose from the division of things into the permanent and the changing: Nouns were said to refer to permanent things; verbs, to changing things.

Obviously, none of these definitions explains the true nature of the verb. The first two definitions are readily seen to be faulty, because they do not state even *what* the verb indicates but only *that with respect to which* the verb indicates—namely, time and person. The last two definitions are even worse, for they exhibit the two greatest vices of definitions: (1) The definitions are too narrow, for they do not apply to all verbs; (2) the definitions are too broad, for they apply to words which are not verbs. Since there are verbs which fail to express the idea of any action or passion and verbs which do not refer to any changing thing—"exists," "reposes," and so on—neither of the last two definitions is correct. Moreover, there are words which are not verbs but which do express the ideas of actions or passions or which refer to changing things—namely, the participles, which are nouns. A participle derived from an active verb expresses the idea of an action whereas one derived from a passive verb expresses the idea of a passion. And a word like "flowing" refers to a changing thing just as much as the verb "flows."

Since there are present, past, and future participles, especially in Greek, we see that participles can function also as time-indicators. The observations that there are words other than verbs which are time-indicators vitiates the first two definitions. Further, nouns in the vocative sense are counterexamples to the claim that only verbs function as subject-suppliers.

A participle is not a verb because a participle does not indicate the activity of assertion. Because a verb indicates the activity of assertion, a verb is an essential part of a sentence. Consequently, a participle cannot be made into a sentence unless a verb is joined to the participle. Why is it that "Peter lives" ("*Petrus vivit*") is a sentence but "Peter living" ("*Petrus vivans*") becomes a sentence only if we add "is" to form "Peter is living"? The answer is simple: The activity of assertion which is indicated by the verb "lives" ("*vivit*") has been removed in transforming "lives" ("*vivit*") into the participle "living" ("*vivans*"), and not until the indication of the activity of assertion is reintroduced by adding the verb "is" does the participial phrase "Peter living" become a sentence. It seems apparent then that the essential nature of a verb is to indicate the activity of assertion.

We add in passing that an infinitive differs from a participle though both often function as nouns. For the participle is an adjectival noun while the infinitive is a substantival noun derived by abstraction from the corresponding adjectival noun, just as "whiteness" is derived from "white." For example, the verb "blushes" expresses the idea of blushing and indicates the activity of asserting blushing of something; the participle "blushing" expresses the idea of blushing without any indication of assertion; the infinitive "to blush" when taken as a noun expresses blushing as the product of the activity blushing.

We have now established the following definition: A verb is a word that indicates the activity of assertion. No word can be found which indicates the activity of assertion and yet is not a verb; nor can we find any verbs which do not indicate the activity of assertion, at least not any verbs in the indicative mood. Were there any word which always indicated the activity of assertion and had no other function—as the verb "is" sometimes does—such a word would still be called a verb. In those sentences which philosophers use to express eternal truths—such as "God is infinite," "Every body is divisible," or "The whole is greater than its parts," the word "is" does nothing but indicate the activity of assertion; for in these sentences no time-indicator is required and the subject is explicit.

The *essence* of a verb is to indicate the activity of assertion. If, however, we want to include in our definition principal accidents of a verb, we would define the copulative verb as a word which indicates the activity of assertion with respect to person, number, and time. A verb which differs from the copulative verb by expressing an idea as well as indicating the activity of assertion can be defined as follows: A noncopulative verb is a word which indicates the activity of assertion with respect to person, number, and time, and which expresses the attribute asserted.

As a final note we may add that the attribute expressed may itself be the attribute of asserting. For example, when I say "I assert," the verb "assert" indicates my activity of asserting and asserts of me the characteristic of asserting. When I say "Peter asserts," the verb "asserts" indicates my activity of asserting that Peter asserts. Thus, there are two "assertings" involved, mine and Peter's. Similarly, when I say "I deny," the verb "deny" indicates an assertion, asserts a negation.

Although not all our judgments are affirmative, verbs indicate only the activity of assertion and not the activity of denial. We indicate denial either by qualifying the verb by means of an adverb or by joining the verb with a noun or pronoun which indicates denial—for example "none" or "no one."

Chapter 5: Simple, Compound and Complex Propositions

Every proposition is expressed by a sentence with at least one subject and one predicate; but it does not follow that a proposition may not be expressed by a sentence having more than one subject or predicate. Propositions expressed by sentences having only one subject and one predicate are called simple propositions, whereas those propositions expressed by sentences having more than one subject or predicate are called compound propositions. In the sentence "Goods and evils, life and death, poverty and riches come from the Lord," "come from the Lord" is predicated not merely of one subject but of several.

Before explaining compound propositions in detail, we must remark that there are some propositions which are simple though they appear to be compound. For a proposition is simple if it is expressed by a sentence having a single subject and a single predicate; and there are complex sentences which have but one subject and one predicate. If either the subject or the predicate of a sentence is a complex expression, then the sentence is a complex sentence. Recall that a complex expression includes as part of itself a subordinate clause joined to the rest of the complex expression by a "who" or a "which"; the function of a "who" or a "which" is to make the subordinate clause a constitutive part of the main sentence. For example, when Christ said, "He who does the will of my father who is in heaven shall enter into the kingdom of heaven," he voiced a complex sentence. Although the subject of this sentence is a complex expression containing two verbs, the sentence has nonetheless a single subject: for the clause "who does the will of my father who is in heaven" is joined to the word "he" to become a constitutive part of the subject. But when we say "Goods and evils come from the Lord," we have uttered a compound sentence; for we predicate "comes from the Lord" of "goods," which is one subject, as well as of "evils," another subject.

A complex expression expresses a single idea, whereas a compound expression expresses more than one idea. A clause joined to the sentence by a "who" or a "which" expresses either an imperfect proposition, as we shall explain subsequently, or else a proposition which was asserted previously and now is conceived as if it were a simple idea rather than a proposition just being asserted. Consequently, the proposition expressed by the subordinate clause can also be expressed (1) by adjectival nouns or participles, as well as (2) by clauses introduced by a "who" or a "which." For example, the same proposition is expressed by "The invisible God has created the visible world" as is expressed by "God, who is invisible, created the world, which is visible." We are not asserting that God is invisible: Rather, this fact is taken for granted as having been previously asserted, and we now assert that God conceived as invisible has created the visible world. A similar analysis applies to the proposition expressed by "Alexander, who was the most generous of all kings, conquered Darius."

If, however, we said that Alexander was the most generous of all kings and the conqueror of Darius, we obviously would have asserted two things of Alexander—(1) that he was the most generous of all kings, and (2) that he was the conqueror of Darius. So with reason such a proposition—as well as similar ones—is called compound, but propositions such as those considered in the preceding paragraph are called simple though complex.

Complex propositions are of two kinds. A proposition may be complex (1) in virtue of the matter of the proposition—that is, the subject-idea or the attribute or both—or (2) in virtue of the form alone.

A proposition is complex with respect to its matter if the proposition has (1) a complex subject-idea, (2) a complex attribute, or (3) both a complex subject-idea and a complex attribute.

1. The subject-idea of a proposition is complex when the subject-idea is expressed by a complex expression. For example, the proposition ex-

pressed by the sentence "Every man who fears nothing is a king" is a complex proposition which has a complex subject-idea. In the next example "happy" is the predicate and all the rest in the subject; the verb "is" is understood.

> Happy he who like the ancient mortal race
> Far from commerce and from trade
> Tills with beast the ancestral fields,
> From all negotiations free.
>
> (HORACE, EPODES II. 1–4)

2. The attribute is complex when it is expressed by a complex expression. For example, the proposition expressed by the sentence "Piety is a good which renders men happy in the greatest adversity" is a complex proposition with a complex attribute.

Note that any sentence containing an active verb along with its object expresses a complex proposition and in one sense two propositions. For example, if we say "Brutus killed a tyrant," we mean that Brutus killed someone who was a tyrant. This proposition is contradicted by saying that Brutus did not kill anyone or by saying that the person whom Brutus killed was not a tyrant. This point is important because when a sentence expressing such a proposition is used in an argument we often prove only part of the sentence while we merely assume the other part. It is often necessary to transform such a sentence from the active to the passive voice in order to put the argument into its most natural form and to express explicitly that which is to be proved. We shall expound this point at greater length when we discuss arguments which consist of complex sentences of this kind.

3. Some propositions have both a complex subject-idea and a complex attribute, each idea being expressed by a complex expression. For example, the proposition expressed by the sentence "The great who oppress the poor will be punished by God who is the protector of the oppressed" is a complex proposition having both a complex subject–idea and a complex attribute.

The first three and a half lines of the following verse express the subject-idea of the proposition expressed; the remaining lines express the attribute, and the verb "sing" indicates the assertion.

> I, who once tuned my song to a slender reed
> But then left the woodland, bidding the neighboring fields
> To serve the landsman, however demanding,
> A servitude welcome to farmers, sing of Mars–bristling
> Arms now and the man who once from the coast of Troy
> Exiled by Fate to Italy and Lavinian shores first came.
>
> (VIRGIL, AENEID I. 1a–d, 1–3)

Chapter 6: *The Nature of Relative Clauses*

Propositions complex in virtue of their form will be discussed later. But first several important observations must be made concerning the nature of subordinate clauses forming part of either the subject or the predicate of sentences expressing propositions complex in virtue of their matter.

1. We have already seen that clauses whose subjects are the relative pronouns "who" or "which" are subordinate clauses. For example, were we to remove the word "men" from either of the expressions "men, who are created to know and to love God" or "men who are pious," what would remain in each case would be a subordinate clause.

Recall what was said in chapter 8 of Part I—namely, that an addition made to an expression in order to form a complex expression may be one of two kinds. When the addition does not alter the idea expressed, the addition is called a simple explication: The idea originally expressed has exactly the same extension as the idea expressed by the complex expression. For example, in the complex expression "men, who are created to know and to love God," the addition "who are created to know and to love God" is a mere explication.

But when the addition restricts the extension and alters the signification of the idea originally expressed, the addition is called a determination. Thus, in the expression "men who are pious," the addition "who are pious" is a determination. So we conclude that a "who" or a "which" may introduce either an explicative or a restrictive clause.

When a "who" or a "which" introduces an explicative clause, the predicate of that subordinate clause expresses an idea affirmed of the idea expressed by the antecedent of the relative word—even though this affirmation is only subordinate to the affirmation asserted by the whole sentence. Because the relative word introduces an explicative clause, we may substitute for the relative pronoun its antecedent without altering the sense of the subordinate clause. For example, in the expression "men, who were created to know and to love God," the subordinate proposition is expressed by "men were created to know and to love God."

But when a "who" or a "which" introduces a restrictive clause, the idea expressed by the predicate of that subordinate clause is not properly affirmed of the idea expressed by the antecedent of the relative word. For example, if in the expression "men who are pious are charitable" we were to substitute for "who" the word "men," we would express the false proposition that man as man is pious. In stating the proposition that men who are pious are charitable, we assert that the characteristic of piety is found neither in men in general nor in any particular man. Instead, we form a complex idea by joining together two simple ideas—the idea of man and the idea of piety—and then we judge that the attribute of being charitable is part of this complex idea. Thus the subordinate clause asserts nothing more than that the idea of piety is not incompatible with the idea of man. Having made this judgment we then consider what idea can be affirmed of this complex idea of pious man.

2. Often there are expressions which are doubly or triply complex, being composed of parts, each of which is complex; and each part may contain either explicative or restrictive clauses. For example, consider the expression "The doctrine which identifies the sovereign good with the sensual pleasure of the body and which was taught by Epicurus is unworthy of a philosopher." The predicate of this sentence is "unworthy of a philosopher"; all the rest is subject. The subject is therefore a complex expression containing two subordinate clauses, the first of which is "which identifies the sovereign good with the sensual pleasure of the body." This first "which" introduces a restrictive clause, since "doctrine," the antecedent of "which," is restricted to refer to that doctrine which identifies the sovereign good with the sensual pleasure of the body. Because the "which" is restrictive, we cannot replace it by the word "doctrine" without arriving at an absurdity. The second subordinate clause is "which was taught by Epicurus." The antecedent of this "which" is the whole complex expression "the doctrine which identifies the sovereign good with the sensual pleasure of the body," an expression which refers to a unique doctrine that may have any number of accidental characteristics—such as being believed by this, that, or the other person. Consequently, the second subordinate clause is explicative rather than restrictive. We may, therefore, substitute for the second "which" its antecedent and say "The doctrine which identifies the sovereign good with the sensual pleasure of the body was taught by Epicurus."

3. Our final remark is this: To determine whether a "which" or a "who" is restrictive or explicative, we must often attend more to a man's intention than to his exact words.

There are complex expressions which fail to appear complex—or at least fail to appear as complex as they are—because not all that the speaker intends by his words is explicitly expressed. The implicit complexity of expressions was explained at length in chapter 8 of Part I. There it was shown that in ordinary discourse general words frequently are used to refer to a unique referent. But we pointed out that there is no danger of a misunderstanding because the circumstances in which the expression is uttered make obvious what the peculiar referent is. For example, on the lips of a Frenchman the word "king" refers to Louis XIV.

In addition to the context the following rule will help us judge whether a general expression is restricted to a distinct and particular idea, even when the restriction is not explicit: *A general word must be taken in a restrictive rather than a universal sense if the word occurs in a sentence which would express an absurdity were the word taken in its general sense.* For example, if I heard a man say "The king gave me a command," I am confident that the word "king" is taken in a restrictive and not a general sense, for it is not kings in general but a particular king that gives a particular command. Or again, suppose that a man says to me "*The Brussels Gazette* of January 14, 1662, treating what happened in Paris, is false." I am certain that he has more in mind than is explicit in his words. In saying that the *Gazette* is false, the man is really speaking of some particular piece of news, say, that the king has received one hundred knights into the Order of the Holy Spirit.

Similar remarks apply to judgments concerning the opinions of philosophers. When we say that the doctrine of such and such a philosopher is false without explicitly expressing the doctrine under question, we are thinking of a specific doctrine of that philosopher. If we say that the doctrine of Lucretius concerning the soul is false, we use the phrase "the doctrine of Lucretius concerning the soul" to refer to a particular teaching of that philosopher. A doctrine is false, not because it is held by a certain author, but rather because the doctrine is contrary to fact. Judgments concerning the opinions of philosophers are of the form: A certain opinion, which was taught by a certain author, is false. More specifically: Two assertions are implicitly made when we assert that the opinion—taught by Lucretius—that the soul is composed of atoms is false. The particular assertion states the necessary truth that it is a great error to maintain that the soul is composed of atoms; the subordinate assertion reports only a point of history, that is, that this error was taught by Lucretius.

Chapter 9: Compound Sentences

We have already said that compound sentences are those sentences which have either a compound subject or a compound predicate. Sentences may be either explicitly compound or implicitly compound. Logicians call implicitly compound sentences exponibles. Explicitly compound sentences are of six kinds: copulatives, disjunctives, conditionals, causals, relatives, and adversatives.

COPULATIVES   Copulative sentences are those sentences which have more than one subject or else more than one predicate and in which these multiple subjects or predicates are joined by an affirmative or negative conjunction, that is, by an "and" or by a "neither/nor." A "neither/nor" functions as an "and" in joining two expressions; [but a "neither/nor" has the additional function of negating the verb. In the sentence "Neither knowledge nor riches makes a man happy," "knowledge" is conjoined with "riches" just as surely as "knowledge" is conjoined with "riches" in the sentence "Knowledge and riches make a man vain."

Three kinds of copulatives can be distinguished:

1. Copulatives with more than one subject:

> Life and death are within the sway of the tongue.

2. Copulatives with more than one predicate:

> He who loves moderation, which is desirable in all things, lives neither sordidly nor opulently.
>
> (HORACE, ODES II. 10.5–8)

> A sound mind hopes for prosperity in adversity and fears adversity in prosperity.
>
> (IBID., 13–15)

3. Copulatives with both more than one subject and more than one predicate:

> Neither homes nor lands nor heaps on heaps of gold and silver can banish fevers from the body nor cares from the mind.
>
> (HORACE, EPISTLES I. 2. 47–49)]

A copulative sentence is true only if each of its predicates can be truly joined to each of its subjects. For example, the sentence "Faith and a good life are necessary for salvation" is true since in fact faith is necessary for salvation and a good life is necessary for salvation. But the sentence "A good life and riches are necessary for salvation" is false since although a good life is necessary for salvation riches are not.

[A contradictory of a copulative sentence is a sentence in which the joining asserted in the copulative is denied. The contradictory of a copulative may take several forms. We may, for example, form the contradictory of a copulative by placing the sign of negation in front of the sentence, as St. Augustine did when he wrote, "It is not the case that you can both love a person and abandon him." Or we may form the contradictory of a copulative by expressly denying the conjunction—as we do when we say "It is not possible that a thing should be at one and the same time both one thing and another."

> One cannot both be in love and be wise.
>
> (P. SYRUS, SENTENTIAE 20)

> Not both love and majesty can be together enthroned.
>
> (OVID, METAMORPHOSES II. 846–847)]

DISJUNCTIVES   Disjunctive sentences are sentences in which disjunctive joining is expressed. Such sentences are very common:

[Friendship either finds friends equal or makes them so.
(P. SYRUS, SENTENTIAE 25)

Whoever lives in complete solitude is either a beast or an angel.
(ARISTOTLE, POLITICS I. 2, 1253a 3).

Men are moved either by self-interest or by fear.

The earth revolves about the sun, or the sun revolves about the earth.

Every deliberate action is either good or evil.]

A disjunctive sentence is true only if one and only one of its parts is true. A disjunctive sentence is *necessarily* true only if one and only one of its parts is true; [but a disjunctive sentence is *morally* true if virtually always one and only one of its parts is true. Since the theologians have made clear that there is no such thing as an indifferent action, the sentence "Every deliberate action is either good or evil" is true. But the sentence "Men are moved only by self-interest or fear" is not necessarily true, since there are men who are not moved by either of these passions but rather by a consideration of duty. What is true is that self-interest and fear are the two motive forces of the majority of men.

A contradictory of a disjunctive sentence is a sentence in which the truth of the disjunction is denied. In Latin the contradictory is formed, as is the contradictory of any compound sentence, by prefixing the sentence with a negating expression: *Non omnis actio est bona vel mala* (Not every action is either good or bad). In our own tongue we prefix the sentence to be negated with the phrase "It is false that" in this fashion: "It is false that every action is either good or bad."]

CONDITIONALS   A conditional is a sentence which is two sentences connected by an "if–then." [The sentence following the "if" is the antecedent, and the sentence following the "then" is the consequent. In the sentence "If the soul is spiritual, then it is immortal," the antecedent is "the soul is spiritual" and the consequent is "it is immortal."

The inference which is claimed to hold from the antecedent to the consequent is sometimes mediate and sometimes immediate. If there is nothing in the antecedent to show why the consequent must follow, then the inference is mediate:

If the earth is stationary, then the sun turns.

If God is just, then the wicked will be punished.

Although the above inferences are quite proper, they are not immediate. The antecedent and the consequent have no term in common; and that the antecedent implies the consequent is seen only in virtue of some unexpressed knowledge present to the mind—namely, that since the earth and the sun are continuously in different positions with respect to one another, it must be that if one is stationary the other is in motion.

If the inference is immediate, one of four things must be true:

1. The antecedent and the consequent have like subjects:

> If death is a passage to a happier life, then death is desirable.

> If you have failed to feed the poor, then you have killed them.

2. The antecedent and the consequent have like predicates:

> If all trials from God should be dear to us, then sickness should be dear to us.

3. The predicate of the antecedent is like the subject of the consequent:

> If patience is a virtue, then some virtues are painful.

4. The subject of the antecedent is like the predicate of the consequent (this condition occurs only when the consequent is a negative sentence):

> If all true Christians live according to the Gospel, then there are not many true Christians.]

We determine the truth of conditional sentences by considering only whether the inference from the antecedent to the consequent is valid. A conditional sentence is true—even though both the antecedent and the consequent be false—provided only that the consequent follows from the antecedent. Consider the following example: "If the will of the creature is capable of keeping the absolute will of God from being accomplished, then God is not omnipotent."

A sentence which is a contradictory of a conditional sentence is a sentence which denies that the consequent follows from the antecedent. In Latin the negation of a conditional is achieved by placing the appropriate negating expression before the conditional:

> *Non si miserum fortuna Sinonem*
> *Finxit, vanum etiam mendacemque improba finget.*
>
> (VIRGIL, AENEID II. 79–80)

> (Nor if Fortune has molded Sinon for misery, then will she also in her spite mold him as false and lying.)

But in our tongue the contradictory of a conditional is expressed by use of an "even though" along with a negating expression: "Even though you eat the forbidden fruit, you will not die." Or we may contradict a conditional simply by prefixing the conditional with an "It is false that"; for example, "It is false that if you eat the forbidden fruit, then you will die."

CAUSALS   A causal sentence is a sentence which is two sentences joined by a word expressing a causal connection, for example, the word "because" or the expression "in order that."

> [Woe to the rich, because they have their comfort in this world.
>
> The wicked are exalted that, falling from a greater height, their demise may be the greater.
>> (CLAUDIAN, IN RUFINUM I. 22–23).
>
> They are able, because they believe themselves able.
>> (VIRGIL, AENEID V. 231).
>
> A certain prince was unfortunate, because he was born under a certain constellation.

Reduplicative sentences can be seen to be equivalent to causal sentences. "Man as man is rational" is equivalent to "Every man is rational, because man as man is rational." "Kings as kings depend only on God" is equivalent to "Every king depends only on God, because kings as kings depend only on God."]

A reduplicative sentence is true only if the equivalent causal sentence is true. And a causal sentence is not true unless the sentences joined by the causal expression are both true; [for the false neither is a cause nor has a cause. Yet both such sentences can be true and still the causal sentence itself may be false if no causal relation holds. For example, a certain prince may both have been unfortunate and have been born under a certain constellation; yet these facts do not prevent the causal sentence "The prince was unfortunate because he was born under that particular constellation" from being false.] So, the contradictories of causal sentences are sentences which deny that one thing is the cause of another: "Being born under that particular constellation did not cause the prince to be unfortunate."

RELATIVES   Relative sentences are sentences which express a comparison or relation:

> Where one's treasure is, there is his heart.
>
> As a man lives, so he dies.

> [You are valued in the world in proportion to your wealth.
> (SENECA, EPISTLES CXV. 14)]

The sentences are true if the relations they express hold; and the contradictory of a relative is a sentence which denies that the relation holds.

> It is false that as a man lives, so he dies.

> [It is false that we are valued in this world in proportion to our fortune.]

ADVERSATIVES   Adversatives are sentences which express contrasts, making use of such particles as "but," "nevertheless," or similar particles, expressed or understood.

> [Fortune can take away one's goods, but it cannot take away one's heart.
> (SENECA, MEDEA 176)

> Rather than being a victim of my circumstances, I try always to rise above them.
> (HORACE, EPISTLES I. I. 19)

> He who crosses the seas changes only his country, not his disposition.
> (IBID., II. 27)]

The truth of an adversative depends upon the truth of the constituent sentences and the truth of the contrast that is made between them. It would be ridiculous to form an adversative from two sentences which, though both true, stood in no relation of contrast to each other; as, for example, if we were to say "Judas was a thief, and nevertheless he could not abide Magdalene's pouring her ointments on Christ."

An adversative can be contradicted in a variety of ways. For example, the adversative "It is not on riches but on knowledge that happiness depends" can be contradicted in these ways:

> Happiness depends on riches and not on knowledge.

> Happiness depends neither on riches nor on knowledge.

> Happiness depends on both riches and knowledge.

Thus we see that copulatives are the contradictories of adversatives, for these sentences are copulatives.

Chapter 10: Implicitly Compound Sentences

Some compound sentences are only implicitly compound, and these are of four kinds: exclusives, exceptives, comparatives, and inceptives and desitives.

EXCLUSIVES   [Exclusives are sentences which express that a characteristic belongs to one and only one entity; such exclusiveness is shown by saying that the characteristic belongs to no other entity. It follows, therefore, that these sentences express two different judgments and as a result are implicitly compound. Exclusiveness is indicated by use of the words "alone," "only," or the like.

The following are some examples of exclusive sentences:

> God alone is worthy of being loved for his own sake.

> The only riches which will remain with you are those which you have freely given away.
> (MARTIAL, EPIGRAMS V. 42.8)

> Virtue is the only true nobility.
> (JUVENAL, SATIRES VIII. 20)

> I know only that I know nothing.

Lucan, speaking of the Druids, gives this disjunctive sentence composed of two exclusives:

> Either only you know the gods, or only you are ignorant of them.
> (LUCAN, PHARSALIA I. 452–453)

Exclusives are contradicted in any of three ways:

1. By denying that the characteristic in question belongs to the entity in question.
2. By holding that the characteristic belongs to other entities also.
3. By holding that the characteristic belongs to several entities but not to the one in question.

Thus we can contradict the sentence "Virtue is the only true nobility" by saying one of the following:

> Virtue is not nobility.

> Not only virtue but birth as well can render a man noble.

> Birth makes one noble, but virtue does not.

Thus, too, the maxim of the Academics, "I know only that I know nothing," was contradicted in one way by the Dogmatists and in another way by the Pyrrhonists. The Dogmatists disclaimed the maxim by holding that it was doubly false: Since there are many things which we know with the utmost certainty, it is untrue that we know nothing but that we know nothing. The Pyrrhonists too said the maxim was false but for a very different reason: Everything is so uncertain that it is doubtful even whether we know that we do not know.

Because there are three ways of forming a contradictory of an exclusive sentence, Lucan's statement about the Druids is in error: It is not necessary that either the Druids alone were correct in their view of the gods or that the Druids alone were wrong. There are many different ways to be wrong about the nature of God. It might well be that although the Druids held opinions about the nature of God which differed from those held by other nations, not only the Druids but the other nations as well held wrong opinions.

Exclusives are only implicitly compound, and, moreover, there are some exclusives in which even the sign of exclusiveness is unexpressed. For example, this verse of Virgil in which the exclusion is explicit

> *Una salus victis nullam sperare salutem.*
>
> (AENEID II. 354)

is well translated by this verse in which the exclusion is understood:

> The hope of the conquered is to expect nothing.

Latin often omits the sign of exclusiveness; and there are many Latin passages whose full import cannot be given in translation unless the exclusion is explicitly stated. For example, in II Corinthians 10:17, the passage, "*Qui gloriatur, in Domino glorietur,*" must be translated as: "He who glories, let him glory in God alone." And in Galatians 6:7, "*Quae seminaverit homo, haec et metet,*" must be translated as: "A man shall reap only that which he sows." Similarly in Ephesians 4:5, "*Unus Dominus, una fides, unum baptisma,*" must be rendered as: "There is only one Lord, one faith, one baptism." And in Matthew 5:46, "*Si diligitis eos qui vos diligunt, quam mercedem habebitis?*" must be translated as: "If you love only those who love you, what reward do you deserve?" And Seneca's words in his *Troades,* "*Nullas habet spes Troja, si tales habet,*" must be translated as: "If Troy has only this hope, it has none."

EXCEPTIVES   [Exceptives are sentences which states that some characteristic belongs to all of a certain kind of entity with the exception of some specified ones of these entities; this exception is indicated by an exceptive particle. An exceptive thus expresses two judgments and as a result is implicitly compound. For example, when we say, "All ancient philosophers except the Platonists failed to recognize that God was incorporeal" we mean two things: First, that the ancient philosophers believed that God was corporeal; secondly, that the Platonists did not so believe. The following are further examples of exceptives:

> A miser does no good but in dying.
>
> (P. SYRUS, SENTENTIAE 59)

> No one thinks himself miserable save through comparing himself with those more fortunate.
>
> (SENECA, TROADES 1023)

> We suffer no wrongs except those we inflict on ourselves.

> But for the sage all men are foolish.

Exceptives are contradicted in the same ways as are exclusives. The last example of an exceptive may be contradicted by any of the following three sentences:

> The sage of the Stoics is as much a fool as any other man.

> There are men other than the Stoic sage who are not fools.

> The Stoic sage is a fool, but other men are not fools.

An exceptive may be very close in meaning to an exclusive. For example, the exceptive of Terence, "Except what he does himself he does not think right," is fairly clearly equivalent to the exclusive of Cornelius Gallus, "He thinks that only what he does himself is right."

COMPARATIVES   A sentence in which a comparison is made expresses two judgments; for in a comparison we say that a thing is such and such and we also say that this first thing is more or less such and such than is some second thing. Comparatives are, therefore, implicitly compound. The following are examples of comparatives:

> To lose a friend is the greatest loss.
>
> (P. SYRUS, SENTENTIAE 33)

> Even in matters of consequence, a bit of good-natured ridicule often achieves more than the best of arguments.
>
> (HORACE, SATIRES I. 10. 14–15)

> Better are the blows of a friend than the treacherous kisses of an enemy.
>
> (PROVERBS 27:6)

Comparatives may be contradicted in many ways. For instance, the maxim of Epicurus that pain is the greatest of all evils was contradicted in one way by the Stoics and in another by the Peripatetics. The Peripatetics acknowledged that pain was an evil but maintained that vice and other disorders of the mind were much greater evils; the Stoics would not even recognize that pain was an evil, must less the greatest of all evils.

There is a question which may be discussed here, namely, whether a comparison implies that the positive of the characteristic be found in both the entities involved in the comparison. For example, is it necessary to assume that two things both be good before we can say that one is better than the other? At first glance we would say, "Yes"; but custom opposes such an answer. The Scriptures use the word "better" not only in comparing two goods, as in "Wisdom is better than force, and the prudent man better than the brave" but also in comparing a good and an evil, as in "A patient man is worth more than a proud one" and even in comparing two evils, as in "It is better to live with a dragon than with a quarrelsome woman." And in the Gospel we find the sentence "It is better to be cast into a millpond with a millstone about one's neck than to scandalize the least of the faithful."

Custom's usage can be justified: A greater good is better than a lesser one because there is more goodness in the greater than in the lesser. And by the same token we can say, although with less propriety, that a good is better than an evil, because a good has more of goodness in it than does the evil—which has none at all. And finally, we may say that a lesser evil is better than a greater one: Since a decrease of evil is a good of a sort, the lesser of two evils has more of this kind of goodness than has the greater evil.

We should, therefore, not burden ourselves needlessly by arguing over these forms of speech. But a Donatist grammarian named Cresconius did not spare himself when he took issue with St. Augustine. Because Augustine had said that the Catholics had more reason to reproach the Donatists with having abandoned the sacred books than the Donatists had to reproach the Catholics, Cresconius thought that Augustine had thereby acknowledged that the Donatists had grounds to reproach the Catholics. Cresconius said:

> If you have *more* reason than we, then we have some reason. For if the comparative of a characteristic is said to be present, this indicates the presence of the positive of the characteristic and not its absence.

But Augustine refutes this specious distinction first of all by citing examples from the Scriptures. Augustine cites the passage from the Epistle to the Hebrews where St. Paul says that the earth which gives forth only thistles is accursed and should wait only to be burned; and then Augustine adds,

> But we hope for better things from you, my dearest brethren. I say better things not because the things I just mentioned—to put forth prickles and thorns and to merit burning—are good and worth seeking, but rather because they are downright evils and once avoided better things—nay, good things—can be chosen and held fast: And here I mean the really good, the very contrary of—not the mere absence of—these great evils.

Secondly, to show that Cresconius was wrong Augustine cites an example from Virgil, the most celebrated of authors:

> With bared teeth they tore and mangled their own limbs.
> Heaven grant a happier fate to the good and such madness to our foes!
> (GEORGICS, III. 513–514)

If Cresconius' method of argument were correct, then just as Cresconius reproached Augustine, Virgil in wishing a "better" fortune to a good people could be reproached for having accepted as a good thing a disease which leads men to tear themselves to pieces—as Augustine noted.

INCEPTIVES AND DESITIVES   A sentence that states that something has commenced or ceased to be such and such expresses two different judgments and hence is implicitly compound. Such a sentence tells us both that the thing was before the time of which we speak as well as what the thing became. Sentences stating that something commences are inceptives; those stating that something ceases are desitives. We treat inceptives and desitives as a single kind, since they are so much alike. Consider the following examples:

> The Jews after the return from captivity in Babylon no longer used their ancient graphic symbols, now called Samaritan characters.

> Five hundred years ago the Latin language ceased to be the common tongue of Italy.

> The Jews did not begin to use dots for marking vowels until the fifth century after Christ.

An inceptive or a desitive sentence may be contradicted by denying either of the two judgments expressed by it. In contradicting the sentence given as the last example, some said—though they were wrong in their contention—that the Hebrews have always used such dots, at least in reading. Others contradict the same sentence by maintaining that the use of dots is more recent than the fifth century after Christ.

GENERAL REFLECTIONS   We have shown that an implicitly compound sentence could be contradicted in several ways; but still it is true that when we deny such sentences in a straightforward way without any further qualification, the negation falls naturally on the exclusion, on the exception, on the comparison, or on the claim of inception or desisting. Consider this illustration. Suppose that a man who does not believe Epicurus placed the chief good in bodily pleasure were told that Epicurus alone placed the chief good in pleasure. If the man denied the proposal in an unqualified fashion, then the man's true opinion would not be fully expressed by his simple denial; for his simple denial would be understood as saying that he thought Epicurus had put the sovereign good in the sensual pleasure of the body but that it was not Epicurus alone who did so. Similarly, if I were asked whether a certain judge with whose honesty I was familiar still sold justice, I could not answer with a simple "No"; although that answer would indicate that the judge sells justice no longer, my reply would at the same time suggest that I acknowledged that he had previously sold justice. We see then that there are some questions for which it would be unjust to demand a simple yes or no answer. Because these questions involve two judgments, we cannot make a proper reply unless we explain ourselves in relation to each of these judgments.]

Chapter 11: Identifying Subjects and Predicates of Sentences

Logic as commonly taught leaves its student with very stereotyped ways of expressing propositions and inferences. Students become familiar with the types of sentences used by the Schoolmen, sentences which mirror only very imperfectly the ways the learned or the untutored man expresses propositions and inferences.

A logic student trained in the ordinary manner has scarcely any idea of subject and predicate except that the subject is the first part and the predicate the last part of a sentence; and his only notion of universality and particularity is that universality is what is indicated by an "all" or by a "no," particularity what is indicated by a "some." And yet these characterizations of subject and predicate, universality and particularity often lead a student astray. A little thought is required to discern what is the subject and what the predicate of a sentence and whether the sentence be universal or particular.

First, let us consider ways of identifying the subject and the predicate of a sentence. The only infallible guide for picking out the subject and predicate of a sentence is to consider the meaning of the sentence. The subject is an expression which refers to that about which the sentence states something; the predicate is an expression which refers to a characteristic which the sentence states to belong to the referent of the subject. And in a sentence a subject may precede or follow the predicate. In Latin, for example, nothing is more frequent than sentences in which the predicate precedes the subject:

> *Turpe est obsequi libidini.*

> (Shameful is he who is enslaved to his passions.)

Obviously the predicate is *"turpe"* ("shameful"), and being shameful is said to belong to him who is a slave of his passions—the referent of the subject. And similarly with the saying of St. Paul:

> *Est quaestus magnus pietas cum sufficientia.*

> (It is a great gain to have piety with contentment.)

the more common order of which would be:

> *Pietas cum sufficientia est quaestus magnus.*

> (Piety with contentment is a great gain.)

And in this verse:

> Blessed is he who has been able to gain knowledge of the causes of things
> And beneath his feet has hurled all fear
> And unbending Fate and the cries of hungry Acheron!
> (VIRGIL, GEORGICS II. 490–492)

"blessed" is the predicate, and the rest of the sentence is subject.

To discover the subject and predicate of complex sentences is often much more difficult: We have already pointed out that sometimes only the context or an explicit expression of the author's intentions can tell us which is the principal part of the sentence, which the incidental. In sentences where an incidental clause precedes the principal one, it is often necessary to change the main verb of the sentence into the passive voice to make apparent the true subject of the principal clause. The first premiss and the conclusion of the following argument are complex sentences of this kind:

> God commands that kings must be honored.
> Louis XIV is king.
> Therefore, God commands that Louis XIV must be honored.

Clearly our principal intention is that the first premiss should state something about kings from which we can conclude that it is necessary to honor Louis XIV. And so "God commands that" is properly only an incidental clause which lends strength to the assertion of the principal clause that kings must be honored. Consequently, "kings" is the subject of the first premiss and "Louis XIV" the subject of the conclusion, though at first sight each of these expressions appears to be only a part of the predicate.

There are also other very common sentences which must be rearranged if subject and predicate are to occur in their natural order. For example, "It is folly to pay attention to flatterers" must be rearranged as "To pay attention to flatterers is folly." Similarly, "It is sleet that falls" becomes "What falls is sleet." And "It is God who redeems us" becomes "He who redeems us is God."

All our examples in this chapter emphasize the necessity of attending to the meaning of a sentence rather than merely to the order of the words in that sentence. Unless we heed this advice, we shall declare certain valid syllogisms invalid. . . .

PART III: REASONING

Chapter 18: Topics Taken from Grammar

The Topics have been classified in various ways. The scheme followed by Cicero in his *Books of Invention* and in Book II of *The Orator* and by Quintilian in Book V of *The Institutes* is well suited for the use of lawyers but is less methodical than is the division of the logicians. Ramus' classification is overly encumbered by subdivisions.

The following is a fairly convenient classification made by the very discerning and reliable German philosopher Clauberg, whose logic we saw only after ours was in press.

The Topics are taken either from grammar, logic, or metaphysics.

1. *Topics taken from grammar.* Under the Topics taken from grammar are: (*a*) arguments based on etymology and (*b*) arguments based on words derived from a common root. For example, to argue in the following way is to argue from etymology:

> Many people are not seriously occupied.
> According to the etymology of the word "divert," "to divert oneself" means to desist from serious occupation.
> Therefore, many people in the world never divert themselves.

Words derived from a common root are often helpful in suggesting arguments; for example:

I am a human; so I deem alien to me nothing of humanity.
Mortal, we flee the mortal enemy.
Who is more worthy of commiseration than the miserable?
And who is more unworthy of commiseration than a miserable one who is proud?

JEAN-JACQUES ROUSSEAU

Essay on the Origin of Languages

CHAPTER ONE

On the Various Means of Communicating Our Thoughts

Speech distinguishes man among the animals; language distinguishes nations from each other; one does not know where a man comes from until he has spoken. Out of usage and necessity, each learns the language of his own country. But what determines that this language is that of his country and not of another? In order to tell, it is necessary to go back to some principle that belongs to the locality itself and antedates its customs, for speech, being the first social institution, owes its form to natural causes alone.

As soon as one man was recognized by another as a sentient, thinking being similar to himself, the desire or need to communicate his feelings and thoughts made him seek the means to do so. Such means can be derived only from the senses, the only instruments through which one man can act upon another. Hence the institution of sensate signs for the expres-

From "Essay on the Origin of Languages" by Jean-Jacques Rousseau, translated by John H. Moran in *On the Origin of Language* (Milestones of Thought series). Copyright © 1966, by Frederick Ungar Publishing Co. Inc. New York.

sion of thought. The inventors of language did not proceed rationally in this way; rather their instinct suggested the consequence to them.

Generally, the means by which we can act on the senses of others are restricted to two: that is, movement and voice. The action of movement is immediate through touching, or mediate through gesture. The first can function only within arm's length, while the other extends as far as the visual ray. Thus vision and hearing are the only passive organs of language among distinct individuals.

Although the language of gesture and spoken language are equally natural, still the first is easier and depends less upon conventions. For more things affect our eyes than our ears. Also, visual forms are more varied than sounds, and more expressive, saying more in less time. Love, it is said, was the inventor of drawing. It might also have invented speech, though less happily. Not being very well pleased with it, it disdains it; it has livelier ways of expressing itself. How she could say things to her beloved, who traced his shadow with such pleasure! What sounds might she use to work such magic?

Our gestures merely indicate our natural unrest. It is not of those that I wish to speak. Only Europeans gesticulate when speaking; one might say that all their power of speech is in their arms. Their lungs are powerful too, but to nearly no avail. Where a Frenchman would strain and torture his body, emitting a great verbal torrent, a Turk will momentarily remove his pipe from his mouth to utter a few words softly, crushing one with a single sentence.

Since learning to gesticulate, we have forgotten the art of pantomime, for the same reason that with all our beautiful systems of grammar we no longer understand the symbols of the Egyptians. What the ancients said in the liveliest way, they did not express in words but by means of signs. They did not say it, they showed it.

Consider ancient history; it is full of such ways of appealing to the eye, each of them more effective than all the discourse that might have replaced it. An object held up before speaking will arouse the imagination, excite curiosity, hold the mind in suspense, in expectation of what will be said. I have noticed that Italians and Provençals, among whom gesture ordinarily precedes discourse, use this as a way of drawing attention and of pleasing their listeners. But in the most vigorous language, everything is said symbolically, before one actually speaks. Tarquin, or Thrasybulus lopping off poppies; Alexander applying his seal to the mouth of his favorite; Diogenes promenading in front of Zeno: do they not speak more effectively than with words? What verbal circumlocution would express the same idea as well? Darius, engaged with his army in Scythia, receives from the King of Scythia a frog, a bird, a mouse, and five arrows. The herald makes the presentation in silence and departs.

That terrible harangue was understood; and Darius returned to his own country as quickly as he could. Substitute a letter for this sign: the more menacing it is, the less frightening will it be. It will be no more than a boast, which would draw merely a smile from Darius.

When the Levite of Ephraim wanted to avenge the death of his wife, he wrote nothing to the tribes of Israel, but divided her body into twelve sections which he sent to them. At this horrible sight they rushed to arms, crying with one voice: *Never has such a thing happened in Israel, from the time of our fathers' going out of Egypt, down to the present day!* And the tribe of Benjamin was exterminated.[1] In our day, this affair, recounted in court pleadings and discussions, perhaps in jest, would be dragged out until this most horrible of crimes would in the end have remained unpunished. King Saul, returning from the fields, similarly dismembered his plow oxen, thus using a similar sign to make Israel march to the aid of the city of Jabes. The Jewish prophets and the Greek lawgivers, by frequently presenting sensate objects to the people, spoke to them more effectively through these objects than they would have by means of lengthy discourse. The way the Athenaeum yields when the orator Hyperides made them acquit the courtesan Phryne, without alleging a single word in her defense, is another mute eloquence, the effects of which are not unusual in any age.

Thus one speaks more effectively to the eye than to the ear. There is no one who does not feel the truth of Horace's judgment in this regard. Clearly the most eloquent speeches are those containing the most imagery; and sounds are never more forceful than when they produce the effects of colors.

But when it is a question of stirring the heart and inflaming the passions, it is an altogether different matter. The successive impressions of discourse, which strike a redoubled blow, produce a different feeling from that of the continuous presence of the same object, which can be taken in at a single glance. Imagine someone in a painful situation that is fully known; as you watch the afflicted person, you are not likely to weep. But give him time to tell you what he feels and soon you will burst into tears. It is solely in this way that the scenes of a tragedy produce their effect.[2]

Pantomime without discourse will leave you nearly tranquil; discourse

---

[1] There remained only 600 men, with no women or children.

[2] I have said elsewhere why feigned misfortunes touch us more than real ones. There is a type that weeps at a tragedy, yet has never had any pity for the suffering. The invention of theater is remarkable for inflating our pride with all the virtues in which we are entirely lacking.

without gestures will wring tears from you. The passions have their gestures, but they also have their accents; and these accents, which thrill
us, these tones of voice that cannot fail to be heard, penetrate to the very
depths of the heart, carrying there the emotions they wring from us,
forcing us in spite of ourselves to feel what we hear. We conclude that
while visible signs can render a more exact imitation, sounds more
effectively arouse interest.

This leads me to think that if the only needs we ever experienced were
physical, we should most likely never have been able to speak; we would
fully express our meanings by the language of gesture alone. We would
have been able to establish societies little different from those we have,
or such as would have been better able to achieve their goals. We would
have been able to institute laws, to choose leaders, to invent arts, to
establish commerce, and to do, in a word, almost as many things as we
do with the help of speech. Without fear of jealousy, the secrets of
oriental gallantry are passed across the more strictly guarded harems in
the epistolary language of salaams.[3] The mutes of great nobles understand each other, and understand everything that is said to them by
means of signs, just as well as one can understand anything said in discourse. M. Pereyra and those like him who not only consider that mutes
speak, but claim to understand what they are saying, had to learn another
language, as complicated as our own, in order to understand them.

Chardin says that in India, traders would take each other by the hand,
varying their grip in a way that no one could see, thus transacting all
their business publicly yet secretly, without a single word being uttered.
If these traders had been blind, deaf, and mute, this would not hinder
their understanding of each other; which shows that of the two senses
by which we act, one alone will suffice to form a language.

It appears again, by the same observations, that the invention of the
art of communicating our ideas depends less upon the organs we use in
such communication than it does upon a power proper to man, according
to which he uses his organs in this way, and which, if he lacked these,
would lead him to use others to the same end. Give man a structure
[organically] as crude as you please: doubtless he will acquire fewer
ideas, but if only he has some means of contact with his fellow men, by
means of which one can act and another can sense, he will finally succeed
in communicating whatever ideas he might have.

Animals have a more than adequate structure for such communication,

---

[3] Many very common items, such as an orange, a ribbon, charcoal, etc., are used as
salaams, the sending of which has a meaning known to all the lovers of the country
in which this language is used.

but none of them has ever made use of it. This seems to me a quite characteristic difference. That those animals which live and work in common, such as beavers, ants, bees, have some natural language for communicating among themselves, I would not question. Still, the speech of beavers and ants is apparently by gesture; i.e., it is only visual. If so, such languages are natural, not acquired. The animals that speak them possess them a-borning: they all have them, and they are everywhere the same. They are entirely unchanging and make not the slightest progress. Conventional language is characteristic of man alone. That is why man makes progress, whether for good or ill, and animals do not. That single distinction would seem to be far-reaching. It is said to be explicable by organic differences. I would be curious to witness this explanation.

CHAPTER TWO

That the First Invention of Speech Is Due Not to Need but Passion

It seems then that need dictated the first gestures, while the passions stimulated the first words. By pursuing the course of the facts with these distinctions we may be able to see the question of the origin of language in an entirely new light. The genesis of oriental languages, the oldest known, absolutely refutes the assumption of a didactic progression in their development. These languages are not at all systematic or rational. They are vital and figurative. The language of the first men is represented to us as the tongues of geometers, but we see that they were the tongues of poets.

And so it had to be. One does not begin by reasoning, but by feeling. It is suggested that men invented speech to express their needs: an opinion which seems to me untenable. The natural effect of the first needs was to separate men, and not to reunite them. It must have been that way, because the species spread out and the earth was promptly populated. Otherwise mankind would have been crammed into a small area of the world, and the rest would have remained uninhabited.

From this alone it follows clearly that the origin of languages is not at all due to people's first needs. It would be absurd to suppose that the means of uniting them derived from the cause of their separation. Whence then this origin? From moral needs, passions. All the passions tend to bring people back together again, but the necessity of seeking a livelihood forces them apart. It is neither hunger nor thirst but love, hatred, pity, anger, which drew from them the first words. Fruit does not disappear from our hands. One can take nourishment without speaking. One stalks in silence the prey on which one would feast. But for moving a young heart, or repelling an unjust aggressor, nature dictates accents, cries, lamentations. There we have the invention of the most ancient words; and that is why the first languages were singable and passionate before they became simple and methodical. All of this is not true without qualification, but I shall return to it in the sequel.

CHAPTER THREE

That the First Language Had To Be Figurative

As man's first motives for speaking were of the passions, his first expressions were tropes. Figurative language was the first to be born. Proper meaning was discovered last. One calls things by their true name only when one sees them in their true form. At first only poetry was spoken; there was no hint of reasoning until much later.

However, I feel the reader stopping me at this point to ask how an expression can be figurative before it has a proper meaning, since the figure consists only of a transference of meaning. I agree with that. But, in order to understand what I mean, it is necessary to substitute the idea that the passion presents to us for the word that we transpose. For one does not only transpose words; one also transposes ideas. Otherwise figurative language would signify nothing. I shall reply then with an example.

Upon meeting others, a savage man will initially be frightened. Because of his fear he sees the others as bigger and stronger than himself. He calls them *giants*. After many experiences, he recognizes that these so-called giants are neither bigger nor stronger than he. Their stature does not approach the idea he had initially attached to the word giant. So he invents another name common to them and to him, such as the name *man*, for example, and leaves *giant* to the fictitious object that had impressed him during his illusion. That is how the figurative word is born before the literal word, when our gaze is held in passionate fascination; and how it is that the first idea it conveys to us is not that of the truth.

What I have said of words and names presents no difficulty relative to the forms of phrases. The illusory image presented by passion is the first to appear, and the language that corresponded to it was also the first invented. It subsequently became metaphorical when the enlightened spirit, recognizing its first error, used the expressions only with those passions that had produced them.

CHAPTER FOUR

On the Distinctive Characteristics of the First Language and the Changes It Had To Undergo

Simple sounds emerge naturally from the throat; and the mouth is naturally more or less open. But the modifications of the tongue and palate, which produce articulation, require attention and practice. One does not make them at all without willing to make them. All children need to learn them, and some do not succeed easily. In all tongues, the liveliest exclamations are inarticulate. Cries and groans are simple sounds. Mutes, which is to say the deaf, can make only inarticulate sounds. Father Lamy thinks that if God had not taught men to speak, they would never have learned by themselves. There are only a small number of articulations; there are infinitely many sounds, and the accents that distinguish them can be equally numerous. All the musical notes are just so many accents. True, we have only three or four in speech. The Chinese have many more; but on the other hand, they have fewer consonants. To these possible combinations, add those of tense and number, and you have not only more words, but more distinct syllables than even the richest tongue requires.

I do not doubt that independent of vocabulary and syntax, the first tongue, if it still existed, would retain the original characteristics that would distinguish it from all others. Not only would all the forms of this tongue have to be in images, feelings, and figures, but even in its mechanical part it would have to correspond to its initial object, presenting to the senses as well as to the understanding the almost inevitable impression of the feeling that it seeks to communicate.

Since natural sounds are inarticulate, words have few articulations. Interposing some consonants to fill the gaps between vowels would suffice to make them fluid and easy to pronounce. On the other hand, the sounds would be very varied, and the diversity of accents for each sound would further multiply them. Quantity and rhythm would account for still further combinations. Since sounds, accents, and number, which are natural, would leave little to articulation, which is conventional, it would be sung rather than spoken. Most of the root words would be imitative sounds or accents of passion, or effects of sense objects. It would contain many onomatopoeic expressions.

This language would have many synonyms for expressing the same thing according to various relationships.[4] It would have few adverbs and

---

[4] It is said that the Arabs have more than a thousand different words for *camel* and more than a hundred for *sword*, etc.

abstract names for expressing these same relationships. It would have many augmentatives, diminutives, composite words, expletive particles to indicate the cadence of sentences and fullness of phrases. It would have many irregularities and anomalies. It would deemphasize grammatical analogy for euphony, number, harmony, and beauty of sounds. Instead of arguments, it would have aphorisms. It would persuade without convincing, and would represent without reasoning. It would resemble Chinese in certain respects, Greek and Arabic in others. If you understand these ideas in all their ramifications, you will find that Plato's *Cratylus* is not as ridiculous as it appears to be.

CHAPTER ELEVEN

Reflections on These Differences

These, in my opinion, are the most general physical causes of the characteristic differences of the primitive tongues. Those of the south are bound to be sonorous, accented, eloquent, and frequently obscure because of their power. Those of the north are bound to be dull, harsh, articulated, shrill, monotonous, and to have a clarity due more to vocabulary than to good construction. The modern tongues, with all their intermingling and recasting, still retain something of these differences. French, English, German: each is a language private to a group of men who help each other, or who become angry. But the ministers of the gods proclaiming sacred mysteries, sages giving laws to their people, leaders swaying the multitude, have to speak Arabic or Persian.[5] Our tongues are better suited to writing than speaking, and there is more pleasure in reading us than in listening to us. Oriental tongues, on the other hand, lose their life and warmth when they are written. The words do not convey half the meaning; all the effectiveness is in the tone of voice. Judging the Orientals from their books is like painting a man's portrait from his corpse.

For a proper appreciation of their actions, men must be considered in all their relationships: which we simply are not capable of doing. When we put ourselves in the position of others, we do not become what they must be, but remain ourselves, modified. And, when we think we are judging them rationally, we merely compare their prejudices to ours. Thus, if one who read a little Arabic and enjoyed leafing through the Koran were to hear Mohammed personally proclaim in that eloquent, rhythmic tongue, with that sonorous and persuasive voice, seducing first the ears, then the heart, every sentence alive with enthusiasm, he would

---

[5] Turkish is a northern tongue.

prostrate himself, crying: Great prophet, messenger of God, lead us to glory, to martyrdom. We will conquer or die for you. Fanaticism always seems ridiculous to us, because there is no voice among us to make it understood. Our own fanatics are not authentic fanatics. They are merely rogues or fools. Instead of inspirational inflection, our tongues allow only for cries of diabolic possession. . . .

Johann Gottfried

J. G. HERDER

Essay on the Origin of Language

SECTION ONE

While still an animal, man already has language. All violent sensations of his body, and among the violent the most violent, those which cause him pain, and all strong passions of his soul express themselves directly in screams, in sounds, in wild inarticulate tones. A suffering animal, no less than the hero Philoctetus, will whine, will moan when pain befalls it, even though it be abandoned on a desert island, without sight or trace or hope of a helpful fellow creature. It is as though it could breathe more freely as it vents its burning, frightened spirit. It is as though it could sigh out part of its pain and at least draw it from the empty air space new strength of endurance as it fills the unhearing winds with its moans. So little did nature create us as severed blocks of rock, as egotistic monads! Even the most delicate chords of animal feeling—I must use this image because I know none better for the mechanics of sentient bodies—even the chords whose sound and strain do not arise from choice and slow deliberation, whose very nature the probing of reason has not as yet been able to fathom, even they—though there be no awareness of

J. G. Herder, "Essay on the Origin of Language" (trans. Alexander Gode), in *On the Origin of Language* (New York: Frederick Ungar Publishing Co., 1966), 87–103; 115–118; 128–138. Some footnotes omitted.

sympathy from outside—are aligned in their entire performance for a going out toward other creatures. The plucked chord performs its natural duty: it sounds! It calls for an echo from one that feels alike, even if none is there, even if it does not hope or expect that such another might answer.

Should physiology ever progress to a point where it can demonstrate psychology—which I greatly doubt—it would derive many a ray of light for this phenomenon, though it might also divide it in individual, excessively small, and obtuse filaments. Let us accept it at present as a whole, as a shining law of nature: "Here is a sentient being which can enclose within itself none of its vivid sensations; which must, in the very first moment of surprise, utter each one aloud, apart from all choice and purpose." It was, as it were, the last motherly touch of the formative hand of nature that it gave to all, to take out into the world, the law, "Feel not for yourself alone. But rather: your feeling resound!" And since this last creative touch was, for all of one species, of one kind, this law became a blessing: "The sound of your feeling be of one kind to your species and be thus perceived by all in compassion as by one!" Do not now touch this weak, this sentient being. However lonesome and alone it may seem to be, however exposed to every hostile storm of the universe, yet it is not alone: It stands allied with all nature! Strung with delicate chords; but nature hid sounds in these chords which, when called forth and encouraged, can arouse other beings of equally delicate build, can communicate, as though along an invisible chain, to a distant heart a spark that makes it feel for this unseen being. These sighs, these sounds are language. There is, then, a language of feeling which is—underived— a law of nature.

That man has such a language, has it originally and in common with the animals, is nowadays evident, to be sure, more through certain remains than through fullfledged manifestations. But these remains, too, are incontrovertible. However much we may want to insist that our artful language has displaced the language of nature, that our civilized way of life and our social urbanity have dammed in, dried out, and channeled off the torrent and the ocean of our passions, the most violent moment of feeling—wherever, however rarely, it may occur—still time and again reclaims its right, sounding in its maternal language, without mediation, through accents. The surging storm of a passion, the sudden onslaught of joy or pleasure, pain or distress, which cut deep furrows into the soul, an overpowering feeling of revenge, despair, rage, horror, fright, and so forth, they all announce themselves, each differently after its kind. As many modes of sensitivity as are slumbering in our nature, so many tonal modes too.—And thus I note that the less human nature is akin to an animal species, the more the two differ in their nervous structures, the less shall we find the natural language of that animal species comprehensible to us. We, as animals of the earth, understand the animal of the earth better than the creature of the waters; and on the earth, the herd animal better than the creature of the forest; and among the herd animals, those best that stand closest to us. Though in the case of these latter, contact and custom too contribute their greater or lesser share. It is natural that the Arab, who is of one piece with his horse, understands it better than a man who mounts a horse for the first time—almost as well as Hector in the Iliad was able to speak with the ones that were his. The Arab in the desert, who sees no life about except his camel and perhaps a flight of erring birds, can more easily understand the camel's nature and imagine that he understands the cry of the birds than we in our dwellings. The son of the forest, the hunter, understands the voice of the hart, and the Lapp that of his reindeer—. But all that follows logically or is an exception. The rule remains that this language of nature is a group language for the members of each species among themselves. And thus man too has a language of nature all his own.

Now, to be sure, these tones are very simple, and when they are articulated and spelled out on paper as interjections, the most contrary sensations may have almost a single expression. A dull "ah!" is as much the sound of languid love as of sinking despair; the fiery "oh!" as much the outburst of sudden joy as of boiling rage, of rising awe as of surging commiseration. But are these sounds meant to be marked down on paper as interjections? The tear which moistens this lusterless and extinguished, this solace-starved eye—how moving is it not in the total picture of a face of sorrow. Take it by itself and it is a cold drop of water. Place it under the microscope, and—I do not care to learn what it may be there. This weary breath—half a sigh—which dies away so movingly on pain-distorted lips, isolate it from its living helpmeets, and it is an empty draft of air. Can be it otherwise with the sounds of feeling? In their living contexts, in the total picture of pulsating nature, accompanied by so many other phenomena, they are moving and sufficient unto themselves. Severed from everything else, torn away, deprived of their life, they are, to be sure, no more than ciphers, and the voice of nature turns into an arbitrarily penciled symbol. Few in number are, it is true, the sounds of this language. But sentient nature, in so far as it suffers only mechanically, has likewise fewer chief varieties of feeling than our psychologies chalk up or invent as passions of the soul. But in that state every feeling is the more a mightily attracting bond, the less it is divided in separate threads. These sounds do not speak much, but what they speak is strong. Whether a plaintive sound bewails the wounds of the soul or of his body, whether it was fear or pain that forced out this scream, whether this soft "ah" clings to the bosom of the beloved in a kiss or in a tear—to establish all such distinctions was not the task of this language. It was to call attention to the picture as a whole. Leave it to that picture to speak for itself. That language was meant to sound, not to depict. Indeed, as the fable of Socrates has it, pain and pleasure touch. In feeling, nature shows its extremes interlinked, and what then can the language of feeling do but show such points of contact?—Now I may proceed with the application.

In all aboriginal languages, vestiges of these sounds of nature are still to be heard, though, to be sure, they are not the principal fiber of human speech. They are not the roots as such; they are the sap that enlivens the roots of language.

A refined, late-invented metaphysical language, a variant—perhaps four times removed—of the original wild mother of the human race, after thousands of years of variation again in its turn refined, civilized, and humanized for hundreds of years of its life: such a language, the child of reason and of society, cannot know much or anything of the childhood of its earliest forebear. But the old, the wild languages, the nearer they are to their origin, the more they retain it. Here I cannot yet speak of a formation of language that might to any extent be regarded as human. I can only consider the raw materials going into it. Not a single word exists for me as yet, only the sounds fit for a word of feeling. But behold! in the languages I mentioned, in their interjections, in the roots of their nouns and verbs, how much has not been retained of these sounds! The oldest Oriental languages are full of exclamations for which we peoples of latter-day cultures have nothing but gaps or obtuse and deaf miscomprehension. In their elegies—as among the savages in their burial grounds—those howling and wailing tones resound that are a continuous interjection of the language of nature; in their psalms of praise, the shouts for joy and the recurrent hallelujahs, which Shaw explains from the mouths of lamenting women and which, with us, are so often solemn nonsense. In the flow and the rhythm of the poems and songs of other ancient peoples echoes the tone which still animates the dances of war and of religion, the songs of mourning and the songs of joy of all savages, whether they live at the foot of the Andes or in the snows of the Iroquois, in Brazil or on the Caribbean Islands. The roots of the simplest, most effective among their earliest verbs are, finally, those initial exclamations of nature, which came to be molded only at a later time; which explains why the languages of all the old and all the savage peoples are forever—in this inner living tone—outside the powers of enunciation of the foreign-born.

The explanation of most of these phenomena must wait for a later context. Here I note only this: One of the upholders of the divine origin

of language[1] discerns and admires divine order in the fact that all the
sounds of all the languages known to us can be reduced to some twenty
odd letters. Unfortunately the fact is wrong, and the conclusion still
wronger. There is no language whose living tones can be totally reduced
to letters, let alone to twenty. All languages—one and all—bear witness
to this fact. The modes of articulation of our speech organs are so numerous. Every sound can be pronounced in so many ways that for instance
Lambert in the second part of his Organon has been able to demonstrate,
and rightly so, how we have far fewer letters than sounds and how im-
precise therefore the latter's expression by the former must needs remain.
And that demonstration was done only for German—a language that has
not even begun to accept into its written form the differences and multi-
plicity of tones of its dialects. What then, when the whole language is
nothing but such a living dialect? What explains all the peculiarities, all
of the idiosyncrasies of orthography if not the awkward difficulty of
writing as one speaks? What living language can be learned in its tones
from bookish letters? And hence what dead language can be called to
life? The more alive a language is—the less one has thought of reducing
it to letters, the more spontaneously it rises to the full unsorted sounds
of nature—the less, too, is it writeable, the less writeable in twenty letters;
and for outsiders, indeed, often quite unpronounceable.

Father Rasles, who spent ten years among the Abnaki in North America, complained bitterly that with the greatest care he would often not
manage to repeat more than one half of a word and was laughed at.
How much more laughable would it have been for him to spell out such
an expression with his French letters? Father Chaumont, who spent fifty
years among the Hurons and who took on the task of writing a grammar
of their language, still complained about their guttural letters and their
unpronounceable accents: "Often two words consisting entirely of the
same letters had the most different meanings." Garcilaso de la Vega
complained that the Spaniards distorted, mutilated, and falsified the
Peruvian language in the sounds of its words, attributing to the Peruvians
the most dreadful things in consequence of nothing but errors of rendi-
tion. De la Condamine says of a small nation living on the Amazon River:
"Some of their words could not be written, not even most imperfectly.
One would need at least nine or ten syllables where in their pronunciation they appear to utter hardly three." And la Loubere of the language
of Siam: "Of ten words pronounced by a European, a native Siamese
understands perhaps no single one, try as one may to express their language in our letters."

But why go to peoples in such remote corners of the world? What

[1] Süssmilch, *Beweis, dass der Ursprung der Menschlichen Sprache Göttlich sey* [*Proof
that the Origin of the Language of Man Is Divine*], Berlin, 1766, p. 21.

little we have left of savage peoples of Europe, the Estonians and the Lapps and their like have sounds which in many cases are just as half articulated and unwriteable as those of the Hurons and the Peruvians. The Russians and the Poles—however long their languages may have been written and molded by writing—still aspirate to such an extent that the true tone of their sounds cannot be depicted by letters. And the Englishman, how he struggles to write his sounds, and how little is one a speaking Englishman when one understands written English! The Frenchman, who draws up less from the throat, and that half Greek, the Italian, who speaks as it were in a higher region of the mouth, in a more refined ether, still retains a living tone. His sounds must remain within the organs where they are formed: As drawn characters they are —however convenient and uniform long usage in writing has made them—no more than mere shadows!

Thus the fact is wrong and the conclusion wronger: It does not lead to a divine but—quite on the contrary—to an animal origin. Take the so-called divine, the first language, Hebrew, of which the greater part of the world has inherited its letters: That in its beginnings it was so full of living sounds that it could be written only most imperfectly, is made quite evident by the entire structure of its grammar, its frequent confusion of similar letters, and especially the total lack of vowels in it. What explains this peculiarity that its letters are exclusively consonants and that precisely those elements of the words on which everything depends, the self-sounding vowels, were originally not written at all? This manner of writing is so contrary to the course of sound reason— of writing the nonessential and omitting the essential—that it would be incomprehensible to the grammarians, if the grammarians were accustomed to comprehend. With us, vowels are the first, the most vital things, the hinges of language, as it were. With the Hebrews, they are not written. Why? Because they could not be written. Their pronunciation was so alive and finely articulated, their breath so spiritual and etherlike that it evaporated and eluded containment in letters. It was only with the Greeks that these living aspirations were pinned down in formal vowels, though these still required a seconding by the spiritus signs and the like, whereas with the Orientals speech as it were was a continuous breath, nothing but spiritus, the spirit of the mouth—as they so often call it in their depictive poems. What the ear caught was the breath of God, was wafting air; and the dead characters they drew out were only the inanimate body which the act of reading had to animate with the spirit of life.

This is not the place to speak about the tremendous importance of such facts for an understanding of their language, but that this wafting reveals the origin of their language is evident. What is more unwriteable than the inarticulate sounds of nature? And if it is true that language is the more inarticulate the nearer it is to its origins, it follows—does it not?—that it was surely not invented by some superior being to fit the twenty-four letters which were invented together with it, that these letters were a much later and only imperfect attempt to provide memory with a few markers, and that language did not arise from the letters of a grammar of God but from the untutored sounds of free organs.[2] Otherwise it would be strange that precisely the letters from which and for which God invented language, by means of which He taught language to the earliest of men, are the most imperfect in the world, that they reveal nothing of the spirit of language but admit through their entire structure that they are not trying to reveal anything of it.

Judged by its worth, this hypothesis of letters would merit no more than a hint, but because of its ubiquity and the numerous attempts to cover up its shortcomings I had to unmask its baselessness and simultaneously show therein a peculiarity for which I for one know no explanation. But let us resume our course:

Since our sounds are destined to serve nature in the expression of passion, it is natural that they appear as the elements of all emotion. Who is he who—in the presence of a convulsive whimpering victim of torment, at the bedside of a moaning fellow in the throes of death, or even before a wheezing beast—when the entire machinery of the body suffers—does not feel how this Ah touches his heart? Who is so unfeeling a barbarian? The more, even in animals, the sensitive chords are strung in harmony with those of others, the more do even they feel with one another. Their nerves are tense in unison, their souls vibrate in unison, they really share with one another the mechanics of suffering. And what fibers of steel, what power to plug all inlets of sensibility are needed for a man to be deaf and hard against this!—Diderot thinks that those born blind must be less receptive to the plaints of a suffering animal than those who can see.[3] But I believe that in certain cases the very opposite is true. To be sure, the entire moving spectacle of this wretched convulsing creature is hidden from the blind, but all examples indicate that precisely through this concealment the sense of hearing becomes less diffuse, more pointed, and more powerfully penetrating. So there the blind man listens in darkness, in the quiet of his eternal night, and every plaintive tone, like an arrow, goes the more keenly, the more penetratingly to his heart. And

---

[2] The best book on this matter, which so far has not been worked out in all its parts, is Wachter's *Naturae et scripturae concordia* [*Concordance of Nature and Scripture*], Hafn. 1752, which differs from the dreams of Kircher and numerous others as a history of antiquity differs from fairy tales.

[3] *Lettres sur les aveugles: à l'usage de ceux qui voyent*, etc. [*Letters on the Blind, for the Use of Those Who See*].

now let him use the help of his slowly scanning tactile sense, let him touch the convulsions, experience in direct contact the collapse of the suffering machinery—horror and pain cut through the organs of his body; his inner nerve structure senses in resonance the collapse and the destruction; the tone of death sounds. Such is the bond of this language of nature!

Despite their cultured forms and malformation, Europeans have everywhere been keenly touched by the crude sounds of lamentation of the savages. Leri relates from Brazil how much his men were softened and moved to tears by the heartfelt, inarticulate screams of affection and good will of these Americans. Charlevoix and others do not find words enough to describe the terrifying impression made by the songs of war and magic of the North Americans. When, in a later passage, we take occasion to observe to what extent early poetry and music were inspired by these tones of nature, we shall be in a position to explain more philosophically the effect exerted on all savages, for instance, by the oldest Greek songs and dances, the old Greek stage, and music, dance, and poetry in general. And even with us, where reason to be sure often displaces emotion, where the sounds of nature are dispossessed by the artificial language of society—do not with us to the highest thunders of rhetoric, the mightiest bolts of poetry, and the magic moments of action come close to this language of nature by imitating it? What is it that works miracles in the assemblies of people, that pierces hearts, and upsets souls? Is it intellectual speech and metaphysics? Is it similes and figures of speech? Is it art and coldly convincing reason? If there is to be more than blind frenzy, much must happen through these; but everything? And precisely this highest moment of blind frenzy, through what did it come about?—Through a wholly different force! These tones, these gestures, those simple melodious continuities, this sudden turn, this dawning voice—what more do I know?—They all—with children, with those who live through their senses, with women, with people of sensitive feelings, with the sick, the lonely, the sorrowful—they all accomplish a thousand times more than truth itself, even though her soft and tender voice were sounding down from Heaven. The words, the tone, the turn of this gruesome ballad or the like touched our souls when we heard it for the first time in our childhood with I know not what host of connotations of shudder, awe, fear, fright, joy. Speak the word, and like a throng of ghosts those connotations arise of a sudden in their dark majesty from the grave of the soul: They obscure inside the word the pure limpid concept that could be grasped only in their absence. But take the word away, and the sound of sentiment sounds on. Dark emotion overwhelms us; the frivolous tremble and shudder—not in reaction to thoughts but to syllables, to the sounds of childhood; and it was the magic power of the

orator, of the poet, that returned us to being children. No plan afore-
thought, no pondered program, a straight law of nature was the basis:
"The tone of sensation shall transpose the sympathizing creature into the
same tone!"

In so far as we may call these immediate sounds of sensation language,
I do indeed find their origin most natural. It is not only not superhuman
but obviously animal in origin: The natural law of a mechanism endowed
with feelings.

But I cannot conceal my amazement that philosophers—people, that
is, who look for clear concepts—ever conceived of the idea that the origin
of human language might be explained from these outcries of the emotions: for is not this obviously something quite different? All animals,
down to the mute fish, sound their sensations. But this does not change
the fact that no animal, not even the most perfect, has so much as the
faintest beginning of a truly human language. Mold and refine and or-
ganize those outcries as much as you wish; if no reason is added, per-
mitting the purposeful use of that tone, I do not see how after the
foregoing law of nature there can ever be human language—a language
of volitional speech. Children, like animals, utter sounds of sensation. But
is not the language they learn from other humans a totally different
language?

The Abbé Condillac [4] belongs in this group. Either he supposes the
whole thing called language to have been invented prior to the first page
of his book, or I find things on every page that could not possibly have
occurred in the orderly continuity of a language in formation. He assumes
as the basis for his hypothesis "two children in a desert before they know
the use of any sign." Why now he assumes all this, "two children," who
must perish or turn into animals; "in a desert," where the difficulties
opposing their survival and their inventiveness are greatly increased;
"before the use of every natural sign"; and, to boot, "before any knowledge thereof," with which no infant dispenses just a few weeks after its
birth; the reason—I say—that such unnatural and mutually contradictory
conditions must be assumed in an hypothesis meant to trace the natural
development of human knowledge, the author of that hypothesis may or
may not know; but that what is built on it is no explanation of the origin
of language I believe I am able to prove. Condillac's two children get
together without the knowledge of any sign, and—lo!—from the first
moment on (2) we find them engaged in a mutual exchange. And yet
it is only through this mutual exchange that they learn "to associate with
the outcry of emotions the thoughts whose natural signs they are." Learn-

[4] *Essai sur l'origine des connoissances humaines* [*Essay on the Origin of Human
Knowledge*], Vol. II.

ing natural signs of the emotions through a mutual exchange? Learning what thoughts are associated with them? And yet being involved in an exchange from the first moment of contact on, even before the acquisition of a knowledge of what the dumbest animal knows, and being able to learn—under such conditions—what thoughts are to be associated with certain signs? Of all this I understand nothing. "Through the recurrence of similar circumstances (3) they become accustomed to associate thoughts with the sounds of the emotions and the various signs of the body. Already their memory is exercised. Already they have dominion over their imagination—have advanced far enough to do by reflection what heretofore they did only by instinct" (yet, as we just saw, did not know how to do before their exchange). Of all this I understand nothing. "The use of these signs extends the soul's range of action (4), and the extended range of action of it perfects the signs: outcries of their emotions were thus (5) what evolved the powers of their souls; outcries of their emotions what gave them the habit of associating ideas with arbitrary signs (6); outcries of their emotions what served them as models in making for themselves a new language, in articulating new sounds, in becoming accustomed to designate things with names." I repeat all these repetitions, and I do not understand the first thing about them. Finally —after the author has built on this childlike origin of language the prosody, declamation, music, dance, and poetry of the ancient languages, making from time to time sound observations (which, however, have nothing to do with our objective), he again takes up the thread: "In order to understand (80) how men agreed amongst themselves on the meaning of the first words they intended to use, it suffices to remember that they uttered them under circumstances where everyone was obliged to associate them with the same ideas, etc." In short, words arose because words had arisen before they arose. Methinks it will not pay to follow further the thread of our guide for it appears to be tied—to nothing.

Condillac, with his hollow explanation of the origin of language, provided Rousseau, as we all know, with the occasion to get the question in our century off the ground again in his own peculiar way, that is, to doubt it.[5] Actually, to cast doubt on Condillac's explanation, no Rousseau was needed; but to deny straightway—because of it—all human possibility of the invention of language, that to be sure did require a little Rousseauesque verve or nerve or whatever one may wish to call it. Because Condillac had explained the thing badly, could it therefore not be explained at all? Because sounds of emotion will never turn into a human language, does it follow that nothing else could ever have turned into it? That it was really only this hidden fallacy which misled Rousseau is

[5] *Sur l'inégalité parmi les hommes*, etc. [*On the Inequality among Men*], Part I.

evident from his own plan: "How language would have had to originate if it is to have originated at all by human means." [6] He begins, as his predecessor did, with the outcries of nature from which human language was to arise. I shall never be able to see how language could have arisen in this way and am astonished that the acuity of a Rousseau could allow it for one moment to arise in that way.

Maupertuis' little essay is not available to me. But if I may trust the excerpts of a man among whose merits reliability and precision were not the least,[7] he too did not sufficiently differentiate the origin of language from those animal sounds. He thus walks the same road with those already mentioned.

As for Diodorus and Vitruvius finally, who—to boot—not so much derived as believed in the human origin of language, they spoiled the matter more obviously than any of the others, in that they first had men, for ages on end, roam the forests as animals with the ability to scream and then invent for themselves language, God knows from what, God knows for what.

Since now most protagonists of the human origin of language have been fighting from so shaky a position, which others—Süssmilch for instance—could attack on so many grounds, the Academy, seeing that this question (with regard to which even some of its past members differed) was still largely unanswered, wished to remove it once and for all from further controversy.

And since this great subject promises such rewarding insights into the psychology and the natural order of the human race and into the philosophy of language and of all knowledge to be found by means of language, who would not wish to try his hand at it?

And since men are for us the only creatures endowed with language that we know and since it is precisely through language that they distinguish themselves from all animals, from where could one set out more safely on the road of this investigation than from the experiences we have about the difference between the animals and men?—Condillac and Rousseau had to err in regard to the origin of language because they erred, in so well known a way and yet so differently, in regard to this difference: in that the former [8] turned animals into men and the latter [9] men into animals. I must, therefore, broaden the base of the discussion somewhat. . . .

[6] *Ibid.*

[7] Süssmilch, *Beweis für die Göttlichheit,* etc. [*Proof for the Divinity*], Appendix III, p. 110.

[8] *Traité sur les animaux.*

[9] *Sur l'origine de l'inégalité,* etc.

SECTION TWO

Man, placed in the state of reflection which is peculiar to him, with this reflection for the first time given full freedom of action, did invent language. For what is reflection? What is language?

This reflection is characteristically peculiar to man and essential to his species; and so is language and the invention of language.

Invention of language is therefore as natural to man as it is to him that he is man. Let us simply develop these two concepts further: reflection and language—

Man manifests reflection when the force of his soul acts in such freedom that, in the vast ocean of sensations which permeates it through all the channels of the senses, it can, if I may say so, single out one wave, arrest it, concentrate its attention on it, and be conscious of being attentive. He manifests reflection when, confronted with the vast hovering dream of images which pass by his senses, he can collect himself into a moment of wakefulness and dwell at will on one image, can observe it clearly and more calmly, and can select in it distinguishing marks for himself so that he will know that this object is this and not another. He thus manifests reflection if he is able not only to recognize all characteristics vividly or clearly but if he can also recognize and acknowledge to himself one or several of them as distinguishing characteristics. The first act of this acknowledgment [10] results in a clear concept; it is the first judgment of the soul—and through what did this acknowledgment occur? Through a distinguishing mark which he had to single out and which, as a distinguishing mark for reflection, struck him clearly. Well, then! Let us acclaim him with shouts of eureka! This first distinguishing mark, as it appeared in his reflection, was a work of the soul! With it human language is invented!

Let that lamb there, as an image, pass by under his eyes; it is to him, as it is to no other animal. Not as it would appear to the hungry, scenting wolf! Not as it would appear to the blood-lapping lion.—They scent and taste in anticipation! Sensuousness has overwhelmed them. Instinct forces them to throw themselves over it.—Not as it appears to the rutting ram which feels it only as the object of its pleasure, which thus— again—is overcome by sensuousness, and which—again—is forced by instinct to throw itself over it.—Not as it appears to any other animal to which the sheep is indifferent and which therefore lets it, clear-darkly,

---

[10] One of the most beautiful treatises to illuminate the nature of apperception on the basis of physical experiments (which only rarely serve to elucidate the metaphysics of the soul) is to be found in the publications of the Berlin Academy of 1764.

pass by because its instinct makes it turn toward something else!—Not so with man! As soon as he feels the need to come to know the sheep, no instinct gets in his way; no one sense of his pulls him too close to it or too far away from it. It stands there, entirely as it manifests itself in his senses. White, soft, woolly—his soul in reflective exercise seeks a distinguishing mark—the sheep bleats! His soul has found the distinguishing mark. The inner sense is at work. This bleating, which makes upon man's soul the strongest impression, which broke away from all the other qualities of vision and of touch, which sprang out and penetrated most deeply, the soul retains it. The sheep comes again. White soft, woolly— the soul sees, touches, remembers, seeks a distinguishing mark—the sheep bleats, and the soul recognizes it. And it feels inside, "Yes, you are that which bleats." It has recognized it humanly when it recognized and named it clearly, that is, with a distinguishing mark. More darkly? In that case it would not have perceived it at all, because no sensuousness, no instinct relative to the sheep could replace for it the lack of distinctness with a more vivid clarity. Distinctly and directly but without a distinguishing mark? In that way no sensuous being can perceive outside itself, for there are forever other feelings which it must repress, annihilate as it were, in order to recognize, as it forever must, the difference between one and another through a third. Thus through a distinguishing mark? And what was that other than a distinguishing word within? The sound of bleating perceived by a human soul as the distinguishing mark of the sheep became, by virtue of this reflection, the name of the sheep, even if his tongue had never tried to stammer it. He recognized the sheep by its bleating: This was a conceived sign through which the soul clearly remembered an idea—and what is that other than a word? And what is the entire human language other than a collection of such words? Even if the occasion were never to arise for him that he should want or be able to transmit this idea to another being, and thus to bleat out with his lips this distinguishing mark of reflection for another, his soul—as it were— bleated within when it selected this sound as a sign of recollection, and it bleated again as it recognized the sound by its sign. Language has been invented! Invented as naturally and to man as necessarily as man was man. . . .

SECTION THREE

The focal point has been found where Prometheus' divine spark ignites in the human soul—with the first characteristic mark there was language. But what were the first characteristic marks to serve as elements of language?

1. Sounds

Cheselden's blind man [11] shows how slowly the sense of vision evolves, how difficult it is for the soul to establish the concepts of space, of form, and of color, and how many trials are needed and what geometric art must be acquired in order to use these characteristic marks with clarity. That therefore was not the most appropriate of the senses to be used in language. Furthermore, its phenomena were so cold and mute while the sensations received by the coarser senses were so indistinct and so intermingled that, by the very nature of things, it was either nothing or the ear that had to become the first teacher of language.

There is for instance the sheep. As an image it looms before the eye with all things and images and colors on a great canvas of nature. How much is there and how difficult to distinguish! All the characteristic marks are finely interwoven, placed together, and all still ineffable! Who can speak shapes? Who can sound colors? Let him take the sheep under his probing hand. This sensation is more secure and fuller, but it is so full and so obscure, with one thing within the other. Who can say what he is thus feeling? But listen! The sheep bleats! Now one distinguishing mark separates by itself from the canvas of the colors wherein so little was to be distinguished. One distinguishing mark has penetrated deeply and clearly into the soul. "Oh," says the learning beginner, like Cheselden's blind man when given the power of sight, "now I shall know you again—you bleat!" The dove coos, the dog barks! Three words have arisen because he tried three distinct ideas. The latter go into his logic as the former into his vocabulary. Reason and language together took a timid step and nature came to meet them halfway—through the power of hearing. Nature did not merely ring out the characteristic mark, it rang it in, deep into the soul. There was a sound, the soul grasped for it, and there it had a ringing word.

So man is a listening, a noting creature, naturally formed for language, and even a blind and a mute man—we understand—would have to invent language if he is not without feeling and is not deaf. Place him at ease and in comfort on a deserted island: Nature will reveal itself to him through the ear. A thousand creatures that he cannot see will still appear to speak to him, and though his mouth and his eye remain closed forever, his soul is not wholly without language. When the leaves of the tree rustle refreshing coolness down upon the poor man in his solitude, when the passing waters of the murmuring brook rock him to sleep, when the

---

[11] *Philosophical Transactions*, abridgment. Also in *Cheselden's Anatomy*, in Smith-Kästner's optics, in Buffon's natural history, in the encyclopedia, and in a dozen small French dictionaries under the key word *"aveugle."*

whispering west wind fans his burning cheeks—the bleating sheep gives him milk, the flowing brook water, the rustling tree fruit—enough of interest for him to *know* the beneficent beings; enough of urgency, without eyes and without speech, for him to *name* them in his soul. The tree will be called the rustler, the west wind the fanner, the brook the murmurer—and there, all finished and ready, is a little dictionary, waiting for the imprint of the speech organs. But how poor and how strange would the conceptions be which this mutilated individual could associate with such sounds! [12]

But now grant man the freedom of all his senses: let him see and touch and feel simultaneously all the beings which speak into his ear—Heavens! What a lecture hall of ideas and of language! Do not bother to bring down from the clouds a Mercury or Apollo as operatic *Dei ex machina*. —The entire, multisonant, divine nature is man's teacher of language and man's muse. Past him it leads a procession of all creatures: Each one has its name on its tongue and introduces itself to this concealed yet visible god as a vassal and servant. It delivers to him its distinguishing word to be entered, like a tribute, into the book of his dominion so that he may, by virtue of its name, remember it, call it in future, and enjoy it. I ask if ever this truth—the truth that "the very power of reason by which man rules over nature was the father of the living language which he abstracted from the tones of sounding beings as characteristic marks of differentiation"—I ask whether in the style of the Orient this sober truth could even be expressed more nobly and more beautifully than in the words, "And God brought the animals unto the man to see what he would call them; and whatsoever the man called every living creature, that was the name thereof." Where, in the poetic manner of the Orient, could there be a more definite statement that man invented language for himself—from the tones of living nature—as characteristic marks of his ruling reason!—And that is what I prove.

If an angel or a heavenly spirit had invented language, how could its entire structure fail to bear the imprint of the manner of thinking of that spirit, for through what could I know the picture of an angel in a painting if not through its angelic and supernatural features? But where does the like occur in our language? Structure and design and even the earliest cornerstone of this palace reveals humanity!

In what language are celestial and spiritual concepts the first? Those concepts which, according to the principles of our thinking mind, too, ought to be the first—subjects, *notiones communes*, the germinal seeds of our cognition, the centers about which everything revolves and to

---

[12] Diderot in his entire letter *Sur les sourds et muets* [*On the Deaf and Mute*] hardly got around to discussing this central point, for he spent his time with inversions and a hundred other details.

which everything leads back—are these living centers to be found as elements of language? It would appear natural that the subjects should have preceded the predicates, that the simplest subjects should have preceded the composed ones, the thing that acts and does the acts and doings of it, essentials and certainties the uncertain and accidental. How much more could one not conclude in this manner, yet—in our original languages it is clearly the very opposite that holds true. A hearing, a listening creature is evident, but no celestial spirit, for—

Sounding verbs are the first elements of power. Sounding verbs? Actions and nothing as yet that acts? Predicates and no subject as yet? The celestial genius would have to blush for it but not the sensuous human being, for what—as we have seen—could move this being more profoundly than those sounding actions? And what else, after all, is the entire structure of language but a manner of growth of his spirit, a history of his discoveries? The divine origin explains nothing and allows nothing to be explained from it. It is—as Bacon said of another thing—a holy vestal, dedicated to the gods but infertile, pious but of no use!

The first vocabulary was thus collected from the sounds of the world. From every sounding being echoed its name: The human soul impressed upon it its image, thought of it as a distinguishing mark.—How could it be otherwise than that these sounding interjections came first? And so, for example, the Oriental languages are full of verbs as basic roots of the language. The thought of the thing itself was still hovering between the actor and the action: The sound had to designate the thing as the things gave forth the sound. From the verbs it was that the nouns grew and not from the nouns the verbs. The child names the sheep, not as a sheep, but as a bleating creature, and hence makes of the interjection a verb. In the gradual progress of human sensuousness, this state of affairs is explicable; but not in the logic of a higher spirit.

All the old unpolished languages are replete with this origin, and in a philosophical dictionary of the Orientals every stem word with its family —rightly placed and soundly evolved—would be a chart of the progress of the human spirit, a history of its development, and a complete dictionary of that kind would be a most remarkable sample of the inventive skill of the human soul. Also of God's method of language and of teaching? I doubt it!

Since all of nature sounds, nothing is more natural to a sensuous human being than to think that it lives, that it speaks, that it acts. That savage saw the tall tree with its mighty crown and sensed the wonder of it: the crown rustled! There the godhead moves and stirs! The savage falls down in adoration! Behold, that is the story of sensuous man, the dark link by which nouns are fashioned from verbs—and a faint move toward abstraction! With the savages of North America, for instance, everything is still animated: Every object has its genius, its spirit, and that the same held true with the Greeks and Orientals is attested by their oldest vocabulary and grammar. They are what all of nature was to their inventor: a pantheon, a realm of animated, of acting beings!

But as man referred everything to himself, as everything appeared to speak to him and indeed acted for or against him; as he thus engaged himself with or against it, as he loved or hated and conceived of everything in human terms—all these traces of humanity appear impressed in the first names! They, too, spoke love or hatred, curse or blessing, tenderness or adversity, and in particular there arose from this feeling, in many languages, the articles! Everything was personified in human terms, as woman and man. Everywhere gods, goddesses, acting beings of evil or of good. The howling storm and the sweet zephyr, the clear source and the mighty ocean—their entire mythology lies in the treasure trove, the verbs and nouns of the old languages, and the oldest dictionary was thus a sounding pantheon, an assembly of both sexes, as was nature to the senses of the first inventor. Here the language of an old unpolished nation appears as a study in the aberrations of human fantasy and passion as does its mythology. Every family of words is a tangled underbrush around a sensuous central idea, around a sacred oak, still bearing traces of the impression received by the inventor from this dryad. Feelings are interwoven in it: What moves is alive; what sounds speaks; and since it sounds for or against you, it is friend or foe: god or goddess, acting from passion as are you!

What I love in this manner of thinking is the humanity of it, the sensuous being in it: Everywhere I see the weak, timid, sensitive being who must love or hate, trust or fear and longs to spread over all existence these sensations in his heart. I see everywhere the weak yet mighty being that is in need of the entire universe and involves everything in war or peace with itself; that depends on everything and yet rules over everything. The poetry and the attribution of sex through language are thus an interest of mankind, and the genitals of speech are, as it were, the means of its propagation. But what, if some higher genius had brought it down from the stars? How would that be? Was this genius from among the stars involved on our earth under the moon in such passions of love and weakness, of hate and fear that he entwined everything in affection and hate, that he imbued all words with fear and joy, that in fine he built everything on acts of copulation? Did he so see and feel as a man sees and feels that the nouns, to him, had to join in the sex and gender, that he brought together the verbs in action and suffering, that he ascribed to them so many true and promiscuous children, in short, that he built all of language on the feeling of human weaknesses? Did he thus see and feel?

To an upholder of the supernatural origin of language it is a matter of divine order "that most stem words are monosyllabic, that the verbs are mostly bisyllabic, and that language is thus divided according to criteria of memory." [13] The fact is not accurate and the conclusion is uncertain. In the remains of the language considered to be the oldest, the roots are all bisyllabic verbs, a fact I can well explain on the basis of the foregoing, while the opposite hypothesis finds no reason for it. Those verbs are built directly on the tones and interjections of sounding nature. They often continue to echo in them, and here and there they are preserved as interjections. Mostly, to be sure, being half-inarticulate sounds, they were bound to be lost as the formation of language progressed. The first attempts of the stammering tongue are thus lacking in the Oriental languages, but the very fact that they are lacking and that only their regularized remnants echo in the verbs, bears witness to the originality and—humanity of language. Are these stems treasures and abstractions from the reason of God, or are they the first sounds of the listening ear, the first tones of the stammering tongue? The human race in its childhood formed language for itself precisely as it is stammered by the immature: it is the babbling vocabulary of the nursery. Where does it survive in the mouth of the adult?

What was said by so many of the Ancients, what in modern times has so often been repeated without understanding, derives from this its living reality: "That poetry is older than prose!" For what was this first language of ours other than a collection of elements of poetry? Imitation it was of sounding, acting, stirring nature! Taken from the interjections of all beings and animated by the interjections of human emotion! The natural language of all beings fashioned by reason into sounds, into images of action, passion, and living impact! A dictionary of the soul that was simultaneously mythology and a marvelous epic of the actions and the speech of all beings! Thus a continuous fabulation with passion and interest!—What else is poetry?

And then: The tradition of Antiquity says that the first language of the human race was song, and many good musical people have hence imagined that man may well have learned that song from the birds.— That indeed is imagining a great deal! A great ponderous clock with all its sharp wheels and newly tensed springs and hundred-pound weights can well produce a carillon of tones; but to put down newly created man with his active mainsprings, with his needs, with his strong emotions, with his almost blindly preoccupied attention, and finally with his brute throat, and to have him ape the nightingale and derive language from singing after it—no matter how many histories of music and poetry say so—is more than I can understand. To be sure, a language through mu-

[13] Süssmilch, 8 [actually, 7, note].

sical tones would be possible—as Leibnitz,[14] too, has thought of it—but for our earliest forebears, still in the state of nature, this language was not possible. It is too artful and refined. In the procession of beings each has its own voice and a language after its own voice. The language of love in the nest of the nightingale is sweet song; in the cave of the lion it is a roar; in the forest it is the troating of the buck deer and in the hiding place of cats a caterwaul. Every species speaks its own language of love, not for man, but for itself, a language as pleasant to itself as was Petrarch's song to his Laura. As little, then, as the nightingale sings—as some imagine—to entertain man, so little can man ever be minded to invent for himself a language by trilling the trills of the nightingale. And what a monstrosity: A human nightingale in a cave or out in the forest with the hunt!

If then the first language of man was song, it was song as natural to him, as commensurate with his organs and his natural drives as the nightingale's song is to the nightingale which is, as it were, a winged lung; and that was—that was precisely our sounding language. Here, Condillac, Rousseau, and others did halfway find the road in that they derived the prosody and the song of the oldest languages from outcries of emotion, and there can be no doubt that emotion did indeed animate and elevate the first tones. But as mere tones of emotion could never be the origin of human language (which, after all, was what this song was), something is still wanting to produce it, and that, once again, was the naming of every creature after its own language. There then all of nature sang and sounded its recital, and the song of man was a concert of all those voices as far as his reason had use for them, as far as his emotions grasped them, as far as his organs could express them.—It was song, but it was neither the song of the nightingale nor the musical language of Leibnitz, nor a mere screaming of animal emotion. It was an expression of the language of all creatures within the natural scale of the human voice!

Even when subsequently language became more regular, more unisonant, and more orderly, it still remained a kind of song, as the accents of so many savages attest. And that this song—eventually sublimated and refined—gave rise to the oldest poetry and music, has by now been proven by more than one. The philosophical Englishman,[15] who in our century took up this matter of the origin of poetry and music, would have been able to progress farthest if he had not excluded the spirit of language from his investigation and if, instead of concerning himself so much with his system of bringing poetry and music to a single focus (in which neither can show itself properly), he had concerned himself more

---

[14] *Oeuvres philosophiques,* publiées p. Raspe [*Philosophical Works,* ed. Raspe], p. 232.
[15] Brown.

with the origin of both from the full nature of man. In any event, since the best samples of the poetry of the Ancients are remnants from the times of the sung language, there are bound to be innumerable instances of misapprehension, of falsifications, and of misalignment and bad taste spelled out from the continuity of the oldest poems, of the tragedies of the Greeks, and of their declamation. How much remains to be said on this point for a philosopher who has learned, among the savages amongst whom that age is still alive, the right tone for reading those pieces! Otherwise and commonly one sees nothing but the texture of the wrong side of a tapestry! *Disiecti membra poetae!*—But I might go endlessly afield if I were to allow myself to make individual linguistic comments. So back to the high road of the invention of language! . . .

SIR WILLIAM JONES

Third Anniversary Discourse of the President of the Royal Asiatick Society ("On the Hindus")

In the former discourses, which I had the honour of addressing to you, Gentlemen, on the *institution* and *objects* of our Society, I confined myself purposely to general topics; giving in the first a distant prospect of the vast career, on which we were entering, and, in the second, exhibiting a more diffuse, but still superficial, sketch of the various discoveries in History, Science, and Art, which we might justly expect from our inquiries into the literature of *Asia*. I now propose to fill up that outline so comprehensively as to omit nothing essential, yet so concisely as to avoid being tedious; and, if the state of my health shall suffer me to continue long enough in this climate, it is my design, with your permission, to prepare for our annual meetings a series of short dissertations, unconnected in their titles and subjects, but all tending to a common point of no small importance in the pursuit of interesting truths.

Of all the works, which have been published in our own age, or, perhaps, in any other, on the History of the Ancient World, and *the first population of this habitable globe*, that of MR. JACOB BRYANT, whom I name with reverence and affection, has the best claim to the praise of deep erudition ingeniously applied, and new theories happily

Sir William Jones, "Third Anniversary Discourse of the President of the Royal Asiatick Society," *Complete Works*, vol. I (London, 1799), 19–28.

illustrated by an assemblage of numberless converging rays from a most extensive circumference: it falls, nevertheless, as every human work must fall, short of perfection; and the least satisfactory part of it seems to be that, which relates to the derivation of words from *Asiatick* languages. Etymology has, no doubt, some use in historical researches; but it is a medium of proof so very fallacious, that, where it elucidates one fact, it obscures a thousand, and more frequently borders on the ridiculous, than leads to any solid conclusion: it rarely carries with it any *internal* power of conviction from a resemblance of sounds or similarity of letters; yet often, where it is wholly unassisted by those advantages, it may be indisputably proved by *extrinsick* evidence. We know *à posteriori*, that both *fitz* and *hijo*, by the nature of two several dialects, are derived from *filius*; that *uncle* comes from *avus*, and *stranger* from *extra*; that *jour* is deducible, through the *Italian*, from *dies*; and *rossignol* from *luscinia*, or the *singer in groves;* that *sciuro, écureuil,* and *squirrel* are compounded of two *Greek* words descriptive of the animal; which etymologies, though they could not have been demonstrated *à priori*, might serve to confirm, if any such confirmation were necessary, the proofs of a connection between the members of one great Empire; but, when we derive our *hanger*, or *short pendent sword*, from the *Persian*, because ignorant travellers thus misspell the word *khanjar*, which in truth means a different weapon, or *sandal-wood* from the *Greek*, because we suppose, that *sandals* were sometimes made of it, we gain no ground in proving the affinity of nations, and only weaken arguments, which might otherwise be firmly supported. That Cús then, or, as it certainly is written in one ancient dialect, Cút, and in others, probably Cás, enters into the composition of many proper names, we may very reasonably believe; and that *Algeziras* takes its name from the *Arabick* word for an *island*, cannot be doubted; but, when we are told from *Europe*, that places and provinces in *India* were clearly denominated from those words, we cannot but observe, in the first instance, that the town, in which we now are assembled, is properly written and pronounced Calicatà; that both Cata and Cut unquestionably mean *places of strength*, or, in general, any *inclosures*; and that Gujaràt is at least as remote from Jezirah in sound, as it is in situation.

Another exception (and a third could hardly be discovered by any candid criticism) to the *Analysis of Ancient Mythology*, is, that the *method* of reasoning and arrangement of topicks adopted in that learned work are not quite agreeable to the title, but almost wholly *synthetical*; and, though *synthesis* may be the better mode in pure *science*, where the principles are undeniable, yet it seems less calculated to give complete satisfaction in *historical* disquisitions, where every postulatum will perhaps be refused, and every definition controverted: this may seem a slight objection, but the subject is in itself so interesting, and the full conviction of all reasonable men so desirable, that it may not be lost labour to discuss the same or a similar theory in a method purely analytical, and, after beginning with facts of general notoriety or undisputed evidence, to investigate such truths, as are at first unknown or very imperfectly discerned.

The *five* principal nations, who have in different ages divided among themselves, as a kind of inheritance, the vast continent of *Asia*, with the many islands depending on it, are the *Indians*, the *Chinese*, the *Tartars*, the *Arabs*, and the *Persians*: *who* they severally were, *whence*, and *when* they came, *where* they now are settled, and *what advantage* a more perfect knowledge of them all may bring to our *European* world, will be shown, I trust, in *five* distinct essays; the last of which will demonstrate the connexion or diversity between them, and solve the great problem, whether they had *any* common origin, and whether that origin was *the same*, which we generally ascribe to them.

I begin with *India*, not because I find reason to believe it the true centre of population or of knowledge, but, because it is the country, which we now inhabit, and from which we may best survey the regions around us; as, in popular language, we speak of the *rising* sun, and of his *progress through the* Z*odiack*, although it had long ago been imagined, and is now demonstrated, that he is himself the centre of our planetary system. Let me here premise, that, in all these inquiries concerning the history of *India*, I shall confine my researches downwards to the *Mohammedan* conquests at the beginning of the *eleventh* century, but extend them upwards, as high as possible, to the earliest authentick records of the human species.

India, then, on its most enlarged scale, in which the ancients appear to have understood it, comprises an area of near *forty* degrees on each side, including a space almost as large as all *Europe*; being divided on the west from *Persia* by the *Arachosian* mountains, limited on the east by the *Chinese* part of the farther peninsula, confined on the north by the wilds of *Tartary*, and extending to the south as far as the isles of *Java*. This trapezium, therefore, comprehends the stupendous hills of *Potyid* or *Tibet*, the beautiful valley of *Cashmir*, and all the domains of the old *Indoscythians*, the countries of *Nepal* and *Butant*, *Camrùp* or *Asàm*, together with *Siam*, *Ava*, *Racan*, and the bordering kingdoms, as far as the *China* of the *Hindus* or *Sin* of the *Arabian* Geographers; not to mention the whole western peninsula with the celebrated island of *Sinhala*, or *Lion-like men*, at its southern extremity. By *India*, in short, I mean that whole extent of country, in which the primitive religion and languages of the *Hindus* prevail at this day with more or less of their ancient purity, and in which the *Nagarì* letters are still used with more or less deviation from their original form.

The Hindus themselves believe their own country, to which they give the vain epithets of *Medhyama* or *Central*, and *Punyabhumi*, or the *Land of Virtues*, to have been the portion of BHARAT, one of *nine* brothers, whose father had the dominion of the whole earth; and they represent the mountains of *Himalaya* as lying to the north, and, to the west, those of *Vindhya*, called also *Vindian* by the *Greeks*; beyond which the *Sindhu* runs in several branches to the sea, and meets it nearly opposite to the point of *Dwaracà*, the celebrated seat of their Shepherd God: in the *south-east* they place the great river *Saravatya*; by which they probably mean that of *Ava*, called also *Airavati* in part of its course, and giving perhaps its ancient name to the gulf of *Sabara*. This domain of *Bharat* they consider as the middle of the *Jambudwipa*, which the *Tibetians* also call the Land of *Zambu*; and the appellation is extremely remarkable; for *Jambu* is the *Sanscrit* name of a delicate fruit called *Jaman* by the *Muselmans*, and by us *rose-apple*; but the largest and richest sort is named *Amrita*, or *Immortal*; and the Mythologists of *Tibet* apply the same word to a celestial tree bearing *ambrosial fruit*, and adjoining to *four* vast rocks, from which as many sacred rivers derive their several streams.

The inhabitants of this extensive tract are described by MR. LORD with great exactness, and with a picturesque elegance peculiar to our ancient language: "A people, says he, presented themselves to mine eyes, clothed in linen garments somewhat low descending, of a gesture and garb, as I may say, maidenly and well nigh effeminate, of a countenance shy and somewhat estranged, yet smiling out a glozed and bashful familiarity." MR. ORME, the Historian of *India*, who unites an exquisite taste for every fine art with an accurate knowledge of *Asiatick* manners, observes, in his elegant preliminary Dissertation, that this "country has been inhabited from the earliest antiquity by a people, who have no resemblance, either in their figure or manners, with any of the nations contiguous to them," and that, "although conquerors have established themselves at different times in different parts of *India*, yet the original inhabitants have lost very little of their original character." The ancients, in fact, give a description of them, which our early travellers confirmed, and our own personal knowledge of them nearly verifies; as you will perceive from a passage in the Geographical Poem of DIONYSIUS, which the Analyst of Ancient Mythology has translated with great spirit:

> "To th' east a lovely country wide extends,
> INDIA, whose borders the wide ocean bounds;
> On this the sun, new rising from the main,

Smiles pleas'd, and sheds his early orient beam.
Th' inhabitants are swart, and in their locks
Betray the tints of the dark hyacinth.
Various their functions; some the rock explore,
And from the mine extract the latent gold;
Some labour at the woof with cunning skill,
And manufacture linen; others shape
And polish iv'ry with the nicest care:
Many retire to rivers shoal, and plunge
To seek the beryl flaming in its bed,
Or glitt'ring diamond. Oft the jasper's found
Green, but diaphanous; the topaz too
Of ray serene and pleasing; last of all
The lovely amethyst, in which combine
All the mild shades of purple. The rich soil,
Wash'd by a thousand rivers, from all sides
Pours on the natives wealth without control."

Their sources of wealth are still abundant even after so many revolutions and conquests; in their manufactures of cotton they still surpass all the world; and their features have, most probably, remained unaltered since the time of DIONYSIUS; nor can we reasonably doubt, how degenerate and abased so ever the *Hindus* may now appear, that in some early age they were splendid in arts and arms, happy in government, wise in legislation, and eminent in various knowledge: but, since their civil history beyond the middle of the *nineteenth* century from the present time, is involved in a cloud of fables, we seem to possess only *four* general media of satisfying our curiosity concerning it; namely, first, their *Languages* and *Letters*; secondly, their *Philosophy* and *Religion*; thirdly, the actual remains of their old *Sculpture* and *Architecture*; and fourthly, the written memorials of their *Sciences* and *Arts*.

I. It is much to be lamented, that neither the *Greeks*, who attended ALEXANDER into *India*, nor those who were long connected with it under the *Bactrian* Princes, have left us any means of knowing with accuracy, what vernacular languages they found on their arrival in this Empire. The *Mohammedans*, we know, heard the people of proper *Hindustan*, or *India* on a limited scale, speaking a *Bhasha*, or living tongue of a very singular construction, the purest dialect of which was current in the districts round Agrà, and chiefly on the poetical ground of *Mat'hurà*; and this is commonly called the idiom of *Vraja*. Five words in six, perhaps, of this language were derived from the *Sanscrit*, in which books of religion and science were composed, and which appears to have been formed by an exquisite grammatical *arrangement*, as the name itself implies, from some unpolished idiom; but the basis of the *Hindustani*, particularly the inflexions and regimen of verbs, differed as widely from both those tongues, as *Arabick* differs from *Persian*, or *German* from *Greek*. Now the general effect of conquest is to leave the current language of the conquered people unchanged, or very little altered, in its ground-work, but to blend with it a considerable number of exotick names both for things and for actions; as it has happened in every country, that I can recollect, where the conquerors have not preserved their own tongue unmixed with that of the natives, like the *Turks* in *Greece*, and the *Saxons* in *Britain*; and this analogy might induce us to believe, that the pure *Hindì*, whether of *Tartarian* or *Chaldean* origin, was primeval in Upper *India*, into which the *Sanscrit* was introduced by conquerors from other kingdoms in some very remote age; for we cannot doubt that the language of the *Veda's* was used in the great extent of country, which has before been delineated, as long as the religion of *Brahmà* has prevailed in it.

The *Sanscrit* language, whatever be its antiquity, is of a wonderful structure; more perfect than the *Greek*, more copious than the *Latin*, and more exquisitely refined than either, yet bearing to both of them a stronger affinity, both in the roots of verbs and in the forms of grammar, than could possibly have been produced by accident; so strong indeed, that no philologer could examine them all three, without believing them to have sprung from some common source, which, perhaps, no longer exists: there is a similar reason, though not quite so forcible, for supposing that both the *Gothick* and the *Celtick*, though blended with a very different idiom, had the same origin with the *Sanscrit*; and the old *Persian* might be added to the same family, if this were the place for discussing any question concerning the antiquities of *Persia*.

SIR WILLIAM JONES

"Preface" to The Persian Language

The Persian language is rich, melodious, and elegant; it has been spoken for many ages by the greatest princes in the politest courts of Asia; and a number of admirable works have been written in it by historians, philosophers, and poets, who found it capable of expressing with equal advantage the most beautiful and the most elevated sentiments.

It must seem strange, therefore, that the study of this language should be so little cultivated at a time when a taste for general and diffusive learning seems universally to prevail; and that the fine productions of a celebrated nation should remain in manuscript upon the shelves of our publick libraries, without a single admirer who might open their treasures to his countrymen, and display their beauties to the light; but if we consider the subject with a proper attention, we shall discover a variety of causes which have concurred to obstruct the progress of Eastern literature.

Some men never heard of the Asiatick writings, and others will not be convinced that there is any thing valuable in them; some pretend to be busy, and others are really idle; some detest the Persians, because they believe in Mahomed, and others despise their language, because they do not understand it: we all love to excuse, or to conceal, our ignorance,

Sir William Jones, "Preface" to *The Persian Language, Complete Works,* vol. II (London, 1799), 121–127.

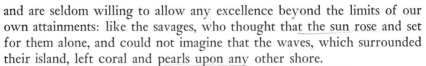

and are seldom willing to allow any excellence beyond the limits of our own attainments: like the savages, who thought that the sun rose and set for them alone, and could not imagine that the waves, which surrounded their island, left coral and pearls upon any other shore.

Another obvious reason for the neglect of the Persian language is the great scarcity of books, which are necessary to be read before it can be perfectly learned, the greater part of them are preserved in the different museums and libraries of Europe, where they are shewn more as objects of curiosity than as sources of information; and are admired, like the characters on a Chinese screen, more for their gay colours than for their meaning.

Thus, while the excellent writings of Greece and Rome are studied by every man of a liberal education, and diffuse a general refinement through our part of the world, the works of the Persians, a nation equally distinguished in ancient history, are either wholly unknown to us, or considered as entirely destitute of taste and invention.

But if this branch of literature has met with so many obstructions from the ignorant, it has, certainly, been checked in its progress by the learned themselves; most of whom have confined their study to the minute researches of verbal criticism; like men who discover a precious mine, but instead of searching for the rich ore, or for gems, amuse themselves with collecting smooth pebbles and pieces of crystal. Others mistook reading for learning, which ought to be carefully distinguished by every man of sense, and were satisfied with running over a great number of manuscripts in a superficial manner, without condescending to be stopped by their difficulty, or to dwell upon their beauty and elegance. The rest have left nothing more behind them than grammars and dictionaries; and though they deserve the praises due to unwearied pains and industry, yet they would, perhaps, have gained a more shining reputation, if they had contributed to beautify and enlighten the vast temple of learning, instead of spending their lives in adorning only its porticos and avenues.

There is nothing which has tended more to bring polite letters into discredit, than the total insensibility of commentators and criticks to the beauties of the authors whom they profess to illustrate: few of them seem to have received the smallest pleasure from the most elegant compositions, unless they found some mistake of a transcriber to be corrected, or some established reading to be changed, some obscure expression to be explained, or some clear passage to be made obscure by their notes.

It is a circumstance equally unfortunate, that men of the most refined taste and the brightest parts are apt to look upon a close application to the study of languages as inconsistent with their spirit and genius: so that the state of letters seems to be divided into two classes, men of learning who have no taste, and men of taste who have no learning.

M. de Voltaire, who excels all writers of his age and country in the elegance of his style, and the wonderful variety of his talents, acknowledges the beauty of the Persian images and sentiments, and has versified a very fine passage from Sadi, whom he compares to Petrarch: if that extraordinary man had added a knowledge of the Asiatick languages to his other acquisitions, we should by this time have seen the poems and histories of Persia in an European dress, and any other recommendation of them would have been unnecessary.

But there is yet another cause which has operated more strongly than any before mentioned towards preventing the rise of oriental literature; I mean the small encouragement which the princes and nobles of Europe have given to men of letters. It is an indisputable truth, that learning will always flourish most where the amplest rewards are proposed to the industry of the learned; and that the most shining periods in the annals of literature are the reigns of wise and liberal princes, who know that fine writers are the oracles of the world, from whose testimony every king, statesman, and hero must expect the censure or approbation of posterity. In the old states of Greece the highest honours were given to poets, philosophers, and orators; and a single city (as an eminent writer[1] observes) in the memory of one man, produced more numerous and splendid monuments of human genius than most other nations have afforded in a course of ages.

The liberality of the Ptolemies in Egypt drew a number of learned men and poets in their court, whose works remain to the present age the models of taste and elegance; and the writers, whom Augustus protected, brought their composition to a degree of perfection, which the language of mortals cannot surpass. Whilst all the nations of Europe were covered with the deepest shade of ignorance, the Califs in Asia encouraged the Mahomedans to improve their talents, and cultivate the fine arts; and even the Turkish Sultan, who drove the Greeks from Constantinople, was a patron of literary merit, and was himself an elegant poet. The illustrious family of Medici invited to Florence the learned men whom the Turks had driven from their country, and a general light succeeded the gloom which ignorance and superstition had spread through the western world. But that light has not continued to shine with equal splendour; and though some slight efforts have been made to restore it, yet it seems to have been gradually decaying for the last century: it grows very faint in Italy; it seems wholly extinguished in France; and whatever sparks of it remain in other countries are confined to the closets of humble and modest men, and are not general enough to have their proper influence.

[1] Ascham.

The nobles of our days consider learning as a subordinate acquisition, which would not be consistent with the dignity of their fortunes, and should be left to those who toil in a lower sphere of life: but they do not reflect on the many advantages which the study of polite letters would give, peculiarly to persons of eminent rank and high employments; who, instead of relieving their fatigues by a series of unmanly pleasures, or useless diversions, might spend their leisure in improving their knowledge, and in conversing with the great statesmen, orators, and philosophers of antiquity.

If learning in general has met with so little encouragement, still less can be expected for that branch of it, which lies so far removed from the common path, and which the greater part of mankind have hitherto considered as incapable of yielding either entertainment or instruction: if pains and want be the lot of a scholar, the life of an orientalist must certainly be attended with peculiar hardships. Gentius, who published a beautiful Persian work called *The Bed of Roses*, with an useful but inelegant translation, lived obscurely in Holland, and died in misery. Hyde, who might have contributed greatly towards the progress of eastern learning, formed a number of expensive projects with that view, but had not the support and assistance which they deserved and required. The labours of Meninski immortalized and ruined him: his dictionary of the Asiatick languages is, perhaps, the most laborious compilation that was ever undertaken by any single man; but he complains in his preface that his patrimony was exhausted by the great expense of employing and supporting a number of writers and printers, and of raising a new press for the oriental characters. M. d'Herbelot, indeed, received the most splendid reward of his industry: he was invited to Italy by Ferdinand II. duke of Tuscany, who entertained him with that striking munificence which always distinguished the race of the Medici: after the death of Ferdinand, the illustrious Colbert recalled him to Paris, where he enjoyed the fruits of his labour, and spent the remainder of his days in an honourable and easy retirement. But this is a rare example: the other princes of Europe have not imitated the duke of Tuscany; and Christian VII. was reserved to be the protector of the eastern muses in the present age.

Since the literature of Asia was so much neglected, and the causes of that neglect were so various, we could not have expected that any slight power would rouse the nations of Europe from their inattention to it; and they would, perhaps, have persisted in despising it, if they had not been animated by the most powerful incentive that can influence the mind of man: interest was the magick wand which brought them all within one circle; interest was the charm which give the languages of the East a real and solid importance. By one of those revolutions, which no human prudence could have forseen, the Persian language found its way into India; that rich and celebrated empire, which, by the flourishing state of our commerce, has been the source of incredible wealth to the merchants of Europe. A variety of causes, which need not be mentioned here, gave the English nation a most extensive power in that kingdom: our India company began to take under their protection the princes of the country, by whose protection they gained their first settlement; a number of important affairs were to be transacted in peace and war between nations equally jealous of one another, who had not the common instrument of conveying their sentiments; the servants of the company received letters which they could not read, and were ambitious of gaining titles of which they could not comprehend the meaning; it was found highly dangerous to employ the natives as interpreters, upon whose fidelity they could not depend; and it was at last discovered, that they must apply themselves to the study of the Persian language, in which all the letters from the Indian princes were written. A few men of parts and taste, who resided in Bengal, have since amused themselves with the literature of the East, and have spent their leisure in reading the poems and histories of Persia; but they found a reason in every page to regret their ignorance of the Arabick language, without which their knowledge must be very circumscribed and imperfect. The languages of Asia will now, perhaps, be studied with uncommon ardour; they are known to be useful, and will soon be found instructive and entertaining; the valuable manuscripts that enrich our publick libraries will be in a few years elegantly printed; the manners and sentiments of the eastern nations will be perfectly known; and the limits of our knowledge will be no less extended than the bounds of our empire.

WILHELM VON HUMBOLDT

"*Introduction*" to *Concerning the Variety of Human Language and Its Influence on the Intellectual Development of Mankind*

The present introduction should, I believe, be devoted to general considerations which will more adequately prepare the transition to the specific facts and the historical investigations. The distribution of the human race into nations and races and the differences of its languages and dialects are directly related to each other, to be sure, but also stand in a direct relationship of dependence on a third, higher phenomenon, namely the production of human spiritual energy in ever new and often intensified configurations. Within this relationship the nations and their languages find their proper valuation but also, insofar as research can penetrate them and grasp their connections, their explanation. The manifestation of human spiritual energy over the course of millennia and the space of the earth, ever diverse in degree and kind, is the highest aim of all movement of the spirit. It is the ultimate idea which world history must strive to enunciate clearly. For this elevation or extension of inner existence is the only thing which an individual, so far as he shares in it, may look upon as his own inalienable property. For a nation, it is the

Reprinted from the "Introduction" to "Man's Intrinsic Humanity: His Language (1830–1835)" by Wilhelm von Humboldt in *Humanist without Portfolio* translated by Marianne Cowan by permission of the Wayne State University Press. Copyright © 1963 by Wayne State University Press, Detroit 2, Michigan.

only thing from which will unfailingly be born again more great individualities. Comparative linguistics, the precise investigation into the diversity with which countless peoples solve the task of language imparted to them by human nature, loses all interest when it does not proceed from the point at which language is connected to the general configuration of the national spirit. But even one's insight into the unique character of a nation and the inner relationships of a language, as well as its relationship to linguistic considerations in general, depends entirely upon one's consideration of the sum total of spiritual characteristics. For only by these, as nature has given them and given situations have affected them, does a national character attain coherence. Upon them, and upon what they produce by way of deeds, institutions, and thoughts, does national character rest, and in it lie all the energies and values which are then handed on to individuals. Seen from its other side, language is the organ of inner existence; in fact it is inner existence as it gradually attains first to self-consciousness and then to utterance. It sinks all its finest multitudinous root fibers into the spiritual energy of the nation, therefore, and the more appropriately the latter reacts back on it, the more lawful and rich is its development. Since in its web of connected elements it is only an effect of the national linguistic sense, the very questions which concern the core of linguistic formation and from which spring the most significant linguistic differences cannot be answered thoroughly unless one assumes the foregoing elevated point of view toward linguistic studies. Of course this elevation yields no materials for linguistic comparisons, which can be had only from a historical consideration, but it does yield the only insight into the original relationships between the various facts, and the realization that language is an inwardly connected organism. This done, it will further even a correct evaluation of the historical details. . . .

GENERAL CONSIDERATIONS OF HUMAN DEVELOPMENT

A careful consideration of our current status so far as political, artistic, and scientific development is concerned, leads us to a long concatenation running through many centuries of mutually determined causes and effects. In following it, we soon become aware that two different kinds of elements hold sway over it and that investigation does not solve them both with equal felicity. For whereas we may explain causally a number of events, from time to time, as every attempt at a cultural history of the human race has amply demonstrated, we hit knots, as it were, which resist all further historical untangling. The reason for this is to be found within that spiritual energy which cannot be wholly penetrated in its nature by us, not calculated in advance. It acts together with what is prior to it and current with it, but treats and forms all such elements in accordance with its own unique character. Any great individual of any period could provide the starting point for all world history; one could show against what background he arose, and how the work of all the centuries before him had contributed to this background. And yet the way in which the background made his thus conditioned and supported activity what it was, what stamped it with his uniqueness, may be described, perhaps represented, surely felt, but never derived from anything outside itself. This is the natural, everywhere recurring phenomenon of human functioning. Originally, everything in the human being is inside him—sensation, feeling, desire, thought, decision, language, and deeds. But as the inside comes into contact with the outside world, it begins to operate independently and determines by its own unique configuration the inner and outer functions of others. In time there grow up security measures for what at first had but fleeting effects, and less and less of the work of prior centuries is lost to future ones. Here is the field in which investigation can examine one level after another. But it is at the same time so crisscrossed by the operations of fresh and incalculable inner powers, and without a proper separation of and deliberation upon this double element the material of one can become so overpowering that it threatens to choke out the energy of the other, that no true appreciation is possible of the noblest products which the history of all times offers us.

The deeper we go into the earliest times, of course, the faster melts the mass of materials transmitted from one generation to the next. But then we meet with another phenomenon which transplants our investigation onto another field of difficulty, as it were. Individuals delineated with certainty become rarer and rarer; we no longer know them in their life situations; their fates, even their very names become uncertain; even whether a given work ascribed to a certain person is truly his, or whether a name has simply become the rallying point for the work of many. Individuals get lost in a collectivity of shadow figures. In Greece this is the case with Orpheus and Homer, in India with Manu, Vyasa, Valmiki, and with so many other celebrated names of antiquity. And as we go still further back, the roundedness of individuality disappears even further. A language as polished as Homer's must for a long time have passed up and down on the waves of song, throughout whole cycles of history of which we have no lore. Even more plainly this is seen in the original forms of language itself. Language is deeply enmeshed in the spiritual development of mankind. It accompanies it on every level of its current progress or lag, and each cultural step is recognizable in it. But there is an epoch in which we see only language; it does not accompany spiritual development but entirely occupies its place. Language, to be sure, emanates from a depth of collective humanity which downright forbids us to locate it as a proper product, as a creation even, of nations. It possesses a force of spontaneity which is perfectly evident to us, though inexplicable, and therefore cannot, with this in mind, be called the product of an activity, but must be considered an unconscious, involuntary emanation of the spirit; not a work of nations but a gift given to them by their inner fate. They make use of it without knowing how they come by it.

Nonetheless it must be true that languages have always developed alongside of and within flourishing national groups, and been spun out of their spiritual character, retaining various of its special limitations. It is no empty play with words if we say that *language* has its spontaneous origin in itself, in divine freedom, but that *languages* are bound to and dependent on the national groups which speak them. For languages have entered upon the field of deterministic limitation. While speech and song flowed free, language formed itself in accordance with the measure of the inspiration and the freedom and the strength of the spiritual energies involved. But this could only emanate from all individuals at once; each single individual had to be carried by all the others, since inspiration attains vitality only from the certainty of being understood and felt. Here opens up, however dimly and weakly, a vista into those times when individuals for us are lost in collectivity, and when language itself is the work of intellectually active energy.

In every survey of world history there lies an advance, here also indicated. But it is by no means my intention to set up a system of teleology or infinite perfectibility; on the contrary, I am on quite another tack here. Peoples and individuals grow lushly like plants, spreading all over the face of the earth, enjoying their existence in happiness and activity. This life which dies with each individual goes on undisturbed at what effects it will produce centuries hence. Nature decrees that all who draw breath shall finish their course to their last breath; the aim of a beneficent and orderly providence that each creature should enjoy its life is attained, and each new generation runs through the same circle of joyful and painful existence, of successful or blocked activity. But wherever man enters the stage, he functions humanly. He socializes with his fellows; he arranges institutions, and gives himself laws. And where these things happen in too imperfect a manner, individuals or groups import or transplant what has been more successful elsewhere. Thus with the very origin of man, the seed of morality is given, and grows together with him. This humanization we can watch constantly advancing; it is partly due to nature itself, and partly to the extent to which it has already advanced, that its further perfectibility can hardly be substantially disturbed.

In the points here mentioned there lies a not to be ignored element of planning; it is no doubt present elsewhere as well, where it may be less obvious. But it must never be assumed; if we look for it we are immediately led astray in our evaluation of facts. The thing of which we are here speaking can least of all be subordinated to the assumption of planning. The appearance of human spiritual energy in its diverse configurations is not bound to progress in time or to the heaping up of what is already accomplished. Its origin is to be explained as little as its effect is to be calculated, and its highest attainments lie not at all necessarily in its latest manifestations. If, therefore, one wishes to investigate these natural formations, one must not project ideas upon them but take them as they are. In all nature's creations she brings forth a certain number of forms which express what has attained reality in any given species and what therefore suffices for the perfectibility of the idea of it. We cannot ask why there are no more forms, or no other forms. There are no others right now: this is nature's only "natural" answer. But this view permits us to consider whatever exists in physical and spiritual nature as the functioning of a basic energy which is developing according to principles unknown to us. If we do not wish to relinquish all possibility of discovering inner connections for the outward phenomena of human life, we must come back to some sort of independent and original cause which is not itself determined and which does not pass away. But the most natural candidate for this is an inner life principle, freely developing in all its aspects, whose various unfoldings are not unrelated just because its outer manifestations seem to stand in isolation. This view is totally different from a teleological one, since it does not aim at an end but only at an origin which is instantly recognized to be unfathomable. It is the only one which seems to me to be applicable to the diverse configurations of human spiritual energy. The ordinary claims of humanity seem to me to be satisfactorily answered by the functioning of natural forces and the somewhat mechanical continuity of human activity. But—assuming this division is a proper one—these forces do not seem to explain by any sufficient derivation the emergence of great individualities, either as individuals or as groups, which suddenly and incalculably intervene in the old ways that are more visibly determined by causally explicable operations.

This view is equally applicable, of course, to the main functions of human spiritual energy, especially to the one to which we limit ourselves here: language. The differences among languages may be considered the result of the striving with which the universal human power of speech breaks through into reality, more or less felicitously, helped or hindered by the spiritual power of a given nation.

For if we examine languages genetically, as a spiritual labor directed toward a definite end, it is obvious that whatever end is stipulated may be attained to a greater or lesser degree of success. In fact the main points appear, in which the unevenness of attainment will consist. A greater success can, for example, be attributed to the strength and fullness of the general spiritual energy which acts upon the language; it may also lie in the degree of special adaptation of the spirit to linguistic formations, for example, in the special clarity and plasticity of its archetypal ideas, or in the depth to which it can penetrate the nature of concepts in order to find instantly their major characterizing element, or in the ready mobility and creative strength of its imagination, or in the properly felt pleasure in harmony and rhythm of tone, to which therefore belong elasticity and mobility of the organs of articulation plus acuteness and subtlety of ear. Further to be observed are the quality of the traditional materials and the historical position in which a nation finds itself during an epoch of significant linguistic change or renewal, midway between its past and the as yet dormant germs of its future development. There are elements, too, in languages which really can be judged only by the effort directed toward them, not by the success of such effort. For languages do not always succeed in following through on a certain effort, however obviously marked. I am thinking here, for example, of such questions as that of inflections versus agglutination, about which much misunderstanding has been current and still is. That nations of happier gifts and under more favored conditions have more excellent languages lies in the very nature of the thing. But we are led to a deeper-lying cause, as well, the one we have just touched upon. The production of language is an inner need of mankind, not merely an external vehicle for the maintenance of communication, but an indispensable one which lies in human nature, necessary for the development of its spiritual energies and for the growth of a Weltanschauung which man can attain only by bringing his thinking to clarity and definition by communal contact with the thinking of others. If one now looks upon each language as an attempt to do this—and it is difficult to look at it otherwise—and upon all languages together as a contribution to the fulfillment of this basic human need, it may well be assumed that the language-creating energy in mankind will not rest until it has brought forth, whether in one place or everywhere, whatever accords most perfectly with its demands. In other words, there may be, even among languages and language groups which show no historical connection, various levels of advance as to this principle of their development. But when such is the case, such connectibility of outwardly unconnected phenomena must be founded on a universal inner cause which can only be the development of the operative energies. Language is one of the aspects from which collective human spiritual energy constantly proceeds into active manifestation. To express it in another way, one can see in language the striving of the archetypal idea of linguistic perfection to win existence in reality. To follow up this striving, and to depict it, is the business in its ultimate simplest analysis of the linguist.

Linguistic studies, incidentally, by no means require this perhaps too hypothetical sounding view for their foundation. But they can and should use it as a stimulus to try to find out whether such a step-by-step approach to perfectibility can be discovered in the various languages. There could be a series of languages, both of simple and of more complex structure, which do reveal to comparative study an advance in the direction of perfect structure. The organism of such languages would have to carry, even in complex forms, a certain order and simplicity which would make their striving for linguistic perfection more easily visible. Progress along this line would be found first in the isolation and perfect articulation of its sounds, hence in the syllabification dependent on it, in the pure segregation of its various elements, and in the structure of its simplest words. Further, we should be able to trace it in the treatment of words as sound units in order to obtain true word units which correspond to conceptual units, and finally, in the proper separation of what should appear independently in language and what should appear as a dependent form which adheres to an independent entity, which of course demands a method that can differentiate between additive compounds and symbolic fusions. For the reasons given above, I do not go into this in any detail, but merely wish my readers to recognize among the various points of view under discussion those which have guided me in my placement of the Kawi language among the Malayan language group. In the consideration of languages to follow, I separate all the changes which can be developed out of each language completely from their forms which to us look like original ones. The sphere of primordial linguistic forms now seems to be closed; the situational development in which we find human energies now does not seem to have the power to repeat itself. For however inward a phenomenon language is, it nonetheless has an independent external force of existence which compels man under its sway. The growth of primordial forms would therefore assume a separation of the peoples in the world which is now no longer thinkable . . . if, indeed—and this is a likelier explanation—there is not a definite period for linguistic breakthrough provided for the human race, as there is for the human individual. . . .

Language, taken as real, is something which constantly and in every moment passes away. Even its preservation in writing is only an incomplete mummified depository which needs, for full understanding, an imaginative oral reconstruction. Language is not a work (*ergon*) but an activity (*energeia*). Its true definition can therefore only be a genetic one. For it is the ever-repetitive work of the spirit to make articulated sound capable of expressing thought. Taken directly and strictly, this is the definition of each act of speaking, but in a true and intrinsic sense one can look upon language as but the totality of all spoken utterance. For in the scattered chaos of words and rules which we customarily call language, the only thing present in reality is whatever particulars are brought forth by individual acts of speaking, and this is never complete. It needs another type of work performed on it in order for us to recognize in it the type of living speech that it is, in other words to yield a true image of a living language. Just the highest and subtlest aspects of language cannot be recognized in its separate elements; they can only be perceived or intuited in connected speech (which demonstrates all the more that language intrinsically lies in the act of its production in reality). Connected speech is what we must hold before our inner ear as the true and foremost manifestation of language, if we are to be successful in any of our investigations into the living essence of language. Beating it down into words and rules is only a dead artifice of scientific analysis.

To designate languages as works of the spirit is a completely correct and adequate expression, if only because the existence of the spirit can only be imagined in the form of activity. The analysis essential to the study of linguistic structure compels us, in fact, to look upon language as a method which pursues certain aims by certain means, and hence to consider it truly a creative formation of a given nation. (I have tried above to prevent the misinterpretations possible at this point. . . .)

I have also drawn attention to the fact that our linguistic studies place us—if I may thus express it—into a historical center, and that neither a nation nor a language now known to us may be considered original or primordial. Since each has already received some of its materials from previous generations in times unknown to us, the spiritual activity above explained as bringing forth thought is always directed at something already given. The bringing forth which is here meant is not so much a purely creative, as a transformative activity.

This activity, now, operates in a constant and uniform manner. For it is the same spiritual power which keeps exerting itself, and it diverges only within rather narrow limits. Understanding is its aim. No one, in other words, may speak to another in a way in which, under similar circumstances, he might not himself be spoken to. And finally, the materials transmitted are not only whatever they are—miscellaneous materials transmitted—but, since they too had a similar origin, they are most closely related to the general spiritual direction. Those elements, in this endeavor of the spirit to lift articulated sound into expression of thought, which are constant and uniform, represented as completely and systematically as possible with full comprehension of their inner connections —constitute the form of language.

In this definition the form appears to be a scientific abstraction. But it would be totally incorrect to look upon it solely as such an existenceless figment of thought. In reality it is the quite individuated urge by means of which a nation creates validity in language for its thoughts and its feelings. Only because it is never given to us to see this urge in the undivided totality of its striving, but merely in its invariably isolated effects, all we can successfully do is comprehend the identical nature of its manifestations with a dead general concept. In itself, the urge is a living whole.

The difficulty facing just the most significant and subtlest linguistic investigations frequently lies in the fact that something which flows through the total impression a language yields is perceived with the clearest feeling of conviction, but is wrecked by all attempts to present it with sufficient completeness of detail and to define it by limited concepts. This is a difficulty which we must also face here. The characteristic form of language depends on each single one of its tiniest elements; each is somehow determined by it, however unnoticeable in detail. On the other hand, it is hardly possible to find certain points of which, taken individually, it could be asserted that the form of the language is specifically and decisively contained in them. Whenever one goes through any given language, therefore, one finds many things in it which one can imagine might be quite different, without their altering the form. To see the form purely differentiated, we are willy-nilly led back to a total impression. And here the opposite instantly takes place. The most decisive individuality lies clear before our eyes, unmistakably convincing to our feeling. Perhaps the least incorrect analogy to languages in this respect is our experience with human physiognomy. Individuality confronts us undeniably; similarities are recognized; but no amount of measuring or describing of the parts, either alone or in relationship to the whole, can weld the evident characteristics into a concept. It rests upon the whole and upon each individual reception of that whole; no doubt, therefore, each physiognomy appears different to each observer. Since language, however we look at it, is always the spiritual exhalation of a nationally characteristic life, the same applies to it. However much we stuff into it or embody in it, however much we abstract and analyze out of it: something unknown is always left over and this, slipping out of the grasp of all direct attack upon the problems language raises, is exactly that wherein it is a unity and the breath of a living entity. Since such is the constitution of languages, then, the representation of their form can never be complete in the sense here indicated, but can only be successful up to a point—which point, however, should suffice us for an over-all view. But this awareness of ultimate failure on the part of the linguist should not render his path any less definite by which he must explore the mysteries of language and seek to reveal its nature. If he loses his way, he will unfailingly miss a large number of investigative clues and must leave unexplained a good many points which are perfectly explicable, for he will take for isolated detail what is in reality joined in a living relationship.

The above introduction makes self-evident that by form in language we do not here mean its so-called grammatical form. The difference that we are in the habit of observing between grammar and vocabulary can only serve practical purposes in connection with learning a new language; it surely prescribes no limits or rules for genuine linguistic research. The concept of form in languages stretches far beyond the rules of syntax and word formation, insofar as one means by the latter the application of certain general logical categories of function, effectuation, substance, quality, etc. upon the roots or bases of words. Form is intrinsically applicable to the formation of roots and bases themselves and must, in fact, be reserved to them as much as possible, in order to clarify the intrinsic nature of language.

Form is opposed, to be sure, to substance. But in order to find the substance of language form, we must pass beyond the boundaries of language. Within them, the only substance that can be found is something which may be only relatively opposed to something else, such as bases, for example, in relationship to declension. A language may borrow words from another and treat them like substances. But again, such words will be substances only in relation to the language that borrowed them, not in themselves. Taken absolutely, there can be no unformed substance—no raw materiality—within language, since everything in it is directed toward a certain aim, namely the expression of thought, and this task already begins with the first element of language: articulated sound. In fact, sound *is* articulated by formal activation. The true material substance of language is on the one hand sound as such, and on the other hand the totality of sense impressions and spontaneous spiritual movements which precede, by the help of language, the formation of concepts.

It is therefore self-evident that the realistic quality of the sounds must be particularly noted, in order to get a notion of the form of a language. Investigation into form begins with the alphabet and this is treated as its major foundation throughout all parts of our investigation. Generally speaking, nothing factual or particular is excluded from our concept of form; on the contrary, all that which can be explained only historically, the most individual aspects possible, are just what is contained in this concept. All the details of language, in fact, if one pursues the method here designated, can only thus be secured for investigation, since they can all too easily be otherwise overlooked. This leads to painstaking and often petty elementary research, to be sure; but it simply is the vast quantity of petty details upon which one's total impression of a language rests. Nothing is as incompatible with linguistic study as the ambition to look only for great things, for spirituality, and predominant factors. Careful search of each grammatical subtlety, painstaking dismemberment of words into their component parts, are absolute necessities if error in all one's judgments is to be avoided. It is likewise self-evident, however, that no detail is taken up into the concept of form as a mere isolated fact, but only insofar as a method of linguistic structure can be recognized in it. By representing to oneself the form, one must recognize the specific way that a language (and with it a nation) has taken in order to express its thoughts. One must be in a position to have an over-all view of its relationship to other languages, both as to its aim and theirs, as well as its reaction and theirs, back upon the spiritual activity of the nations involved. . . .

Whatever identity or relationship two languages may have must rest on the identity or relationship of their forms. . . . Form alone decides the relationship among language groups. This applies to Kawi, for example, which does not stop being a Malayan language just because it contains a great many Sanskrit words. The forms of several languages may be collected under a still more general concept of form, and this in fact happens as soon as one looks only at the most general characteristics, such as the interrelationships of the ideas necessary for the designation of concepts and the exigencies of syntax, the sameness of the organs of articulation whose extent and nature permit of only a certain number of articulated sounds, the relationships, finally, between certain consonants and vowels to certain sense impressions, from all of which springs identity of form without necessarily cognate relationship. For the individuation of languages, within a most universal sameness is so marvellously great that one might say with equal propriety that the entire human race has but one language, or that each human being has his own. Among the linguistic analogical similarities, however, first and foremost is that which is due to the family relationship among nations. How great and of what quality such similarity must be in order to justify the assumption of cognation when it is not otherwise historically vouched for, we cannot examine here. We are concerned here only with the application of our concept of linguistic form to cognate languages. It should be clear by now that the form of various cognate languages must be found in the form of the entire linguistic family. Nothing may be contained in them which is not in harmony with the more general, generic form; as a rule one will find each special characteristic of the individual language at least hinted at in the generic form. And there will usually be one or more languages in each family which will contain the original form more purely and completely. For we are speaking here of languages one of which has grown out of the other, where, in other words, a given material substance (always taken, as above specified, in a relative sense only) passes over from one nation to another and is transformed in passing. This happens in a definite sequence and order, which can usually not be accurately determined, however. But the transformations themselves, given the similar ideational complexes and directions of the operative spiritual energy, the sameness of the speech organs and the transmitted speech habits, and finally the many similar historical influences, can only be closely related.

THE NATURE AND ATTRIBUTES OF LANGUAGE IN GENERAL

Since the difference in languages rests upon their form, and this form is related to the spiritual constitution of the nations and the particular energy coursing through them at the moment of their creation or transformation, it now becomes necessary to develop the concepts underlying these in greater detail and to pursue at least several of the main directions of language. For this purpose I shall pick out the most consequential ones which clearly show how basic inner energy reacts upon language and language in turn upon it.

Two principles come to light as one reflects upon language in general and the analysis of specific differences among languages in particular: phonetic form and the uses made of it for the designation of objects and the interrelation of thoughts. The latter is founded on the demands made upon language by thought, from which originate the general rules of language, and this aspect is therefore the same among all peoples, within the limits of their national characteristics or its subsequent developments. The phonetic form itself, on the other hand, is the truly constitutive and guiding principle of the diversity among languages, both in itself as well as in the helping or hindering effect it has on the inmost tendency of language. It is of course likewise closely related and dependent upon the total constituent characteristics of a nation, being a part of the human organism that is closely connected with the sum total of inner spiritual energy, but the types of connection and the reasons for them are shrouded in an obscurity which hardly permits of any clarification. These two principles now (phonetic form and its application), in all the intimacy of their mutual interpenetration, yield the individual form of every language. They form the points of reference which linguistic analysis must investigate and attempt to represent in all their connectedness. The indispensable ingredient in such investigation is that the undertaking be founded on a correct and worthy estimate of language as a whole, of the depth of its origin, and the vastness of its extent. We shall therefore need to tarry once more in order to ascertain that we are working with these requirements well in mind.

I am taking the linguistic process in its widest sense, not merely in its reference to speech or to the accumulation of its verbal elements as the immediate products of speech, but also in its relationship toward our thinking and feeling functions. Under consideration, therefore, is language's entire path, emanating from spirit, reacting upon spirit.

Language is the formative organ of thought. Intellectual activity which is totally spiritual, totally inward, which passes without a trace, as it were, becomes externalized and perceptible to the senses by means of the sounds of speech. It and speech are therefore one and indivisible. But aside from this, intellectual activity has a reason implicit in itself for entering into relationship with the sound of speech; if it did not, thinking could not reach clarification; imaginative representation could not be conceptualized. The indivisible connection between thought, the organs of speech and the organs of hearing lie unalterable and intrinsic in the arrangement of human nature, to be explained no further than to state that it is so. The harmony of sound with thought presents a clear enough image. Just as thought, comparable to a flash of lightning or a blow, collects all imaginative representation into a single point which excludes everything not belonging to it, so does sound resound with incisive acuity and singleness of purpose. Just as thought seizes the entire psychic constitution, so does sound possess a power which penetrates and shivers every nerve. What makes sound different from and unique among all sensuous impressions is that the ear (which is not true or not equally true of the other sense organs) receives the impression of actual movement, of an action in the case of the sounds of voice, and that this movement or action emanates from the inmost core of a living creature—a thinking creature in the case of articulated sound, a feeling creature in the case of unarticulated sound. Just as thinking in its most intimately human aspects is a yearning from darkness to see the light, from restrictedness and constraint toward infinity, so sound streams outward from the depths of the breast and finds in air a wonderfully appropriate mediating material, the subtlest and most mobile of all elements, whose seeming incorporeality accords with even the sensuous conception of spirit. The incisive acuity of speech sounds is indispensable to the understanding as it grapples with a conceptualization of objects. The objects of external nature as well as the internally stimulated activity press in upon man all at once, with a multitude of distinguishing marks. But he strives for comparison, analysis, synthesis, and—in his loftier moments—for the development of an ever more comprehensive organic development into unity. He demands, therefore, to conceive even of separate objects in a well-defined form, forcing the unity and clear definition of sound to replace the object. But such sound never displaces any of the other impressions made by objects on man's outer or inner senses, but instead becomes their carrier, adding a new significance which is the joint result of its own individual nature and the individual reception the object impressions have received from the speaker. At the same time the acuity of the sound permits an undefined number of modifications which are cleanly separable from the original imaginative representation and which are equally separable from each other. This is nowhere nearly as true in any of the other sense impressions. Since intellectual endeavor does not only occupy the understanding but stimulates the entire human being, this fact too is reflected by the sound of the human voice. As living sound, like the breath of life itself, it comes forth from the human breast, accompanying, even without language, his pains and joys, his loathings and his desires, thereby breathing the life which produces it into the sense which accepts it as part of itself, just as language itself always reproduces the represented object together with the feeling which it stimulates, thereby relating over and over again in repeated separate acts the world with humanity or—in a different formulation—man's spontaneous activity with his receptivity. Finally man's upright posture, denied to the animals, is a singularly fitting accompaniment to the sound of speech which evokes it, as it were. For speech does not care to die away along the ground; it longs to pour forth from the lips of the speaker directly toward the recipient, to be accompanied by the expression of his eyes and countenance as well as the gesture of his hands, thus being surrounded by all the typically human aspects of human beings.

After this preliminary consideration of the appropriateness of sound for the operations of spirit we may now have a closer look at the connections between thinking and language. In thinking, a subjective activity forms itself an object. For no type of imaginative representation may be considered a merely receptive apperception of an already existent object. The activity of the senses must be synthetically joined with the inner action of the spirit. From their connection the imaginative representation tears itself loose, becomes objective in relation to the subjective energy, and then returns to it, having first been perceived in its new, objective form. For this process language is indispensable. For while the spiritual endeavor expresses itself through the lips, its products return through the very ears of the speaker. The representation is therefore truly transformed into actual objectivity without therefore being withdrawn from subjectivity. Only language can accomplish this, and without this constant transformation and retransformation in which language plays the decisive part even in silence, no conceptualization and therefore no true thinking is possible. Without reference, therefore, to the communication between persons, the act of speaking is a necessary condition of thinking even in a single individual in complete solitude. So far as actual reality is concerned, of course, language develops only socially and man understands himself only by having tested the understandability of his words on others. For the objectivity is intensified when the word which one has formed oneself re-echoes from someone else's mouth. And yet nothing is robbed from the simultaneous subjectivity because every human being feels humanly allied to other human beings; it is, in fact, likewise intensified since the representation now transformed into language no longer belongs exclusively to a single subject. By being imparted to others, it joins the collectivity of the entire human race, of which each individual carries a single modification which longs for the wholeness which can only come through the others. The greater and more varied the social operations on language, the more it gains, other conditions being equal. What makes language necessary in the simple act of thought production, is repeated over and over in man's spiritual life; social communication through language affords man conviction and stimulation. The thinking function requires something like itself and yet separated from itself. It is kindled by the sameness; the separateness gives it a touchstone for the validity of its inner products. Although the epistemological ground for truth, for absolute permanence, can only lie within the human being, his spiritual efforts to attain it are ever accompanied by the danger of delusion. Immediately feeling as he does only his ephemerality and his limitations, man must actually look upon this epistemological ground as something lying outside himself. And one of the most powerful means for drawing near it, for measuring its distance from himself, is social communion with others. All speech, beginning with the simplest, is a relating of that which is separately sensed and felt to the common nature of mankind.

It is no different so far as understanding is concerned. It is present in the psyche only by its own activity. Understanding and speaking are but different operations of the same linguistic capacity. Communal speech is never to be compared with the handing on of a given material. The materials of speech must be developed by the intrinsic capacity of listener as well as speaker; what the listener receives is only the stimulus that attunes him harmoniously to the other. It is very natural for human beings to give out immediately with what they have just heard. Thus the whole of language lies within each human being, which only means that each of us contains a striving, regulated by a definitely modified capacity, which both stimulates and restricts, gradually to produce the entire language, as inner or outer demands dictate, and to understand it as it is produced by others.

Understanding as we have just discussed it, however, could not rest upon inner spontaneous activity, and communal speaking would have to be something other than merely mutual awakening of the linguistic capacity of the listeners, if human nature did not lie in the diversity of its individuals, split off from the basic unity of nature, as they are. The comprehension of words is something quite different from the understanding of unarticulated sounds, and comprises a great deal more than the mere mutual evocation of sounds and the objects they signify. Words, to be sure, may also be taken as indivisible wholes, just as in writing one sometimes recognizes the sense of a word group without as yet being certain of its alphabetical composition. It is possible that the child's psyche operates like that when it first begins to understand. But just as not merely the sensory understanding which we share with animals but also the specific human linguistic capacity is stimulated (and it is far more probable that even in an infant there is no moment when this does not hold true, in however small a degree), so the word, too, is perceived as articulated. Now that which is added to the mere evocation of a word's significance by the articulation is that it presents it directly through its form as part of an infinite whole—that of a language. For it is a language that gives us the possibility, even if we know only individual words of it, to form from its elements a truly unlimited number of other words, in accordance with feelings and rules which define them, and thereby to create a relationship among concepts. But our psyche would lack all comprehension of this artful mechanism, it would comprehend articulation no better than a blind man color, if it did not contain an intrinsic capacity to realize that latent possibility. For language simply cannot be looked upon as though it were a collection of materials lying visible and gradually communicable before us, but must be considered forever in process, where the laws of generation are constant but the extent and in a sense even the kind of product remain wholly indefinite. When infants learn to speak, the process cannot be described in terms of the simple addition of words of vocabulary, their retention in memory, and the subsequent attempts at repetitive babbling, but only as a growth of the child's linguistic capacity, judged by age and practice. What has been heard does more than merely communicate itself; it imparts skill to understand more easily what hasn't yet been heard; it casts sudden light upon what was heard long ago but not understood at the time; it sharpens the urge and the capacity to draw more and more of what is heard into memory and to let less and less of it roll by as mere sound. Progress in linguistic capacity is therefore not measurable in even advances, as is progress in —say—vocabulary learning . . . but is constantly intensified and stepped up by the mutual interaction of the material and the child's ability to handle it. A further proof that children do not mechanically learn their native language but undergo a development of linguistic capacity is afforded by the fact that all children, in the most different imaginable circumstances of life, learn to speak within a fairly narrow and definite time span, just as they develop all their main capacities at certain definite growth stages. But how could the listener master the spoken word just by the developmental process of a separate isolated capacity growing in him if there did not underlie speaker and listener alike the same nature, merely divided into mutually corresponding individuality, so that a signal as subtle but as profoundly rooted in nature as is articulated sound is sufficient to stimulate both and mediate a harmony between them!

An objection to this argument might be found by pointing out that if children are transplanted before they learn their native tongue, they develop their linguistic capacity in the foreign one. This undeniable fact, it might be said, clearly shows that language is the mere reproduction of what is heard, depending entirely on social intercourse without consideration of the unity or diversity of the people involved. In the first place, however, it has by no means been determined by exact tests that the inclination toward such children's native speech did not have to be overcome at some cost to the finest nuances of skill in the adopted language. But even disregarding this possibility, the most natural explanation is simply that human beings are everywhere human and the development of linguistic capacity may therefore take place with the aid of any given individual. That doesn't mean that it comes any less from the individual's innate nature; only, since it always needs outer stimulus as well, it must become analogous to whatever stimulus it receives. This it can do, since all human languages are interrelated in some sense. Nonetheless the binding force of closely related origins is plain enough to behold in the division of nations. Nor is it difficult to understand, since national origins are so predominantly powerful in their effect on individuality, and the various languages so intimately related with these origins. If language were not truly connected through its origins in the depths of human nature with even the physical hereditary processes, how then could one's native tongue have so much power and intimacy for the ear of the uneducated and educated alike, that after a long separation from it it greets one like the sound of magic and creates deep yearning for itself during one's separation from it? This obviously is not a matter of the spiritual content of any language, of its expressed thoughts or feelings, but of the most inexplicable and individual element in it: the sound. When we hear the sound of our native tongue it is as though we heard a part of our self.

And even when we consider the products of language, the notion that it consists but of the designation of perceived objects is not confirmed. With this function alone, the profound and full contents of language can never be exhausted. Just as no concept is possible without language, so no object is possible without it for the psyche, since even external ones receive their intrinsic substance only through language. But the entire method of subjective perception of objects goes necessarily into the development and use of language. For words are born of the subjective perception of objects; they are not a copy of the object itself but of the image of it produced in the psyche by its perception. And since subjectivity is unavoidably mingled with all objective perception, one may —quite independently of language—look upon each human individuality as a singuler unique standpoint for a world-view. But it becomes far more so through language, since words when confronted with psyche turn themselves into objects, an intrinsic significance being added to them, and thus produce a new characteristic quality. This, being one which characterizes the sound of speech, presents thoroughgoing analogies within a language, and since the language of a given nation is already characterized by a similar subjectivity, each language therefore contains a characteristic world view. As individual sound mediates between object and person, so the whole of language mediates between human beings and the internal and external nature that affects them. Man surrounds himself by a world of sounds in order to take into himself the world of objects and operate on them. What I am here saying outdistances in no way the simple truth. Man lives with objects mainly, in fact exclusively, since feeling and acting depend on his mental images, as language turns them over to him. The same act which enables him to spin language out of himself enables him to spin himself into language, and each language draws a circle around the people to whom it adheres which it is possible for the individual to escape only by stepping into a different one. The learning of a foreign language should therefore mean the gaining of a new standpoint toward one's world-view, and it does this in fact to a considerable degree, because each language contains the entire conceptual web and mental images of a part of humanity. If it is not always purely felt as such, the reason is only that one so frequently projects one's own world-view, in fact one's own speech habits, onto a foreign language.

One must not think of even the earliest origins of language being limited to a sparse number of words, as one frequently does if one thinks of language not originating in free human sociality, but rather as limited to acts of mutual assistance—a point of view facilitated by the reduction of early humanity to an imaginary status of "children of nature." These notions are among the most erroneous views one could possibly form regarding language. Man is not as helpless as all that, and besides, inarticulated sounds would suffice for the purpose of mere mutual aid in trouble. Language is human even in its very beginnings, and extends broadly without special purposes to all objects of random sensory perception or inner operation. Even (and especially in fact) the languages of so-called savages, who after all should be fairly close to a state of nature as we think of the phrase, show a fullness and diversity of expression which far exceeds simple needs. Words well up from the breast of their own free will, without need or intention, and there doubtless never was a wild wandering horde in any of the earth's desolate places which did not already have its songs. For man, as an animal species, is a singing creature, though one who joins thoughts to the tones.

But language does not merely transplant an undefined number of material elements from nature into the psyche. It also acquaints it with the aspects of form which come to us from the whole complex. Nature unfolds before us a bright many-colored diversity, rich with configurations affecting all our senses, and irradiated by a luminous clarity. Our power of reflection discovers in this richness a regularity or conformity to law which suits our spirit form. Quite apart from the corporeal existence of things there clings to their outlines a magic haze of outward beauty, as though it were made for man's sake alone, in which the conformity to law is wedded to the sensory material in a way which moves and overwhelms us but which we cannot explain. All these things we find again in the analogical echoes of language, for language can represent the state of affairs as we find it. For by entering the world of sound with the aid of language, we do not leave the real world that surrounds us. The conformity to law found in nature is related to that found in linguistic structure, and by stimulating man to perform his loftiest, most human activities, it furthers his understanding of the formal impression that nature makes, since it too cannot be considered other than a development of spiritual energies, however inexplicable. Through the rhythmic and musical form inherent in related sounds, language—affecting yet another human field—heightens the impression of natural beauty in man, but even independent of this, affects the psyche's mood by just the accents of speech.

Language, being the mass of its products, is different from whatever fragment is spoken at a given time. And before we leave this chapter we must tarry awhile at that difference. A language as a whole contains everything transformed by it into sounds. But just as the materials of thought and the infinitude of its connections can never be exhausted, neither can the number of things to be designated and related by language. A language therefore consists of not only its already formed elements but above all of a methodology for continuing the spiritual labor for which it designates the orbits and the forms. The firmly composed elements form a certain kind of dead mass of language, but this mass carries the living germ of never-ending definability. At each given point and in each given epoch, therefore, language just like nature appears to man as an inexhaustible reservoir, in contrast to all he has already thought and known, a reservoir in which his spirit may still discover the unknown, and his inward sensation may still become aware of things not felt this way before. Each time language is used by a truly original and great genius, that is what happens. And the human race needs for the inspiration of its constantly advancing intellectual efforts and the unfolding of its spiritual life-stuff, the ever open vista beyond what has already been achieved, the assurance that the infinite entanglements yet remaining may gradually be dissolved. But language contains a dark unrevealed depth, as well, and a depth which reaches in two directions. For backwards as well as forwards, it flows out of (or into) an unknown wealth of materials which may be recognized only up to a point and then vanishes from view, leaving the feeling of unfathomable mystery. Language has this infinity, with neither end nor beginning except for a very brief past, in common, so far as our view is concerned, with the whole existence of the human race. But we feel and intuit in language plainly and vividly how even the remote past is related to the feeling of the present, since it has passed through the human sensations of former generations and has retained their living breath. But these same generations are nationally and familially related to us in the same sounds of their native tongue which becomes the expression of our own feelings.

This double aspect of language, partly firm and partly fluid, produces a unique relationship between it and the generations that speak it. They produce within it a depository of words and a system of rules by which it grows in the course of the centuries into an independent power. Our attention was earlier focused on the fact that a thought taken up by language becomes an object for the psyche and thus exerts an effect upon it from the outside. But we have been looking at this object mainly as it has developed from the subject, at the effect, in other words, as emanating from that upon which it reacts. Now we must also look at the process from the opposite point of view, according to which language is truly a foreign object, its effect actually emanating from something quite other than that upon which it reacts. For language must necessarily belong to a twosome and at the same time it is truly the property of the entire human race. Since in writing, too, it holds out slumbering thought to be awakened by the spirit, it builds for itself a unique existence which can only attain validity in any given act of thought, but which in its totality is nonetheless independent of thought. The two contradictory views here suggested—that language is both extrinsic to the psyche and a part of it, that it is both independent from it and dependent on it—pertain to it in reality and make out the individuality of its nature. Nor must we seek to solve the contradiction by saying that language is in part extrinsic and independent, and in part neither. For language is objective and independent to precisely the same degree that it is subjective and dependent. For it has no abiding place anywhere, not even in writing;

what we called its dead part must always be newly generated in thought; it must always transfer itself alive into speech or understanding, in other words become wholly transferred to the subject. But this same act of regeneration is what makes it also into an object. To be sure, it experiences the entire operative influence of the human individual, but this same operative influence is bound by what it is and has been. The true solution of the paradox lies in the unity of human nature. Whatever originates with what is one and the same with myself, dissolves the concepts of object and subject, of dependence and independence. Language is mine because I produce it as I do. And because the reason I produce it as I do lies in the speaking and having spoken of all the generations of men, insofar as uninterrupted linguistic communication reaches, it is the language itself that gives me my restrictions. But that which restricts and confines me came into language by human nature of which I am a part, and whatever is strange in language for me is therefore strange only for my individual momentary nature, not for my original, true nature as a human being. . . .

Bibliography

This bibliography contains not only references cited in the text and introduction, but also suggestions for further reading in areas of the history of linguistics not covered herein: the Hindu grammarians and the nineteenth and twentieth centuries, for example.

I. GENERAL WORKS

Aarsleff, Hans, *The Study of Language in England: 1780–1860*, Princeton, N. J., 1967.

Carroll, John B., *The Study of Language*, Cambridge, Mass., 1953.

Hamp, Eric P., Fred W. Householder, and Robert Austerlitz (eds.), *Readings in Linguistics*, vol. II, Chicago, Ill., 1966.

Haugen, Einar (ed.), *First Grammatical Treatise*, Austin, Tex., 1953.

Joos, Martin (ed.), *Readings in Linguistics*, 4th ed., vol. I, Chicago, Ill., 1966.

Lehmann, W. P. (trans. and ed.), *A Reader in Nineteenth-Century Historical Indo-European Linguistics*, Bloomington, Ind., 1967.

Mohrmann, Christine, F. Norman, and Alf Sommerfelt (eds.), *Trends in Modern Linguistics*, Utrecht, 1963.

Mohrmann, Christine, Alf Sommerfelt, and Joshua Whatmough (eds.), *Trends in European and American Linguistics 1930–1960*, Utrecht, 1961.

Pedersen, Holger, *The Discovery of Language: Linguistic Science in the 19th Century* (trans. J. W. Spargo), Bloomington, Ind., 1962. (reprint of Harvard University Press edition, 1931).

Robins, R. H., *Ancient and Mediaeval Grammatical Theory in Europe*, London, 1951.

Robins, R. H., *A Short History of Linguistics*, London, 1967.

Sebeok, Thomas A. (ed.), *Portraits of Linguists* (2 vols.), Bloomington, Ind., 1966.

Waterman, John T., *Perspectives in Linguistics*, Chicago, Ill., 1963.

II. SPECIALIZED WORKS

(Note: In general, works excerpted in the text have not been included here.)

Abercrombie, D., "Forgotten Phoneticians," *TPS* (1948), 1–34.

✓ Allen, W. Sidney, *Phonetics in Ancient India*, London, 1953.

Bursill-Hall, G. L., "Mediaeval Grammatical Theories," *Canadian Journal of Linguistics*, IX (1963), 40–54.

Chomsky, Noam, *Cartesian Linguistics*, New York, 1966.

Colaclides, P., "On the Stoic Theory of Tenses," *QPR* of the RLE (M.I.T.), no. 80 (January 15, 1966), 214–216.

Colson, F. H., "The Analogist and Anomalist Controversy," *Classical Quarterly*, XIII (1919), 24–36.

Downer, G. B., "Traditional Chinese Phonology," *TPS* (1963), 127–142.

Emeneau, Murray B., "India and Linguistics," *JAOS*, LXXV (1955), 145–153.

✓ Faddegon, B., *Studies on Pānini's Grammar*, Amsterdam, 1936.

Forbes, P. B. R., "Greek Pioneers in Philology and Grammar," *Classical Review*, XLVII (1933), 112.

Fowkes, Robert A., "The Linguistic Modernity of Jacob Grimm," *Linguistics*, VIII (1964), 56–61.

Gaudefroy-Demombynes, J., *L'Oeuvre linguistique de Humboldt*, Paris, 1931.

Heintel, Erich (ed.), *Johann Gottfried Herder: Sprachphilosophische Schriften*, 2d ed., Hamburg, 1964.

Hirschfeld, H., *Literary History of Hebrew Grammarians and Lexicographers*, London, 1926.

Hunt, R., "Studies on Priscian in the Eleventh and Twelfth Centuries," *Mediaeval and Renaissance Studies*, I (1941–1943), 194–231; II (1950), 1–56.

Langendoen, D. Terence, "A Note on the Linguistic Theory of M. Terentius Varro," *Foundations of Language*, II (1966), 33–36.

Langendoen, D. Terence, *The London School of Linguistics*, Cambridge, Mass., 1968.

Lersch, L., *Die Sprachphilosophie der Alten*, Bonn, 1838–1841.

McCawley, James D., "Sapir's Phonologic Representation," *IJAL*, XXXIII (1967), 106–111.

McCawley, James D., "The Phonological Theory Behind Whitney's Sanskrit Grammar," in *Languages and Areas: Studies Presented to George V. Bobrinskoy*, Chicago, Ill., 1967.

Ó Cuív, Brian, "Linguistic Terminology in the Mediaeval Irish Bardic Tracts," *TPS* (1965), 141–164.

Postal, Paul M., "Boas and the Development of Phonology," *IJAL*, XXX (1964), 269–280.

Robins, R. H., "The Development of the Word Class System of the European Grammatical Tradition," *Foundations of Language*, II (1966), 3–19.

Sapir, Edward, "Herder's *Ursprung der Sprache*," *Modern Philology*, V (1907–1908), 109–142.

Schaade, A., *Sibawaihi's Lautlehre*, Leiden, 1911.

Seeman, Khalil I., *Linguistics in the Middle Ages: Phonetic Studies in Early Islam*, Leiden, 1968.

Shefts, Betty, *Grammatical Method in Pānini*, New Haven, Conn., 1961.

Staal, J. F., "Context-sensitive Rules in Pānini," *Foundations of Language*, I (1965), 65–72.

Staal, J. F., *Word Order in Sanskrit and Universal Grammar*, (Foundations of Language, Supp. Series vol. V), Dordrecht, 1967.

Steinthal, H. (ed.), *Die sprachphilosophischen Werke Wilhelm's von Humboldt*, Berlin, 1883.

Steinthal, H., *Geschichte der Sprachwissenschaft bei den Griechen und Römern*, 2d ed., Berlin, 1890.

Voegelin, C. F. and F. M., "On the History of Structuralizing in 20th Century America," *Anthropological Linguistics*, V (1963), 12–35.

Wilamowitz-Moellendorff, U. von, *Geschichte der Philologie*, Leipzig, 1959 (reprint of 1st ed., 1921).